THE COVER

"A TYPICAL BROOKLYN WALKUP"

THE DAY STALKERS

BY JOE RAINONE

ACKNOWLEDGEMENTS

The first person I would like to acknowledge is my wife, Joanne, who stood by me through thick and thin, who put up with my madness. Who also cooked many meals for me. Meals that were missed because I was involved in an arrest and was unable to make it home for dinner. I thank her for her patience and understanding. I would also like to thank my three children, Felicia A, Dora A, and Joseph J, who missed having dinner with their father because he was too busy with his second love, the NYPD (My first love is my family). I would also like to acknowledge my father, who encouraged me to become a cop, a dream he never lived to see. Also, my mother and sister (who are not here), my mom was so proud of her son, the cop, that she carried around the news clipping every time I made an arrest, and it made the newspaper. She did this so she could show her lady friends what a great cop her son was. (A typical good mother).

Also, my nephew Joseph Gallo, for whom I believe I was his inspiration to become a cop. When he did, he eventually made Detective 2nd and was a dam good one, a raise he well deserved. Which made his family and my family proud of him. Also, my adopted nephew Sam Consolazio, another one who made me and everyone proud of him. Both of whom thought I had the power of the Police Commissioner. I would also like to acknowledge all the great Anti-Crime cops that I worked with both as a Cop and as a Sergeant. All great cops with whom we made many great arrests. Arrest that if we didn't make them right, then when the crime was committed, the arrest would most likely never been made. They made my time on the NYPD an enjoyable time. Last but not least, I would be remiss if I didn't mention Cliff Bieder, who was more like a partner to me than one of my team members. Cliff, who was in my Anti-Crime team, as well as my module in Auto-Crime. Cliff always thanked me for getting his Detective Shield. A shield that he well deserved. He always told me, "Joe, this is not just my shield, but it's our shield." It's the shield you deserved but never got. So, I have to say Thank You, Cliff, you made me feel like all my work and dedication paid off.

I would also like to thank my unofficial East New York Historian who showed me certain landmarks that were in East New York. My good friend Artie Molinelli was not only an Anti-Crime Cop and Detective in the 75th precinct, but also grew up in East New York. Ironically, when he became a cop, he was assigned to patrol the very streets he grew up in. Growing up, he knew all the history of the racial problems that existed in the sixties in the changing neighborhood. There are a couple of sights that he pointed out to me at the time that I must have passed a thousand times and never realized they were there. I would bet that most of the young cops who are there now have no idea they are there. So, the history regarding East New York comes from someone who has firsthand knowledge of it. As they are described in my book.

I also say thanks to all my Anti-Crime Team, Joe Campanella, Bill Campisi, Cliff Bieder, Mike Graziose, Danny Mahoney, Dave Hurst, Jerry Keuchler, George Klouda, and Tony Farneti, all of whom were a great team, and a great bunch of Cops. I am proud to say I worked with them. All who told me, "Sarge, with all the stories you know, you should write a book." Well, guys, I listened to you, and I finally did. I have memories that will last a lifetime. I could fill a separate book with stories and all of the great cops (too many to mention) I met along the way, so I say to all who made my time on the NYPD the best job in the world, tanx. I could tell you about my worst day on the NYPD as well as my best day, but that's for another book.

TANX TO ALL OF YOU

FOREWORD

For those of you readers who have never been in the Police Department, at the beginning of the Day Stalkers, I will explain the partnership of the District Attorney's office and Detectives and Police Officers of the NYPD, including court proceedings.

There is also a little Brooklyn and E.N.Y. history in this book.

These stories take place in the mid-1970s; each story is true. The names of the victims have been changed to protect them and their families. The families who have suffered enough pain. However, the names of the guilty have also been changed to protect them. I say protect the guilty because it is possible that while serving their sentences in jail, they may have found GOD. Upon being released, they are living a life free of crime. Their names have been changed to also protect their families, who should not suffer shame for their misdeeds. Families who were more than likely law-abiding people.

DISCLAIMER: Any similarities of the names, either living or dead, mentioned in any of these stories are purely coincidental, whether they are victims, defendants, or Police Officers. The author shall be held harmless.

During this period, New York State did not have a sentence of Life Without Parole or Execution. So, after serving the minimum sentence (e.g., 25 to life after 25 years, they are eligible for parole). After reviewing their records, the Parole Board may grant them freedom, or not. Upon release, they may now be living a normal, productive life. They have paid their debt to society. However, this may not be fair to their victims or their families, but this is the law, whether we like it or not. We live and abide by the LAW of the LAND.

THE DAY STALKERS

With regards to the Day Stalkers in the first story, it was strange how some people were murdered, some were violently assaulted, and yet others were just threatened or frightened and not injured. The question always remained why some were treated more harshly than others. Why were some murdered, and others were brutally assaulted? Yet others were just threatened, but no violence was used against them.

NEW PATTERN SCRU

(Senior Citizen Robbery Unit)

In the case of the new pattern, in the Senior Citizen Robbery Unit (SCRU), this culprit was extremely careful, apparently learning from a family member's mistake. He didn't get caught until he changed his M.O. (Method of Operation).

THE SENIOR CITIZEN ROBBERY UNIT

Eventually, in 1978, I was assigned to the Senior Citizen Robbery Unit, where I did my own investigation with tips I learned from the Detectives of the 12th Division Homicide Squad, as well as the 69 Squad Detectives. One thing I learned is that you can do all the reading you want to learn about certain things in life. But firsthand knowledge by an experienced person is the best teacher, along with hands-on experience.

THE ULTIMATE MORTAL SIN

This was the story of the robbery of a church that went bad, where an elderly priest was killed. However, it took four and a half years to solve and bring the skells to justice.

FIFTY YEARS LATER

Now, fifty-some-odd years later, the streets are much safer in NYC. The Homicide/Assault, Robbery/Burglary, and Grand Larceny Stats are all well below what they were in the 70's.

The Pink Houses, as well as the Boulevard Houses, are a much safer place to live, with the crime stats down as they are. NYC has come a long way since the "FEAR CITY" days of the 70's-80's. The makeup of the Police Department has also changed from the 70's when most of the Police Officers were White.

Now there are many different ethnic groups from many different countries, and they speak many different languages, that makes the NYPD, which is now, a White, Black, Brown, and Yellow more diversified Police department. For the most part, as it stands today, the Hispanics of the different ethnic Hispanic groups make up the largest part of the NYPD. As opposed to the Irish or Italian officers of yesteryears. The NYPD is now what the makeup of New York City is, and probably the most diversified Police department in the United States. Which makes it the greatest Police Department in the USA.

These stories are actual true crimes that occurred. I wrote about them based on my recollection from the Detectives I talked to. I was also on the scene of some of these crimes. I also read some of the reports the detectives prepared, and by reading newspaper articles of these events. Even though some were almost fifty years ago, I have a vivid recollection of them. I came across many different crimes in my 26+year career, several of which were Homicides. But these cases were embedded in my mind like they were committed recently. I can picture the crime scenes I saw, as well as the detectives interviewing the victims/

witnesses, like it was yesterday. I was also privy to how the detectives solved these cases. How they proceeded to make the arrest. I am not perfect, but I have a great recall of certain events and incidents that I will never forget. I have friends who encouraged me to write about certain events on the job that I have come across. These stories are part of them. I wanted to write about them for a long time, and now I have finally found time to do so.

This story starts out in Brownsville, Brooklyn, but reaches out to the hearts of all NYC residents.

FIRST A WORD ABOUT

THE DETECTIVES

THE ANTI-CRIME COPS

THE DISTRICT ATTORNEYS

This section is for those who have never been with the Police Department. So, I will try to describe what the Police Officers, as well as the Detectives, and the District Attorneys/ ADA's do. I will take you from arrest to prosecution to sentencing, finally to appeal. This will hopefully give you a better understanding of these stories and the procedures.

THE DETECTIVES

It should be noted that the Detectives that were involved in these homicide cases were all seasoned Detectives. This was especially true with the Detectives that were assigned to the Homicide Squad; a few had close to 20 years, but most were well over 20 years. The Detectives that are assigned to the Homicide Squad have seen some of the worst crime scenes of their entire career and worked to solve some of the most difficult Homicide cases. The homicide squad is one of the most prestigious jobs in the Detective Bureau. It ranks on par with the Major Case Squad, which is also a prestigious position. Most of the

Detectives that are assigned to the homicide squad are usually handpicked. They are the ones who excel in their job as precinct detectives. The job is desired by many detectives, but as previously stated, only the ones who excel are selected. However, there are a few of those for one reason or another, slip in the backdoor so to speak. This is a part of the job that was, and still is, part of the NYPD, and probably will be until the end of time. It's nothing new and has been going on since the beginning of the formation of the Police Department. As the old timers would say, he is here because "he/she has a hook." Meaning he/she has someone in a position of authority who spoke up for her/him. Or others would say he is here because "he/she has a Rabbi in his/her corner." This is just a saying and has no bearing on one's ethnic background; it's just another way of saying someone has a hook or has someone in authority in his/her. But they are still the Greatest Detectives in the World

THE ANTI-CRIME COPS

Sometime around late 1971, early 1972, the NYPD created the precinct Anti-Crime units, which were drawn from the uniformed patrol officers within the precinct. They worked in plain clothes and had unmarked cars. Prior to that, they had a City-Wide Anti-Crime Squad (CWACS); they were all young plainclothes cops who worked all over the city. Especially high-crime areas battling street crimes. They were the ones who got that robber, or burglar, right in or right after the act of committing a crime. They also took many guns off the streets. The concept of the Street Crime

Unit (CWACS) worked well, so the higher-ups in the department decided to try it on a precinct level. First, they tried it as a pilot project in certain precincts around the city. When they saw that the results proved to be successful, they decided to expand it to all precincts. The Commanding Officer of each command handpicked his team for this assignment. Only the best ones were assigned. I was one of the lucky ones, although many cops didn't want it due to having to use your own car in the beginning. At first, cars were scarce, so you were forced to use your own car. You would be reimbursed with one gallon of gas for every ten miles you put on, a limit of five gallons. Once the department got funds (some of which were Federal), more cars were obtained, and you rarely used your own car.

The purpose of Anti-Crime, when it was performed right was to arrest people committing street crimes. Crimes such as Robberies, Burglaries, Grand Larceny from the person I.E. (Purse Snatch) and Grand Larceny Auto. These were the crimes that people feared the most; they were the crimes that kept some people off the streets for fear of getting mugged. Or kept them home to protect their houses from being burglarized, cars had double/triple locks on them. Ignition, steering wheel locks, and cutoff switches. During the 70s there were many of those crimes committed against the average person. Those were the targets of Anti-Crime cops. A good Anti-Crime cop was a nosy cop, always looking, always getting to know his street urchins, skells. Even when he saw a fellow officer arrest someone, he would take notice of the person's name, where he lived, what he looked like, what he/she was arrested for, and if he had a Knick name. This proved very beneficial at times. Many times, the Detectives may have had a case where they had just a nickname. The Detective would go to a sharp Anti-Crime cop and ask if he knew the true name, which many times the A-C cop did know; we knew our skells. Eventually, the department started a file where they stored nicknames. But going to a precinct Anti-Crime Cop was the much shorter way. Because he may even supply you with additional info, like where he hangs out and who he hangs out with. He may also be able to tell the detective what kind of crimes the skell is capable of. The department didn't have a nickname unit, but after a person got arrested and the cop put it on the arrest report, it would be entered into the nickname file. Many of the suspect's true name was discovered by his nickname. The detectives were mostly stuck in the station house doing a lot of paperwork, while the Ant-Crime cops were out patrolling all day. Searching, hunting for the bad guys, getting to know who they were. Where they frequented, who they associated with, and what kind of crime they specialized in. Although many were opportunists, meaning if something was easy for them, no matter what it was, they would jump on it if it was something they could make money from.

The Anti-Crime cops sometimes would be the eyes and ears for the Precinct Detectives. The Anti-Crime cop was the greatest tool the department created to combat local street crimes. Many times, when an elderly woman is walking home late from a bingo game or shopping, and is noticed by the A-C cops, they would carefully follow her home, watching from a distance to make sure she didn't become a victim. So, in essence, the person, unbeknownst to them, had a police escort getting to her home.

STOP QUESTION FRISK

The Stop Question and Frisk form (UF 250) had to be filled out each time a person was stopped. When used properly, that was another great tool used by the police department. The form is filled out when a person who is stopped has committed a crime, is about to commit a crime, or the person fits the description of a person who committed a crime. Most of the time, if the cop notices a bulge that could possibly be a gun, the suspect is usually stopped and given a pat-down for a gun. If no weapon is found, a UF 250 would be filled out, and the reason the stop was made. Many guns were taken off the street, which saved a possible homicide/ robbery, or assault. This kept the bad guys in check, for fear of carrying a gun and getting frisked by an Anti-Crime cop or any Police Officer, for that matter. Most of the bad guys feared getting stopped and frisked, especially when the cop did the UF 250(stop and frisk form), which had to be filled out. This also helped keep crime down by keeping guns off the street. Because the bad guy was afraid of getting stopped and frisked. Sometimes, it may have useful information when a UF 250 was filled out, which may aid a detective in solving a sometimes-serious crime. As you will see, as the story progresses.

THE DISTRICT ATTORNEY

With regards to the (D.A.) District Attorney, it is an elected position. He/she is the Chief Law Enforcement Officer for the County to which he/she was elected. Each D.A. has several Assistant District Attorneys (ADA) working for him/her. There are several different units in the D.A.'s office, one of which is the Homicide Bureau. The DA's Homicide Bureau has a chief in charge of it. Each Chief has several ADAs assigned to the bureau. When a homicide occurs, the DA will assign an ADA, usually with another to assist him/her with an investigation. Which will be their assignment all the way to a trial, if need be. The Chief usually feels confident of the ADAs that are prosecuting the case, as well as the Detectives from the Homicide Squad, who are usually experienced Detectives who work with the ADAs. The D.A. knows that when dealing with the Detectives from the Homicide Squad, they have an experienced officer who knows what he/she was doing. So, the ADA had no problem or fear of what the Detective may say on the stand to jeopardize the case. They knew most detectives had experience testifying. Testifying at times can be very stressful, with an experienced trial lawyer hammering away at you. Trying at every step of the way to get the detective to foul up or break down. One must realize all that was needed for an aspiring Police Officer to be appointed to the Police Department back in the 60s, all you needed was a High School Diploma or G.E.D. equivalent. (College credits came later.)

So here you have a Detective/Police Officer with nothing more than a High School diploma going against a lawyer, who has a college degree, as well as a Law Degree. Who is trained in law school, be it Civil or Criminal, how to question a person who is testifying and cross-examine after the ADA has finished. The Lawyer, who had training in Law School, who is well versed in the law, is questioning a Detective/Police Officer whose training cannot be compared to the lawyer's training. At the time, very little training was given on testifying in the Police Academy to the probationary Police Officers. The NYPD Detectives who usually testify in a Murder case most likely have previous experience in testifying. Sometimes they go up against a high-priced lawyer, who is paid extremely well to defend his client. The lawyer who is always looking to trick the person testifying into saying the wrong thing, anything that will aid him/her win their case. Many times, they use an intimidating line of questioning to put the person testifying on the defensive. A good detective usually does not get shaken up. Considering all the facts, the officers do a pretty dam good job testifying, as can be judged by their conviction rate.

With regards to the Detectives, as well as any Police Officer in the Police Department, they tell you to never take your cases home with you. Don't take them personally. Also, don't take the sight of any crime scene home with you.

(Unfortunately, I did, this is why I wrote this book, 50 years later, I never forgot some of the crime scenes I witnessed.) It's time to let them go.

This is taught to you right at the beginning of your career, right in the Police Academy. Don't take them personally; it was not good for you or your family to get emotionally involved. But unfortunately, many Detectives/Police Officers did, and sometimes it disrupted their family life. The crime scenes they saw sometimes left a lasting image in their mind that, as hard as they tried, could not be forgotten. It was said that some of the Detectives who investigated these cases had dreams about them (as I did) and in some cases nightmares. While other Detectives took it as just another case and didn't let it bother him/her. It doesn't mean they weren't good Detectives, for lack of a better word, they were just a little hard-core, colder. Because everyone is an individual and has their own mindset, as well as personality, opinion, and tolerance level. But each gave it their all to solve a difficult homicide that was just about almost impossible to solve. Nevertheless, it would be addressed with just as much zeal and aggressiveness, no matter who the victim was or what the circumstances were.

Whether it was a wealthy Wall St. Banker, or was just an average every day working stiff, or a retired senior citizen. Or maybe it was the homicide of a Drug Dealer or homeless person, the case had to be addressed and given the same attention as that of the Wall St. Banker. Even Drug Dealers or homeless people have families that want closure. In some cases, the Media might have obtained information about the homicide, and if they felt it was newsworthy, they would print a story about it. If the Police Department felt the need, they would have a press conference regarding the homicide. The press conference was to assure the public that no matter who the victim was, it would be thoroughly investigated. No matter what the circumstances were.

There were also cases that were called "ground ball cases"; these were cases where the suspect was known. This could be a family member murder, husband vs wife, or vice versa, or just friends. Friends that maybe went a little too far with their anger. Either way, it was just a matter of putting the cuffs on him/her. Usually, in an arrest situation like this, a confession comes with the arrest, where the suspect tries to justify what he/she has done. This is sometimes known as a self-serving statement. However, it is not always guaranteed that the suspect will make a statement of any kind. Thereby invoking the "Fifth Amendment, of the Constitution, "The Right to Remain Silent, and not make any Incriminating Statements." In the eyes of the law, everyone has the presumption of innocence until proven "GUILTY BEYOND A REASONABLE DOUBT." The result will be after being tried by a jury of his/her peers, or a bench trial (judge only). Unless a self-plea of guilt is given by the defendants themselves after conferring with counsel (lawyer).

TRIAL OR NO TRIAL

In cases like the ones noted, most times the defendant doesn't opt to go to trial. Usually, the defense attorney will sit down with the ADA who is handling the case to try to hammer out the best deal for his client. Depending on the circumstances and the strength of the evidence, the ADA will then inform the defense attorney what sentence he is going to request from the judge. The judge can go along with it or set his own sentence for the defendant; this can go either way. The ADA will also have to confer with the D.A. (boss)and explain the reason for wanting to make the deal. After explaining his reason to the D.A., he/she (the D.A.) will make a final determination as to approval or disapproval of the deal. The D.A. usually will accept the deal by trusting the judgment of his ADA. Instead of taking the chance of going to trial and possibly having the case thrown out on some kind of technicality or an acquittal by a jury. In accepting the plea, a conviction is guaranteed. This keeps the D.A.'s conviction rate up. Or as the Police call it, keeping the "batting average up." However, usually, before the judge accepts a plea, he will ask for an allocution from the defendant. Which is an explanation of what happened. This is usually followed by the judge asking the defendant, are you pleading because you are in fact guilty? Which is usually followed by "YES." If the defendant says "No," then the proceeding is immediately stopped. Assuming he answered in the affirmative. The next question by the judge would be, did anyone threaten you or promise you anything to take this plea, which is usually answered with a "NO" by the defendant. When there really was a deal made with the promise that by taking this plea, the sentence would be substantially lower than if he/she was convicted at trial. However, this is a normal procedure in probably every courtroom in New York City, and most likely just about every courtroom in the United States. The plea bargain is a necessary evil/tool in the court system. Not only does it conclude a case, but it also helps alleviate the backlog and helps clear the court calendar of cases in the entire system. If a defendant prefers to go to trial, the defendant has the option of having a jury trial, which means being judged by twelve, and hope that he can gain an acquittal completely, or maybe be found not guilty on some of the lesser charges. However, the defendant can ask for a Bench Trial, which means the defendant will be judged solely by one person, the judge. E.G., the defendant is charged with Murder, Manslaughter 1, and Manslaughter 2, hoping that they don't convict on the top charge, which usually comes with a twenty-five to life sentence, as opposed to Manslaughter One, which is usually fifteen to life. However, in Manslaughter Two, the sentence could be as low as five to fifteen years. This means that he/she can get out in as little as five years.

In the case of a judge trial, some attorneys, as well as defendants, feel that a judge is more familiar with the law than a jury of twelve civilians, who, for the most part, know very little of the law. Also, the judge may be more understanding and sympathetic as to why the crime was committed, or may even justify the crime, thereby dismissing the case.

But as one learned attorney has said, "Who would you want deciding your case, one person or twelve?" With twelve people, the vote must be unanimous, meaning all twelve must agree on the outcome of the case. If there is as little as one holdout for not guilty/guilty and that person refuses to change his/her vote, the judge will usually tell the jury they must go back, talk it over, and try to reach a unanimous verdict. If, after a period of time, the jury comes back again and tells the judge they still can't reach a verdict and are hopelessly deadlocked, the judge will then declare a mistrial.

A mistrial means the ADA can try the case again or just dismiss it outright. Usually, the ADA will poll the jury and see how they voted. If the majority voted for conviction, the ADA will more than likely retry the case. However, if it was eleven to one for acquittal, then more than likely the ADA may make a request to the judge that the charges be dropped, and the case dismissed. The poll isn't an automatic decision maker; it's usually a barometer of what the jury was feeling. It may also send a signal to the ADA that the way he may have been presenting his case was not convincing enough. This may also indicate what he/she was doing wrong. Which may get him/her to change his/her strategy. There have been cases where the jury voted 10-11 to one for acquittal, but regardless of the change of strategy, the ADA may opt to retry the case. There is the possibility that he or she may have realized his/her mistakes and is now using a different strategy. By the same token, a different makeup of the jury can also change the outcome of the case. In retrying the case the second time around, the ADA may win a conviction.

When a jury is deadlocked and can't reach a decision, they are discharged, and a mistrial is declared. If the ADA wants to retry the case, a new jury will have to be picked. Now using a different strategy, or maybe even the fact that with a different jury of twelve people, they may see the facts of the case in a different light. Twelve different people saw the facts and the evidence differently from the way the first jury saw them. This is not really an unusual occurrence, as it has happened many times in the past. With regards to the judge, he/she will usually remain, throughout the re-trials, which can sometimes be as many as three or more if the ADA desires, the choice lies with the ADA.

TABLE OF CONTENTS

CHAPTER ONE

THE DAY STALKERS

CHAPTER TWO

THE PLAN

CHAPTER THREE

THE FIRST HOMICIDE

CHAPTER FOUR

HOMICIDE NUMBER TWO

CHAPTER FIVE

THE PATTERN

CHAPTER SIX

HOMICIDE NUMBER THREE

CHAPTER SEVEN

THE FOLLOW-UP HOMICIDE #3

CHAPTER EIGHT

THE BIG BREAK

CHAPTER NINE

THE FIRST

ARREST

CHAPTER TEN

THE STATEMENT

CHAPTER ELEVEN

SOLVING HOMICIDE NUMBER #3

CHAPTER TWELVE

ARREST OF THE OTHERS ON HOMICIDE #3

CHAPTER THIRTEEN

ARREST ON HOMICIDE ONE/TWO

CHAPTER FOURTEEN

THE PROSECUTION

CHAPTER FIFTEEN

THE TABLES ARE TURNED

CHAPTER SIXTEEN

SUMMATION OF THE DAY STALKERS

CHAPTER ONE

THE DAY STALKERS

Just about every Monday through Friday morning, a group of anywhere from two to six young kids would meet sometime between 8:30 and 9:30 am on a specific street in Brownsville, Brooklyn. The size of the group varied; at times it was as many as six, other times it was as few as two. They ranged in age from as young as 13 to 18 years of age. There was no rhyme or reason why the group varied in size, possibly because some didn't feel like getting up early that morning to join up with the others at that time. Which is more than likely the reason. One of these youths was a kid named Ben. Ben spent some time in Rikers Island, a NYC Jail. Rikers Island was like a training ground for young criminals. It was there that you learned how to hot-wire a car, do a burglary, or commit robbery. You learned from criminals who were in jail for any one of those crimes. You learned it all for free, there were no real classes to attend, and no correspondence fees to pay. While Ben was staying there, he met two brothers who, between the two of them, had almost one hundred arrests between them. They were the Simmonds brothers; they were Transit Recidivists. They told him that when you get out of jail, you must rob those old people. They all have money, and they have bad eyesight; they are too afraid of us to identify us. So, when he gets out of jail, he picks his crew, a couple of street skells who will go along with his leadership.

These youths were known in Police jargon as Skells. A skell is derived from the word Skellum, which is a word from yesteryear that describes a rascal, and not a good one. To most cops on the job, especially the newer, younger ones, it was just a word that was passed down from the old-time cops. It has been passed down for decades. So, for the most part, most cops had no idea what the word meant, and no one cared or bothered to find out what it meant. It was passed on from older officers to younger officers. To them, it meant they were locking up or dealing with a person who was not a nice person. It was just a cop's normal way of talking. To the civilians who had no knowledge of police jargon, the word would be foreign to them. But someone who worked with the Police like an ADA or an EMS worker, may know or have an idea of what the word meant. Because in dealing with the Police on a regular basis, the word would be used by the Police as a normal figure of speech. So, they would either figure it out or were told by the Police, it wasn't a term of endearment. So right to this day, through generations of Police Officers, the word is still used by modern-day Police, even though most don't know or even care what the true meaning is. Simply put, they had no intention of finding out what it meant either.

THEIR JOURNEY

Once the crew grouped up, they formulated their plan, even though it was basically the same routine. They went over it, so everyone knew their part. They had it down to science. Once this was done, it was time for these young thugs (skells) to start out on their journey. But what was their journey, going to work, going to school, looking for a job, going to a sporting event, going to a park, meeting other friends, no, not any of these things.

Then what were they doing? Were they looking for a car to steal to do a drive by robberies out of it? Or maybe stripping it and selling the parts to make a few bucks. Again, it was none of these things. What they were doing would shock a normal person's mind. They were hunting for victims, the weak, defenseless, the elderly human victims. The older, the weaker, the better they make for a victim. They were not just a group of kids walking around enjoying the fresh air. They were really Serial Killers, searching for a victim. People seeing a couple of kids ranging in age from thirteen to eighteen had no idea what was on their minds or in their hearts. There is the possibility that if anyone did observe them didn't realize they may have been following a victim at that time. Because their walk was just a casual walk, no one would suspect what they were up to. Also, given the fact that their victims were old and didn't walk fast. So, it was easy for them to just slowly drift along, never having to worry about losing sight of the victim.

Their journey took them to other parts of Brooklyn, Canarsie, East Flatbush/Remsen Village, and sometimes their home base, which was Brownsville. They were all young and healthy, so walking was no problem for them; in fact, it was a good exercise. They needed no getaway car after committing their crime; it was not needed to make good their escape, and they didn't need to run either. Just walking and blending in with the public. This was the same way they walked when they stalked their victims. The walk would be just a normal walk where they would pass many potential victims, or someone who could be a victim. But it had to be the right victim, someone who was elderly, someone who was weak and wouldn't, or couldn't fight back. They would keep walking until they found the right victim. When they found their victim, they would eventually Rob, Assault, torture, and yes, sometimes Murder them. (This will be explained as the story progresses.) Even though they were between the ages of 13 and 18 years old, they were all streetwise and vicious kids. They were kids who grew up on the streets of a tough neighborhood, so they knew the ins and outs of the law, and knew it quite well, so they thought. They got their education through the school of Hard Knocks in a tough neighborhood. These kids were your typical High School dropouts, and in one case, a Junior High dropout.

However, many kids also grew up in this same neighborhood who were streetwise too, but in just the opposite manner. They were kids who saw that looking up to a criminal was not the right way to go. Seeing those going in and out of the justice system was not the way they wanted to grow up. Whether this was instilled in them by good parenting or just knowing this was not the life they wanted to lead. They did not look up to the criminals as role models. Whereas our stalkers apparently did. The role models for the good kids were people who succeeded in life. They attended school, kept out of trouble, and didn't look up to the criminal element, nor did they hang around with them. Some went on to become professionals in one field or another, while others became civil service workers. While others just stood away from the life of crime and held normal, everyday jobs. They raised families and made sure that their offspring were brought up to follow in their footsteps. Some moved on to other neighborhoods while others remained behind. Whichever they chose, it was a life that was crime-free for them and their families. It was a life that rose above the poverty of the environment that surrounded their neighborhood. It was a life of clean living and hard work. They made sure that their offspring didn't hang around with the skells, who, when they wanted something, they just took it by force. It didn't matter if they hurt the person or not; they just took what they wanted. When they wanted it.

CHAPTER TWO

THE PLAN

Their M.O. (Method of Operation or Modus Operandi) was to stalk a victim who was out shopping or coming from a bank where they had cashed a Social Security check or maybe just taking a daily morning constitutional walk. Sometimes they would go to a bank and watch to see if anybody (a senior citizen) would cash a Social Security check or withdraw any money. (This was long before the days of Direct Deposit and ATM machines.) This made it easy to sometimes find a victim.

How the scheme worked, sometimes they would go to a bank and scan it to see if there were any seniors in it who were standing in line. If there were any seniors standing on the line, they would go into the bank and pretend they were filling out a withdrawal or deposit slip so they would be able to watch the potential victim. Or sometimes they would stand in the next line to a victim to see if the victim would withdraw money or cash a check. If they got to their window before anyone withdrew any money or cashed a check, not to arouse suspicion, they would produce a dollar bill and ask for a roll of pennies. The victims who were at least 65 years of age or usually much older, sometimes well into their 80s, were easy targets. But if the victim was right for them (had money), it didn't matter how old the victim was as long as he/she looked elderly and weak, or if he/she was black or white. But many times, they were usually elderly Jewish people, as statistics would show. Although the NYPD did not keep accurate statistics like that showing the race or ethnic background of the victims. At least at that time, they didn't. But by reading the reports and interviewing the victims, the Detectives ascertained who the victims were, their age, and ethnicity.

During their journey, sometimes they would walk for hours without finding a victim. After spending the day with no fruits of their search, they would return home, so to speak, empty-handed. "Tomorrow was another day." However, while on their way home, sometimes they would run into an easy type of crime, a larceny or an easy robbery, and they would jump on it. Sometimes, when they couldn't find a victim to rob, they would go by a school in their own neighborhood. They would then grab the much younger, not-so-tough kids and shake them down for their lunch money or any money they had on them. Most of these kids would give it up willingly because they feared they would be hurt by them. Some of the kids would hide the money in their shoes, but if the stalkers found out, they would not only take their money but also take their shoes too. Because they were opportunist, meaning if something easy came up, even though it wasn't in their plans they would jump on it. But on other occasions, they may hit a jackpot, which means that they found the right victim. After carefully picking their victim and feeling sure that this wasn't someone who might offer any resistance, or it wasn't a Police Decoy, it was time to strike. However, they were careful because they knew the Police Department also had a unit called the "Street Crime Unit/ City Wide Anti-Crime

Squad (CWACS)." These officers specialized in street robberies. The men in this unit also dressed as elderly people or sometimes as Hasidic Jews or women. Reason being, Hasidic Jews, sometimes because of their dress, which was usually black clothing, hats, jackets, pants, shoes, and a white shirt. That was their standard dress code. They never wore anything with gold or brass buttons because it reminded them of when they were captured by the Nazi' and put in concentration camps. The sight of the bright brass buttons that were on the Nazi uniforms was frightening to them. They would be reminded of the times when they were tortured by them. So, because of the Nazi's wearing their shiny buttons while they were torturing them, they would never wear anything shiny on their clothing. It just brought back many bad memories. So, Hasidic Jews, because of their dress code, which was always black, were considered weak. They felt they were considered easy targets. The Hasidim would also wear black Felt hats trimmed with fur. Sometimes the kids would rob them just for their hats with the Fur trim. These hats were expensive and would be worn by Hasidim who could afford them. The kids who would be following them and stalking them when the time was right would run up and snatch the hat right off the victim's head. At the time, the Felt hat was the style for some of these young kids; it was a Homberg style. Buying one was too costly, so the next thing was to go out and snatch one. Once they obtained one, they would then trim the fur off and shape the hat to their liking and wear it.

ALWAYS ON THE ALERT

One of the things they learned in jail was that the Police Department had undercover cops in the street. They were known to the stalkers as "DTs". So obviously, through the word on the street and through information ascertained through people in jail, they knew that the Police had cops, dressed as old people. These undercover cops were from the Street Crime Unit (CWACS). At one time, the Street Crime Unit had the saying of "We Own the Night." To the liberals in their minds, the words were too harsh and sounded threatening, like the Police were bullies who just picked on people randomly. But other people thought differently of it. To them, it means the Police are out there and are there to protect us from the violence of the evil miscreants (skells) that prey on the innocent victims. Which meant the Police were out there and the streets were safe because of their presence. Meaning the Police owned the night, not the skells.

The Street Crime Unit would also have their decoys out, trying hard to blend in with the everyday people in hopes they would get robbed/mugged, whereas the public prayed not to. The unit specialized in street robberies, hoping that the miscreants saw them as potential victims. They would be dressed as the people in the area they were assigned to were dressed. Sometimes it would be a male decoy, other times it would be a female, depending on what the pattern was in the area they were assigned. However, prior to 1973, there were very few females on patrol, so most of the decoys were males who tried their best to impersonate females. In 1973, the female Police hopefuls won a court battle where they would be considered equal to the males that took the test prior to 1973. So sometime in mid-1973, the females were put on patrol full duty alongside their male counterparts. Prior to that, the females were considered matrons and were assigned menial duties, non-patrol. Hopefully, the decoy will become a victim, and the backup team will be able to pounce on him/her and arrest the perpetrator right in the act.

So, the crew, being they were street wise, would scan the area where they were looking for anything they could associate with a Police Officer (DT). This could be a Police Department looking car (taxi, unmarked car) or some younger people in the area who didn't look like they belonged there. Even though the Street Crime Officers blended well into the neighborhood and dressed in normal, regular street clothes, these miscreants were very cautious about doing their misdeeds if they suspected the cops were in the area. Sometimes they would say that they could actually smell a cop.

Being streetwise made them extra careful. So, anybody or anything that they thought, or they associated with the Police would immediately put an end to their plan. Because these guys were more than hat snatchers, they were much more dangerous, much more aggressive, even though they participated in hat snatches that was small-time stuff. They were big-time robbers. So, once they were sure their victim wasn't a decoy, and there were no Police in the area, and it was just another old, weak person, it was time to execute their plan.

Note: Most of the incidents happened in 1975-76, and although the females won full Police Officer status in 1973, there still weren't that many on patrol. However, on July 1, 1975, the city furloughed many city workers. This was because the city was in a fiscal crisis, and as hard as it was to do, the furloughs had to be done. Among the layoffs were 5000 Police officers. This was also hard, but again, it was something that must be done. Many of them were females who were recently hired. Some of those who were lucky to come back within the year were lucky because of some prior city time, or were of any age where they could have taken the test when they were eligible at 21, but were unable because of gender restrictions. But for the most part, many others didn't come back until 1979, which included mostly male officers.

It is also to be noted that the name of the test was changed from Patrolman (PTL) NYPD to Police Officer NYPD. Although on roll calls at the time, the names were carried as POM (Police Officer Male) and POF (Police Officer Female), this was done to identify their gender.

During this period, they committed many street robberies, most of which were what the police called strong-arm robberies. Where they would surround a victim and maybe punch him or threaten him with force. Putting fear in the victim made it much easier to take whatever property they had. The victim, who may have just come from a bank or check-cashing establishment where he may have cashed his Social Security check, would give the money up willingly for fear of getting hurt, or maybe killed. Although they were successful at these types of robberies, they were also taking a chance of being caught. Because they were on the street, there was a chance they would be caught while doing the robbery by an Anti-Crime team. Or maybe getting caught as they were making their escape based on a description. So, the robbery on the street, although it was successful, was risky. There had to be a safer way. It was then that they decided to do the robberies off the street, out of view of the public. First, they did a couple in the hallways of apartment houses. Once they saw how easy it was, they got the idea of doing it right in the victim's apartment. This is when the Push In robbery was born to them. It may have been used by others, but it was new to them. It was off the street, out of view of the public, where there were no witnesses or Police Officers. After the first one, they saw how easy it was, and it became part of their M.O. There were many after the first.

CHAPTER THREE

THE FIRST HOMICIDE

January 9, 1975, was the date of the first Push-In-Robbery that would turn into a Homicide. The victim is a male, white, 82 years of age, and apparently lives alone. Even though they did other Push-ins before this one. This is the first case where the victim died because of the robbery. Now they hit the big time. The stalkers, who were 3-4 or sometimes as many as 6 of them, would follow the victim who had just come from cashing his Social Security check at the bank or check-cashing establishment. However, in this case, he was not coming from a bank or check-cashing store, so what was the reason they picked him? Was it just the fact that he was elderly and frail, an easy target? No one knows for sure why they picked him; did he look like he had money? He did not look wealthy by any means, by the way he was dressed. Whatever their reason was, this was their victim. They would follow him, maybe half/three quarters of a block behind him. The victim, who was elderly, walked slowly as most old people do, so it was easy to follow him. When the victim went into his building, which was a walkup they would speed up to easily catch up to him. At the time, most of these front doors were unlocked. As he walked up the stairs, they would follow a flight behind. As he climbed slowly, it was easy to keep up with him. Once he got to his landing, they would rush up quietly and wait at the threshold of the doorway of his floor. Watching him as he fumbles for his keys and unlocks the door, which usually has two locks, and in some cases, some even have three locks. As soon as he opened the door, they all rushed him, attacking him like a pack of hyenas would attack a wounded animal. They all knew their part as they went over it many times. One would knock him down and would immediately jump on him. Another would then cut a lamp cord to tie him with. If, for some reason, they couldn't cut the lamp cord, they would wrap the wire around his hands and leave it attached and lay it right on top of the body. They would also gag him and blindfold him. While another would immediately lock the door. This all occurred in seconds. Once he was secure, and after searching him and taking whatever valuables he had on him, the ransacking would start. They would search his whole apartment looking for anything of value that they could put in their pockets. The big money they were looking for did not exist because this victim had very little. Because most of these people were old and poor people living at the poverty level on Social Security and food stamps, and very few had pensions, if any at all. While they were doing their searching, the vic (the word they used for victim) would be lying there tied and gagged, having difficulty breathing, which ultimately caused his death. Did they not notice him struggling to get some air into his system? Apparently, they didn't care if he was getting or not getting air as his life was slipping away. You would think that one of them would have compassion and pull the gag away from his face so he could breathe, but apparently, this was not the case. They just continued with their ransacking as the victim slowly expired.

Once they were done with their marauding, they would leave the building, walking out one at a time, not to arouse suspicion. It wouldn't be unusual for them to be walking out of the building, because it was a multi-racial building, as was the neighborhood. They would walk away casually like nothing ever happened. They would then regroup once they were away from the building. The next day, a neighbor who hadn't seen or heard from the victim tried calling him on the phone. When she didn't get any answer, she went to his apartment to see if he was alright. Knocking on the door, she still didn't get an answer, so she opened the door, which was unlocked, and was shocked by what she saw. Her neighbor, all trussed up, was lying on the floor. She immediately ran back to her apartment and called the Police.

When the uniformed Police arrive and observe the scene, they immediately call for EMS and the Patrol Sergeant. The Patrol Sergeant's job is to make sure that the officers keep the crime scene secure for the Detectives. Another part of his job is to make an Unusual Occurrence (U.O.) report. This report goes all the way up through the chain of command to the Chief of Department and eventually the Police Commissioner, informing them of the circumstances of this death.

NOTE: You can imagine the first cops on the scene, especially if they were rookies and never had the experience of dealing with a DOA. A sight like this may be a horrifying experience: the body of an elderly man lying on the floor, all trussed up. It could possibly cause one who is not callous of heart to puke. This could be one of their fathers or maybe even a grandfather. A sight like this may have a lasting, horrible image in his/her mind that can last throughout his/her career.

However, even the most calloused Homicide Detective who has seen some of the worst crime scenes you can imagine may have the same effect. Given the fact of a homicide detective's age, this could be a father or even an older brother. They may have possibly seen the bloodiest crime scenes in their career. However, in this murder, not a drop of blood was shed, due to the fact that he was asphyxiated. It was just the sight of the elderly man, fully clothed, his hands and feet tied, lying face down, helpless, right in his own apartment. At the time, it is unknown that this will be the first of three gruesome murders by these calloused, ruthless skells.

The body is examined by the EMS team. The body, which is faced down, is fully clothed with his outer garments still on. When the body is turned over, they find a paper bag with two bagels, a pack of cream cheese, and a package of lox underneath him. Apparently, he just went out shopping for breakfast at the local grocery store, where he may have been followed from. The EMT member, after examining the body, made the official pronouncement that the victim is DOA (Dead on Arrival). The sergeant has already called for the precinct detectives as well as the Detective Squad Boss.

The Homicide Squad is also called as well as the Crime Scene unit.

The Crime Scene Unit's job is to search the scene to try to find any evidence that would aid in solving this crime. Part of their job is to dust with powder for fingerprints as well as photograph the scene, which includes the victim. This is done to preserve the crime scene for future reference if there is an arrest made; the photos may be used in the court proceedings to describe the scene to the judge/jury. Fingerprints were not found because these stalkers may have been smart enough to wear gloves, or they did a good job of cleaning up anywhere they possibly may have left prints.

NOTE: The Crime Scene Detectives are well-trained and do an excellent job of searching the scene. If there were prints to be found, they surely would have.

The case is assigned to a Detective in the Homicide Squad. He is taken off the chart and is given 3 sets of tours to work exclusively on the Homicide. Seeing the groceries under his body gives them a starting point. They do a canvas of the area and find the grocery store where he bought the items. The store is only one and a half blocks away from his building. They interviewed the owner, who does remember the little old man, but he saw nothing out of the ordinary; the old guy (as he called him) didn't appear to be in distress or nervous. It was just an ordinary sale.

There were very few credit cards used back then, so it was a cash sale. But he doesn't remember what time he came into the store. But at least now they have a starting point. They apparently followed him, most likely right from the store. They do a canvas of the block, but no one remembers the old guy walking or being followed. So, they come up empty-handed, as they would say. They didn't find any witnesses; the fact that it's a normal neighborhood, and seeing the old man walking, or by the same token, young kids walking around, would not arouse suspicion in anyone, especially since they were not following him closely.

Note: Sometime in the late seventies, the Detective Bureau underwent reorganization. Whereby specialization came into effect. The Precinct Detective Squad would be taken out of the Detective Bureau and put under patrol. The precinct detectives would be known as P.I.U. "Precinct Investigating Unit." They would be under the supervision of the uniformed precinct commander. All other Detectives would be put into specialty squads I.E. Homicide/Assault, Robbery/Burglary, Auto Squad, (Rape Sexual Abuse Squad). Later, it was changed to the Special Victim Squad. These specialized detective units were in the Detective Bureau. So, when a case comes into the precinct detective squad, and it was in one of those categories, it would have to be referred to the specialty squad concerned. This sometimes caused animosity to some of the Detectives who were in the PIU, because the feeling was that they were not part of the prestigious Detective Bureau, and they were not good enough to handle these cases. After a short period of time, the Detective Bureau underwent another reorganization, apparently because the prior reorganization was akin to rearranging the Deck Chairs on the Titanic. The P.I.U Detectives were back in the Detective bureau, now to be named the Precinct Detective Squad (PDS), with them catching all cases except for Homicides, and Rapes/Sexual Abuse, which went to the Rape/Sex Squad, as previously stated, later to be known as the Special Victim Squad.

This Homicide is in the confines of the 69 precinct, and a detective from the 12th Davison Homicide Squad is assigned. The Detective from the Homicide Squad is assisted by Detectives in his team to work with him on the case.

(It should be noted that in the 70s, the Homicide squad was broken into divisions. This was in the Twelfth Division, which was made up of the following precincts, 63,67,69,71,75 precincts.) It wasn't until sometime in the 80s that specialization came in, and the Homicide squad was reorganized again and formed on a Borough basis. This would eliminate the Homicide squad Detectives working in different divisions. Everyone would be working out of one office under one umbrella in whatever borough it was in.

With the case being assigned to the Homicide Detective, if the case is not solved within the allotted 3 sets of tours, if another homicide came into his team and he was, as the detectives would say (at bat) he would catch another Homicide. Either way, it would be a joint effort with his whole team working on the case with him. As the precinct detectives would say, we catch everything from Dis Con (Disorderly Conduct) up to homicide, and there are no shortages of cases in the NYPD. Each Homicide would be logged into the precinct of occurrence and given a precinct 61 number (UF 61 is a Uniformed Complaint report of a crime or occurrence). The Homicide Squad would also give it their own number, I.E. Homicide # 1, etc., etc. The investigation would be done by the Homicide Squad where the saying was back in the days of the 70s and 80s "Give Me Twenty Minutes and I'll Give You A Homicide". Or as the 12th Division Homicide Squad would say "Our Day Begins When Your Life Ends" As previously stated it was a team effort every time a team member or the assigned officer did any type of work on the case the detective would have to document it on a DD5 (Detective Division 5 the name of the form.) It was a follow-up report on the investigation. It was put into the folder along with the other 5s, the reason being to let the catching/assigned detective know what was done to avoid a duplication of effort. This was the mid-seventies, when the Homicide rate was just starting to grow; eventually, in the eighties, NYC would have the distinction of logging over 2000 homicides in one year. Where some of the busier precincts would contribute to it by logging in over 100 Homicides for the year.

Once the body is pronounced by the EMT (Emergency Medical Technician), it is removed to the Morgue by the Morgue attendants in the Morgue vehicle, which some cops call the (meat wagon.) It will be delivered to the O.C.M.E. (the OFFICE of the CHIEF MEDICAL EXAMINER). At the morgue, the Medical Examiner will perform an autopsy to determine the exact cause of death.

THE MEDICAL EXAMINER'S DIAGNOSIS:

Victim Harry Kittler Male White 82

Cause of Death: Asphyxiation

Manner of Death: Homicide

The M.E. performs an Autopsy to find the true cause of death. The M.E. can also give the detectives a timeline on the approximate time of death. This is usually ascertained by the condition of the body. If it is not in the Rigor Mortis state, the death is usually before twelve hours. If it is in the Rigor Mortis state, the victim would be dead sometime between twelve and thirty-six hours. After thirty-six hours, the body goes into a relaxed state, so to speak. When it starts deteriorating and lets off noxious odors, you will know then that it is past 36 hours. Judging from the condition of the body, which was still in the state of Rigor Mortis, the homicide was committed within the last thirty-six hours. Unfortunately, the M.E. can only give an approximate time of death, not an exact time. Which means less than twelve hours, or more than twelve hours.

The cause of death in this case was determined to be that the victim was gagged by these cold-hearted thugs. This ultimately caused him to choke to death. The instrument that caused his asphyxiation was his own Pray Shawl.

A Pray Shawl is a religious garment that is worn over the outside of the clothing. It would be draped over the shoulders when the person went to pray at the local Schul/Synagogue. The Shawl is worn by religious Jewish men to show their faith in God. Apparently, the shawl was wrapped around his face and stuffed in his mouth, which made him unable to breathe, thereby causing his death. So, in this case, even though it was his devotion to God that he would wear it, it was the instrument that caused his death. In this Homicide all they got was a few dollars, hardly worth killing anyone for; to them, it would be what they considered Chump Change.

Note: No matter what condition the body is (I.E.) gunshot to the head /heart, only the Medical Examiner (M.E.) or the designated Emergency Medical Technician (EMT) can make the final determination that the victim is dead. Also, what is the cause of death is. This is protocol and is mandated by the Police Department as well as the D.A.'s office.

Now the Detectives have the official diagnosis of the homicide, even though it was obvious, now it's confirmed. They start their investigation by interviewing everyone in the building. The building is a walk-up, which is a large apartment house with many apartments in it. Every door is knocked on, and everyone is interviewed, but they come up empty. No one can supply any useful information. While another team reinterviews the owner of the grocery store where he bought the items. The owner remembers the little old guy who is a regular customer. As previously stated, he didn't seem like he was in distress or nervous. They would also try to get a timeline of when he left the grocery store. But he doesn't remember exactly what time he left. Did he leave alone, or was he with anyone? He answers no to both questions. They interview people on the street near the grocery store. They also interview people in the surrounding buildings, once again unable to gain any positive results. Did anyone see him on the street, at a store, or at a bank? Anything he did prior to being killed may aid in solving this mystery. But again, they are coming up with nothing; they can find no witnesses.

But with the stalker's life went on as usual, they would meet and roam the streets searching for a victim. It was just about a daily routine; however, it was not always the same group, some days there were more youths than on other days. Again, it was possibly because on some days one or two may not have wanted to get out of bed; it was not that they were remorseful or didn't want to be involved, just lazy, or maybe coming down from last night's high on drugs? But the others couldn't wait to get started in their search for victims. But when they didn't find a victim, as previously stated, they would find some other mischief to get into. Like maybe break into a car or a quick purse snatch, they were more than opportunists; you might say they were multitaskers. But that was small-time stuff to them; their real goal was the Push In Robbery, hoping to hit that jackpot as the way they were told "all these old people have money.

The building where this Homicide occurred was a walk-up building, but the ideal robbery would be one where the victim lived in a building with an elevator; this is what they preferred. They like the elevator one the best because having their point man on the elevator, they knew exactly what floor the vic was going to. Most of these elevators were old and installed maybe 60 to 75 years ago when the building was built. They were worn out, probably from making a million or so trips up and down. Even though they were maintained, it didn't make them any faster; it just kept them in good working order. In fact, some were quite slow. But what it came down to was that if the victim was old and weak and possibly had money, it didn't make a difference what kind of building it was.

If it were in a building with an elevator, the plan would be as follows.

As previously stated, one would get on the elevator with the (vic) and see what floor he/she was going to. While he is getting on the elevator, his cohorts will remain out of sight. They were waiting for a signal as to which floor the victim was going to. He would push the button for the vic and say loudly you are going to four, I am going to three. His cohorts then knew exactly which floor to go to. They, in turn, would then run up to that floor and wait at the threshold of the doorway on the victim's floor. If this was not possible, they would run up to each floor and wait in the threshold of the doorway of the floor for their co-conspirator to join them. This was because he was getting off the floor below the victim. Once he joined them, they would all run up one more flight and wait for the victim to arrive with the elevator. They rarely encountered anyone on the stairway, because most of the tenants were elderly, so walking upstairs was too difficult and stressful, and some were just too scared to walk upstairs for fear of getting mugged. So, the elevator was the perfect means of conveyance. Also, most of these robberies occurred at mid-morning, so there was very little traffic on the elevator, as opposed to late afternoon when people were coming home from work or shopping. The victim, now alone on the elevator, felt completely safe because he/she was alone. He/she would feel safe because of the threat, if it was in fact a threat, he got off the elevator. His/her threat was no threat at all; at least that's what the victim thought. The victim figured that possibly the person was visiting someone else in the building, or maybe even lived in the building. As most of these buildings were multi-racial. So, there was no fear or concern. The victim would walk to the apartment, not realizing what was about to occur. Not realizing the monstrous act that was about to be perpetrated on them. As they were elderly, they didn't walk fast; in fact, most would just shuffle along. When they got to their door, most had two, sometimes as many as three locks on the door. Taking his/her keys out, fumbling to unlock the door, gave the miscreants even more time to set up and attack. As previously described, this was their plan; they had it down to a science because of prior discussion and planning, and prior experience.

As soon as the apartment door opened, like a pack of hyenas attacking a wounded deer, they would attack. Immediately, they would run silently up to the victim, push him/her in, and immediately lock the door behind them. The victim never knew what happened; it just happened that quickly. Now, the beginning of their plan was being executed. They were safe to continue with their plan. This was a home invasion, later termed a push-in robbery. The victim, who was usually old and frail, would fall to the floor, as previously described. One would then immediately jump on the victim's back while another would cut a lamp cord or anything they would be able to bind them with. They would tie the victim's hands behind his/her back. Or sometimes they would even tie the victim who was face up with the hands in front of the body, and then one of them would sit on the victim while the others did their ransacking. Most times, they would gag the victim, so they weren't able to scream. They also would blindfold the victim, usually by covering the victim's eyes by laying a cloth of some kind over their face. But either way, the victim was never left alone; there was always someone guarding him/her. If one didn't sit on the victim, then he would just stand guard over the victim to make sure he/she remained quiet. The ransacking would start as soon as the victim was securely tied, which was within seconds of him being pushed in. They also searched his body for any valuables he may have had on him. The apartment search would be done methodically. They went through every drawer, cabinet, closet, and under the couch. In some cases, they even turned the couch over and cut the bottom of the cloth lining to see if there was anything hidden in there. This was a trick they apparently learned from drug dealers who sometimes hid their money or drugs in there. They looked under mattresses, anywhere, any place where someone may hide anything of value. They even went through books to see if the victim had any cash hidden in the books. This was done by holding the book upside down and thumbing through the pages to see if any currency fell out, as witnessed by a surviving victim. If they didn't get enough cash or jewelry, they would sometimes torture the victim to get him/her to talk. This was done to try to get him/ her to tell them where anything of value was hidden. They did this by punching/slapping the victim numerous times in the face. In one instance, one of the suspects threatened to stab the victim in the neck with a fork that he had gotten from the kitchen. This was done sometimes before the victim was gagged; there was never a rhyme or reason for who was treated more harshly than others. Possibly, they were higher on drugs than they were on their other Push Ins. Sometimes the torture worked, but most times it didn't. It didn't work because most of the people were poor elderly people living on nothing but Social Security and food stamps. If it was money or expensive jewelry they were looking for, they were targeting the wrong people. Because they had nothing to give up. Some of these victims were survivors of the Holocaust who were lucky to be alive, only to be tortured in their final years of life in America.

These incidents took place in the early to mid-seventies by this group. Although there were similar type robberies, this type was unique in that the victims were all in the same age range. They were, for the most part, in the same area, which was approximately one mile from each other. When the victim survived, it was eventually reported to the Police, usually through a 911 report. However, it was usually reported as a crime in the past, which it was. The reason it was considered in the past is that sometimes it would take hours, sometimes many hours, to loosen their bindings. In some cases, the report wasn't made until a day later. Because sometimes the victim would be unable to break free of his bonds. But was found by a neighbor who was unable to get in touch with the victim and checked in on him/her. Only to find the victim tied and gagged on the floor. You can just imagine the fear that went through their minds lying there helpless for several hours. Unable to even call out for help due to being gagged. So, by the time the victim called the Police, and the job was dispatched, it would be considered a past Robbery/ Burglary. When the Police received the assignment, there was no rushing through the streets to the scene, no sirens blaring, lights flashing; it was just a routine, as the police would call it, "radio run." It was just a regular, ordinary crime in the past, of which there were many during that period. When they arrived, it was a normal report of a past crime with a report to be taken, a UF 61, which is a report of a crime, which would be filled out by the uniformed officer on the scene. During this period, NYC was overburdened with senior citizen robberies. Precincts and Detective Units were overwhelmed with all kinds of cases. Cases meant paperwork, and lots of legwork doing canvases and interviews, which take time. Also, another reason why the Detective units were overwhelmed was that most of the Detective squads in New York City were working shorthanded. The reason, on July 1, 1975, as previously stated, the Police Department was forced to lay off 5000 cops. To help save the city, as hard as it was to do, it had to be done. Eventually, some of the officers came back within a year, but most of them didn't come back until 1979. So, between 1975 and 1979, other than the few previously furloughed officers who came back, there were no new hires. There was very little movement into the detective squad; the main reason was to keep the patrol force as strong as possible. For they do the bulk of the work. During this period, the department tightened its belt; they tried many ways to cut O.T. in any manner they could. One way was when an arrest was made on a day tour (8 am x 4 pm), when the (4 pm x 12 am) crew came on, the arrest was assigned to an officer on that tour. In theory, it worked fine. But it rarely worked. Because when the assigned officer went down to the D.A.'s office to draw a complaint up, the ADA would ask him, "What happened, officer?" The cop would usually say, "I don't know, they just told me to process this". I didn't make the actual arrest, so I really don't know what happened. Or they told me to say this is what happened. This was third-hand information; in some cases, it was considered "HearSay," which meant it was something told to you by a third party. So, most of the time, the cop would give a not-so-accurate version of what happened based on what he heard third-hand. This resulted in the A.D.A. marking the case 343. This means the case is being deferred. Deferring Prosecution of the case (D.P.) means the D.A.'s office is declining to prosecute, under the Criminal Procedure Law. This meant that at this time, they weren't proceeding with the prosecution of the arrest. But it left open the door that if more evidence or more information, other than what the cop told them, were developed and submitted, it would allow them to reopen the case and prosecute it. However, when the arrest involved a really serious incident, the D.A. had been known to call the precinct and tell them to get the arresting officer "back here now." This resulted in more overtime than would have happened to begin with. This procedure was instituted to save O.T., but it backfired; it just caused more O.T. Because the cop may be home already and had to come all the way back in from his home, the O.T. would start right from his home.

The Detective Bureau also did the same thing; again, this also resulted in one big mess. The Detective boss sometimes would ask the precinct desk officer from patrol if he/she could spare a uniformed cop to process an arrest. This also usually ended up with the same results. There were other times when the Detective Squads were so low on manpower that they would ask the precinct desk officer if he could spare a car to transport their prisoner to court. This was a courtesy that was always done. Also, for a short period of time, they even tried a pilot project where if a Detective was working alone, they would assign an Anti-Crime Cop who would fill in the squad for the day. (He was called, like the TV show back then, "Queen for a DAY"). (This was before the days when it was considered not to be gender correct to joke in this manner).

He caught no cases and did no investigating; he was just a body for the Detective so he could answer the phones for him and take messages. Also, if the Detective had to go out on a case, he wouldn't have to go alone. Even though most of the Detectives were good, hard-working Detectives they just didn't have the time and the manpower due to the shortage to do a thorough investigation. It was all about closing your cases; no Detective wanted to have a folder full of open cases. But the fact was that it was hard to make an arrest on a senior citizen robbery, since all the victims were elderly. Most of them couldn't ID or sometimes were just too afraid to ID. Even interviewing residents of the building was of no aid to the Detectives. Usually, when the crime was committed, it was done stealthily with no witnesses. Even though they may have been in the apartment for a couple of hours. No one knew there was a heinous crime taking place right in the victim's apartment, not even the next-door neighbor. Because they were smart enough to work quietly, and they kept the victim quiet. So, no one knew there was a violent robbery taking place right in their building. When they left, they were smart enough to walk out of the building separately so as not to arouse suspicion. When the suspects left the building, even if people saw them leave, they had no idea that two, three, maybe four were together and what they had just perpetrated. But possibly seeing three or four youths leaving the building at the same time, not usually a normal event, may have aroused some suspicion. However, with them leaving separately, it made it a lot easier for them to just walk away without anyone realizing what a monstrous act they had just committed. No one knew or suspected what a heinous crime they just perpetrated. So, for the most part, they left unnoticed. Also, most of these buildings, as well as the surrounding area, were a multi-racial neighborhood, so they were able to blend right in. As soon as they were well away from the building (crime scene), they would once again regroup. It was just a regular, everyday occurrence of people coming and going. This also added to the complication of getting a suspect identified. The fact that no one knew a crime had even been committed, at least not until an hour or even several hours later. Or in some cases, maybe even a day or two later. So, unfortunately, most people didn't even pay attention to who was leaving the building as they were completely unaware of what had just happened. So, with no witnesses, very little physical evidence, and no fingerprints found. (Either they wore gloves or did a thorough job of cleaning anywhere they may have left prints.) With the complainant unable to identify the suspects, the detective would eventually mark the case closed, with negative results (N/R). Whereas with a Homicide the case is never closed until a successful conclusion is reached. So, until then, it's put "on the back burner" until any new information or evidence is developed, and the case would come to life again.

Even though the Precinct Detective did the best he/she could do, sometimes they were just overwhelmed with cases. This just increased their workload. Wherever the crime was committed, that's what the Detective Squad got the case. Even though most cases were committed in the East Flatbush/Remsen Village section of Brooklyn, there were other similar robberies committed in other parts of Brooklyn. However, even though the crimes were spread out among different precincts, apparently in Brooklyn South, a pattern was developing. At first, it went unnoticed. One of the reasons it went unnoticed was that all the victims were elderly, and they didn't realize how they were set up. Another reason they gave was that the uniformed officer who took the report had very little information on how they were robbed. They simply did not realize that the person who was in the elevator with them was part of the wolf pack that attacked them. Or they were followed into the building, and the wolf pack walked up the stairs slowly behind them. So now this is down in the books as Homicide number one of the Push In pattern.

CHAPTER FOUR

HOMICIDE NUMBER TWO

On February 4, 1975, the stalkers committed their second Homicide. This was in a City Housing Project in the 73 precinct, Brownsville, Brooklyn, which was in the Brooklyn North Area of Brooklyn. This was just over the border of the 69 precinct, which was in the Brooklyn South Area. After a discussion between the Chiefs of Brooklyn North and Brooklyn South, it was decided that, even though it was in Brooklyn North, a decision was made to put the case into the pattern with the Brooklyn South Homicide. This was done because of their previous Push in homicide. Also, there were other push-ins in Brooklyn South that were not homicides but were still part of the pattern. The reason is that the manner of crime fits the Push In pattern in Brooklyn South, and the proximity was within one mile or so.

 The victim was a male, white, 86 years old, living alone. This push-in was in an elevator building, so the plan went as previously described, with one of them riding the elevator with the victim, as the others went up the stairs. The victim was apparently pushed in and was face up. He was tied with his hands in front of him, and a pillow was placed over his face so he couldn't see. This also stopped him from being able to breathe, which caused him to be asphyxiated and ultimately led to his death. Did someone intentionally hold the pillow tight to his face, or was it just placed there without being held? That is unknown currently. Either way, it wouldn't make any difference; this is what caused his death. The ransacking would proceed as previously described; when they were done, they would casually stroll out of the building. However, in this homicide, the perpetrator unknowingly gave the police their first tip. Apparently, they knew the victim was dead. After they left the scene, the ringleader, Ben (last name unknown at the time), bragged to some local kids by saying what we did today, "you will see on the news tonight". He then apparently told them what building it was and the apartment number of his braggadocios deed. Kids being kids, went to the apartment to see for themselves what would be on the news. After seeing the victim on the floor, tied and apparently dead, you would think they would flee the building and call the police. But they didn't; what they did do was tell other kids. Now they all came to see what this was all about. Some came as gawkers; others came and ransacked what was left of the apartment. There was no way of telling just how many kids were going in and out. Eventually, with all the traffic coming and going out of the apartment, the neighbors down the hall sensed something was wrong and called the police. They know no one lives there but an elderly man. By the time the police got there, the kids were gone, but the victim, DOA, was discovered, and the apartment was in a shambles. So now the usual starts with the notification to the Sergeant, the precinct Detectives, as well as the Homicide Squad. The EMS and the Crime Scene Unit are also notified. The EMT pronounced the victim DOA, and the Crime Scene Unit does its search. Once the body is pronounced dead, it can be removed to the morgue by the attendants in the morgue wagon. Once at the O.C.M.E., the Medical Examiner will perform an Autopsy to determine the exact cause of death.

The Detectives start by interviewing people who called, as well as other tenants of the building. Basically, the callers stated that they saw kids going in and out of the apartment and knew something was wrong. Because they knew the occupant of the apartment was an elderly man. There was no reason for young kids to go in and out. There were also many others in the building interviewed, but no one could identify anyone who entered the apartment. Saying they were just "a bunch of young kids". The only thing is now the whole building knows there was a Homicide and now everyone is in panic mode. Some people are so frightened that if they see kids in the lobby, they are afraid to enter it to get on the elevator and will not even attempt to walk up the stairs. They would wait until other people came and then enter with them. Apparently, feeling safe being with other people on the elevator, safety in numbers. These are people who lived in the area their whole life but were never afraid as they are now. Now that they know of this homicide, they feel it is far more dangerous living there than it ever was. Because these kids put a whole new outlook on their view of crime in their neighborhood. These kids were terrifying, so much so that many of the residents were afraid to even go out shopping and depended on neighbors to bring them groceries.

The building manager was also interviewed. He told the detectives that he had warned his workers not to go into certain areas alone. If you see kids hanging out in the building lobby, don't go in. He also stated that the victim confided in him once that he feared that he was going to be attacked. He also tells the Detectives that the victim had relatives, but they were afraid to visit him because of the crime in the area. He said he offered the victim a chance to move to another building, but for some unknown reason, he turned it down. He never said why. So once again, the detectives start with their investigation as previously described. The Detectives start interviewing some of the younger kids in the neighborhood, all of them denied they were in the apartment.

Eventually, they did find a couple of kids who they say they heard a guy named Ben say, "What we did today you will see on the news tonight". However, they all deny that they knew what his last name was or where he lived; they just knew of him from the area. They also denied that they were ever in the apartment. Was this a half-truth? Did they really know more about him? But we were too afraid to say so for fear of getting beaten up or maybe even killed by him or his crew or maybe even a member of his family.

As the saying in the Ghetto goes, "Stitches for Snitches who end up in Ditches," which is the code of the street in some neighborhoods. So, what it amounted to was that even these kids feared them. Were they loyal to them or just really scared of them? Either way, they offered no other information to the Detectives. But now the Detectives have another piece to the puzzle, another little bit of information. Possibly the first name of one of the killers, and more than likely, he is a local kid, most likely from Brownsville. Before computers, index cards were made out when they got a tip of some kind. So, another index card is made out and put into the case folder. The info would also be put on a DD5.

The fact that this is a city Housing Project, which is usually patrolled by a lone housing cop. Or sometimes it has no officer assigned to patrol it. The building is a quiet building, so the officer may be assigned to a much busier nearby housing project. This is the only building that is a dedicated building for Senior Citizens. So, it may have been one cop patrolling the area, or maybe no one on that day. However, once again, this was during the year of the Fiscal Crisis, and the Housing Police were also working shorthanded as they also felt the budget crunch. The Housing Police have their own Homicide Squad, which, even though it is a much smaller unit than the NYPD Homicide Squad, the Housing Detectives worked hand in hand with the NYPD. They try to pick a starting point where the old gentleman may have been followed from, but they are unable to find any. They check the local area stores; no one remembers seeing the old gent walking or shopping in the area. The theory was developed that maybe the stalkers, if they were from the neighborhood, knew the building was a Senior Citizen building. Possibly, they were just hanging out in the lobby or in front of the building, waiting for a victim. So once the victim came home and got on the elevator, they put their plan into action. Which has previously been described.

With the robbery/burglary taking place, but now Homicide number two has taken place. It is added to the Push In pattern, and there is more pressure on the Police to solve them.

CHAPTER FIVE

THE PATTERN

This is the second Homicide in two months where the victim is elderly and lives alone. He is found tied and smothered with a pillow over his face in his own apartment. He is also still wearing his outer garments, which is obvious because he was pushed in as soon as he opened the door. Even though it is two different boroughs (Brooklyn North/Brooklyn South), it had all the ear markings of the same group of thugs. The similarities were just too close to dismiss as two random killings. If this is the case, that it is two Homicides that are committed by the same group, they would now be considered serial killers. So, as previously stated, it was decided that this Homicide would be put into the pattern that is being handled by the Brooklyn South Homicide Squad. Being the first Homicide occurred in Brooklyn South, and one of the many other push-ins in the Brooklyn South area.

There is a Task Force formed consisting of one Lieutenant, one Sergeant, and eight Detectives. They also set up a 24-hour tip hotline seeking any information about these cases. Word is spreading regarding this homicide, as well as fear. It wasn't long after that the tips started coming in. It was just in bits and pieces, a first name, a Knick name. Possibly lived on a certain street. One may possibly live at this address. Bad groups of kids hang out here. Bad kids just terrorize the neighborhood. All little tips, but also all anonymous. Because these neighborhood people were obviously terrified of these kids. These were people, most of whom lived here all their lives, and had no place to go. So, this is why they made their reports anonymously for fear of retaliation. Each time a tip came in, it was recorded on an index card (before computers), and the cards were then put into the case folder. It was all bits and pieces, not enough to make an arrest, but enough to point the detectives in the right direction and have some possible suspects. These task force detectives would work exclusively on these two homicides. The detectives theorized it was all young kids because experienced older burglars would not rip the apartments apart. They would take what they wanted and leave, get in and out quickly. But what also made any gathering of evidence harder was the fact that several other younger kids had gone to the crime scene and trampled over it. Some were as young as 12–13-year-olds, and it was unlikely that they were ever fingerprinted. Also, the fact that young children's prints do not last long because their sweat glands are not fully developed. Even if they left fingerprints, they would most likely not be on file because they weren't fingerprinted at that age unless it was for a really serious crime, like murder, etc. If there was any evidence that may have helped, it was trashed away by these younger thugs. These younger kids invading this building made the people who lived there even more frightening knowing they went into the apartment while the victim was lying on the floor dead, with no regard; they had no respect for the dead person. They just continued thrashing the apartment. The thinking was amongst these older residents, who will be next? Could I be next? Will my next-door neighbor be next? This is what went through their minds; it was just a frightening way to live life for them. Especially since most were old and lived there most of their lives and had nowhere else to go, because most were just too poor to move.

THE MEDICAL EXAMINER'S DIAGNOSIS

Victim: Julius Bernstein M/W/ 86 years old

Cause of death: ASPHYIXATION

Manner of death: HOMICIDE

The autopsy reveals that the cause of death was asphyxiation. The victim was found face up with his hands tied in front of him, with a pillow on his face. This restricted the victim's ability to breathe, which ultimately caused his death. The M.E. was able to provide the Detectives with a timeline for the death, which had previously been described in Homicide number one. This, too, was apparently within thirty-six hours. Once again, it gave the Detectives a starting point for their investigation. Again, they start backtracking, but this time they cannot find a starting point where he was last. They check the local stores; they even check the local Synagogue, but they also come up empty. This was apparently an elderly man walking alone, like he did many days. As it was his norm, he did not realize that he was being stalked. The people in the neighborhood did not really pay attention to him walking by himself. It was just a normal sight of an elderly person walking alone. The Detectives also feel there is a possibility that maybe he wasn't even stalked. The miscreants may have been hanging out around the building and saw an easy mark. So, they put their plan into action and followed him onto the elevator. As previously stated, they were opportunists.

THE INVESTIGATION CONTINUES

The Detectives reinterviewed victims of other push-ins, hoping to get some information to aid them in the Homicide investigation. But because they were hit from behind and were face down, and they were blind folded, not only did they not see their faces, but also in some cases they didn't even know how many there were. They knew it was more than one by one holding him/her, and the other tying the victim up. Also, by the movement in the apartment, they could tell it was more than one, but did not know exactly how many. It soon appeared that it was basically the same M.O. Although the victim did not know just how many suspects there were. After each victim was interviewed and their statements were taken, the statements were then analyzed by the pattern unit and Homicide as well as Squad detectives. It was obvious from the statements given that they were just about the same. They came up the elevator, or walked up the stairs after shopping, or came from their usual walk. When they got on the elevator, there was a young male who got on the elevator with them, but he got off at the floor below. He was a gentleman, even pushing the button for their floor. Or they didn't realize they were closely followed if they were walking up the stairs. The next thing you know is when they opened their door, without realizing it, they were about to be pushed into their apartment. They had no idea where this band of marauders came from. It was like a swarm of bees appeared out of nowhere, immediately attacking them. They never saw them, but once the door was open, they were immediately pushed in, tied, gagged, and blind folded, all within a minute or so.

The NYPD had a pattern unit in each Borough. Brooklyn South Detectives had such a unit, with a Detective assigned to it. This assigned detective would peruse all the cases from the precincts in Brooklyn South to see if there were any similarities that would form a pattern. They took notice of several Home Invasions: push-in robberies in the Brooklyn South area, specifically East Flatbush/Remsen Village. They took note of where all the robberies were happening, inside or outside; if it was inside, what type of building it was. The location of where the robbery took place, I.E. the lobby, stairway, hallway, elevator, or in the apartment itself. Also, what time of day, what day of the week, if the victim was just coming home, where was the victim coming from? They would also try to get them whenever possible to give them a description of the suspects. This was usually met with negative results. In some cases, the victims could not even tell what color or ethnic background the suspects were. They were being hit from behind and were face down, and in most cases, they were being gagged as well as blind folded and tied up. This also contributed to making it harder to get a good description of the suspects, or even how many there were.

THEY STRIKE AGAIN

On about February 26, 1975, the stalkers struck again, this time it was a 77-year-old woman, Ida Teitelbaum. Apparently, the stalkers followed her home to her building, which was a walk-up in the Remsen Village neighborhood. As soon as she opened her door, the usual happened, she was pushed in. However, in this case, for no apparent reason, she was severely beaten. She was being beaten so badly that she lost consciousness and fell to the floor. When she woke up, they were gone, so she immediately called the Police, as well as EMS. She was taken to the hospital because her eye was badly damaged, so much so that it couldn't be saved, and she lost sight in it. The flurry of punches was apparently coming so hard and fast that she wasn't even able to scream. When questioned by the Detectives she was understandably shaken up. So shaken that she didn't know how many there were, because as soon as she opened the door, the assault started. The only thing she could tell them there was more than one person.

When the first uniformed cops arrived, they immediately called for the patrol Sergeant and EMS. The Sergeant called for the Crime Scene Unit, as well as the Precinct Detectives and the Homicide Task Force. The Task Force was called, even though it was not a Homicide; the M.O. was the same pattern as the Push In Homicides. Once the victim was interviewed, the detectives were analyzing all the information, and once again, the similarities were there. This led to this case also being put into the pattern case. However, after interviewing the victim, the detectives couldn't determine if she resisted or if they beat her to try to get her to tell them where she hid her valuables. She was too injured, as well as confused and disoriented, to know exactly what happened. Days later, she was re-interviewed, but she still couldn't add or remember anything else. So more than likely, they struck again, and once again, leaving no evidence behind. With another victim who could not aid the police in any manner. Just another victim of a brutal assault for no apparent reason. So, this incident is added to the list of unsolved push-ins that are attributed to this group of stalkers (skells).

A CHANGE UP

With most of the Robberies/Burglaries happening in apartment houses, one day they apparently deviated from their normal routine. As previously stated, they were also opportunistic, as well as multitaskers. Early one morning at the start of their journey, sometime between the hours of 9:00 and 9:30 am, not far from Brownsville. Near the border of East Flatbush and the Remsen Village section, the stalkers observed an elderly gentleman pulling out of the driveway in the rear of his one-family home. Being that they were opportunists, among other things, they figured this would be an easy score. Knowing the male just left the house. They broke into the house by entering through a rear window on the second floor after boosting themselves up on a garbage pail and shimming up some electrical conduit. Being that it was in the rear of the house and in the back yard/ driveway, it was out of public view. Apparently, other thieves used this manner of entry many times, knowing people rarely observe their backyards, and it is not visible from or to the street. They then entered through an unlocked window, as it was above street level; the window was apparently left unlocked. The average homeowner was so lackadaisical, never dreaming that someone would enter in this manner. Especially since it was one story above the ground. Once inside, roaming around the house, they eventually wound up in the bedroom, where the wife of the gentleman who had just left, and she was still asleep. They immediately woke her up and tied, gagged, and blind folded her. They told her they saw her husband leave, but asked if there was anyone else in the house. She used her head and said yes, my son is asleep downstairs, which was a total lie. It was a lie because there was nothing but a garage underneath that her husband just pulled the car out of. They then told her to be quiet, and you and your son won't get hurt. They then started ransacking the room as one of them sat on her. After a few minutes, she told him with a muffled voice, "If you don't get off me, you will have a dead woman on your hands because I can't breathe". Apparently, the miscreant, for whatever reason, had compassion and brains, and he obliged her and got off her. But he kept her blindfold and the gag in place. The blindfold sometimes would be just a towel or any kind of cloth, laid over their eyes so they couldn't see. He then sat next to her. In doing so, he noticed she had a couple of diamond rings on her fingers that had been overlooked before. He tried taking them off, but couldn't as they had been on for years, as she stated through her gag, "I can't even get them off." He then told one of his coconspirators to go to the kitchen to get a pot of warm water and some soap. He then untied her hands with a warning not to try anything now that her hands were untied. He then patiently sat there as he made her keep soaking her hand in the soapy warm water. Eventually, he was successful and was able to slip the rings off. As soon as he got the rings off, he immediately re-tied her. His partners in crime also found other jewelry as well as some cash that she told them where she had hidden before being gagged. As they methodically searched the house, she had a bookcase containing several books. They held up each book upside down and thumbed through the pages to see if any cash fell out. She observed this for a second when her blind fold slipped down as he was untying her hands. After an hour or so, as quickly as they appeared, that's as quickly as they disappeared. Apparently, walking right out the front door separately, which again went unnoticed by any neighbors. Once they left, she was able to free herself and call the Police. When the Uniformed Police arrived, they immediately called the Patrol Sergeant, as well as the Detectives and Anti-Crime, who arrived with them. They also called the Homicide Squad Task Force . There were apparently three or four youths who had tied her up and searched the house. They could possibly fit the pattern. The Crime Scene Unit was also notified. When they arrived, they did their usual investigation.

The detectives who had arrived tried to glean as much info out of her as possible. However, she said she couldn't identify them other than they were young boys, there were at least three or maybe even four, maybe 16 to 18 years of age. They were basically all dressed alike. She also said they really weren't bad boys, as they didn't harm her in any way, especially when she asked him to get off her, and he complied. The feeling by the Detectives was that there was no need to hurt or torture her. Given the fact that she was cooperative and told them where some money was hidden, they made a really nice score. Besides, the cash as well as the jewelry from her hands, and some they found in her jewelry box. So, after interviewing her, the detectives felt this, too, would be added to the pattern case. The reason being there were three, maybe four of them, they tied her up, blindfolded her, gagged her, and methodically searched her house. The only difference was that they really didn't hurt her, and it was a private house.

However, she did add one fact: she stated she was glad her husband had just left because he was a supervisor in the U.S. Customs Agency. She further stated he was armed, and if he was home, who knows what could have happened. So maybe it was their good luck all the way around that he just left for work, or maybe his good luck? Because there were possibly four, they may have overpowered him before he could get to his gun, and they got it first. She also stated that her husband had just turned sixty-five, and was considering retiring and moving to a senior development in N.J. This was the straw that broke the camel's back; they were going.

Now that a pattern was already established within the Brooklyn South area, this one would also be added in. After analyzing all the facts due to the similarities, there were three or four suspects, and they tied the victim up/gagged and blind folded her. They then methodically searched the house. The only difference was that they really didn't hurt her, and the fact that it was a private house and not an apartment house. The Detectives theorized that the fact that they made a nice score probably saved her from a beating. The Robbery/Burglary fit the pattern of the push-ins, other than the fact that this was in a private house. Once again, the Crime Scene Detectives found no fingerprints; either they wore gloves or wiped clean everything they touched. So, each time there was a Push In Robbery in one of the precincts in Brooklyn South, or Brooklyn North, the Patrol Borough office, as well as the Detective Borough, had to be notified by the precinct of occurrence. This way, the Police Department knew exactly how many there were and where these Robberies/Burglaries were occurring. Also, what the method was and if it should be added to the pattern. The department took the usual steps in trying to combat this crime. They posted the pattern on the precinct crime bulletin board so the precinct cops, as well as the Anti-Crime cops, could see where and what was happening. They also flooded the area with extra cops and created special posts they called Robbery Posts. At times, these posts were filled by officers who were ordered to work overtime. This was done by officers who were drawn from other precincts to augment the precinct officers. With all this extra manpower, the push-ins continued, as previously noted, all were in a building and off the street, out of the view of the public. Being these miscreants (skells) moved so fast that before the victims even knew what hit them, they were tied and gagged. If they weren't gagged, one guy just sat on the victim, who was threatened with injury if they tried to scream. But for the most part, they were gagged. As previously stated, most of the time it would be hours, or even a day or two, before a crime was even reported. So, the suspects were long gone from the area. Even if there was a cop on the local foot post, they would walk right past him with the thought that was possibly in their mind, "screw you," you don't know what we just did. In some cases, the crime was not even reported; either the victim was too scared, or the attitude was, why report it? You're not going to get my property/money back. Or if I report it and the Police make an arrest, and I press charges, the suspect or his friends would come back and hurt me, maybe even kill me.

When a case was reported, it was put on the Police Radio as a crime in the past, so there was no urgent rush to get there. No lights flashing, no sirens blasting, no adrenaline or hearts pumping, just the cop driving in a normal manner to take a report. Whereas if it came over as a crime in progress, it was a completely different story; then all the stops get pulled out, and you go as quickly as you can to get there. Usually, flashing lights and sirens are blasting. But as previously stated, these crimes were in the past. Now that the cases against the elderly were increasing, it was soon noticed that other parts of the city had similar problems with elderly victims. As the cases came in and the elderly victims were interviewed in Brooklyn South, they basically all gave the same statements previously noted.

"I took the elevator up to my floor. There was a young man on the elevator with me, but he got off the elevator before mine. He was a nice young man who even pushed the button for my floor. He got off the floor before mine." I was alone on the elevator. Never realizing that the skell who got off was one of the marauders. "If it was a walkup, "I was walking up the stairs by myself, never realizing they were being followed up the stairs close behind by the stalkers. It didn't take long for the Detective to figure out how this pattern worked. Once it was established, it was elementary. They knew they were dealing with a vicious group of individuals who had no respect for the elderly and no respect for human life in general. Picking on the weakest people, the elderly. It made no difference whether it was a male or a female. The older they were, the more vulnerable they were; in fact, it made it easier to deal with them, the less chance that they would fight back. The pattern was the same; the group would follow the victim to his/her building, one would get on the elevator, or if it was a walkup, they would follow him/her up the stairs. In one of the cases, the victim only went up one flight to the 2nd floor. The point man went to the opposite end of the hallway and fumbled at a door, pretending to reach for his keys. His cohorts just waited in the threshold of the doorway until the victim opened the door. Then the usual happened: the victim opened the door to the apartment and was pushed in, and the marauding began. It was also noted that in some of the cases, the victims were beaten as well as tortured; this was done apparently to try to get them to give up any information where they may have valuables hidden.

In another one of the cases, they beat up an 87-year-old man and his 73-year-old nephew, who was living with him. Apparently, they followed the 73-year-old home from shopping when he entered his apartment, however/ they didn't realize he was living with his 87-year-old uncle. Possibly one of them, more than likely the 73-year-old, resisted, so they used force against them. They beat the two of them so badly that they had to be hospitalized. But again, the victims were unable to identify anyone, and once again, it was within the apartment of the victims. So, it would be another case added to this crime wave, another one to add to the mystery list.

Now the pattern was complete as far as the M.O. went. All the detectives needed now was a break in the case, some information received, or an arrest made, even if it was made by a uniformed officer. Even though tips were coming in from the public, it was just not enough to break the case wide open. Hoping to identify the mysterious Ben before they did another homicide. Maybe they would get some information from an informant. Or maybe someone arrested for something else wanted to get him/herself off the hook by giving whatever info they had. As far as on a precinct level, each precinct's Crime Analysis person was given a copy of the pattern. It was their job to pick out any similar robberies/burglaries that would fit the pattern. They would then immediately notify the pattern unit.

Particularly in the Brooklyn South area, the Patrol Officers were notified, as well as the precinct Anti-Crime units. The Street Crime Unit was also notified and sent to work in the area. The additional officers on the Robbery overtime post (O.T.) were also apprised of the pattern. But even with all this effort being put into it, there were still no positive results. As previously stated, the fact that these occurrences were off the street and not visible to the patrol units, the anti-crime units, or the public made it difficult to make an arrest. Compounding this was the fact that the victims could not identify their assailants, and at times weren't even sure of how many there were. The Chief of the borough was aware of the situation and gave the investigating units all the tools that were needed to put an end to this terrorizing crime wave. This includes the extra manpower in the form of overtime (O.T.) robbery post. Also, as part of the investigation, the Crime Scene Unit was called to every scene that had the possibility that it might be connected to the pattern. Anything that may be connected to their M.O., if it was in East Flatbush, Remsen Village, Brownsville, or Canarsie. Which hopefully would lead to an identification of the miscreants (skells). But as previously noted, apparently the suspects were smart enough to wear gloves or wipe the area clean so prints were never found. If they weren't wearing gloves, then they did a good job of wiping down everything they touched. Because the crime scene detectives were experts at finding prints, sometimes in places where you least expect to find them. But so far, they have had no luck. Pull out all the stops to end it. This was the order from the Boro Commander. This was also the sentiment of the Chief of Detectives, who formed the Task Force and made sure these cases were given special attention. The Borough Commander, as well as the Chief of Detectives, wanted an end to this crime wave before there was another Homicide. For this crime wave went all the way to the Police Commissioner's office, so it had to be stopped. The press had gotten some info on this crime wave and wrote articles in the local newspapers, which also added to the fear in the neighborhood. In cases like this, once it hits the news, it's usually protocol that the Police Department must let the public know that the problem is being addressed. This was done by holding a press conference that was usually held to assure the public that the situation was being addressed. Because once it hit the newspaper, the community knew, and when the community knew, there would be pressure from various groups in the neighborhood. The Police Commissioner or Chief of Dept would be forced to answer many questions from the press. One of the questions would be the obvious "Is this part of a pattern?" This would have to be addressed carefully so it would not alarm the public. For obvious reasons, the department did not want to create fear in the neighborhood. Especially in the elderly Jewish Community as well as the community in general. Although they kept it out of the press for as much as possible, fear was already spreading in the neighborhood. Victims of past Push Ins told their neighbors, who then told their neighbors. Soon, word was spreading in the community, and many people in the immediate area heard or knew of what was happening. Fortunately, most of the elderly didn't roam too far from home, so they didn't know if one happened a mile away. The only problem was the fact that detectives were doing canvases in the buildings, which contributed to the fact that the word was spreading of a serious crime being committed right in their own neighborhood. No matter how hard the Police Department tried to keep it quiet, they could not stop the word of mouth by the residents of the neighborhood, or its victims. But at the same time, anonymous tips were still coming in, although each one was not enough to run out and make an arrest; each one was put on an index card and into the case folder. As previously stated, it was just bits and pieces, but they were all pointing in the same direction. As the tips were coming in from long-time residents of the community, people who knew who the bad kids were, as well as from the good ones. So, they were just giving whatever info they had on this small group of miscreants (Skells) and not just all the kids. But as usual, it was always anonymous. More than likely, these anonymous informants knew more but were too scared to divulge any more information. Afterall, they lived right in the neighborhood and were concerned about themselves becoming victims. Because these kids respected no one.

CHAPTER SIX

HOMICIDE NUMBER THREE

There were many street robberies during this period, and there were also many residential Burglaries but again, most of them were in the daytime when there was no one home. It was possible they took part in these other crimes because, as noted, they were opportunists. But these cases did not fit into the pattern; they were just your normal, everyday type of crimes. It was the push-in-residence type robbery that the Task Force Detectives were interested in; all other robberies and burglaries would be handled by the precinct detectives. There were many arrests made for street robberies as well as the burglaries by the precinct Anti-Crime Cops, but apparently, they were not connected to the Day Stalkers. (Or so they thought at the time.) In all the arrests, not one arrested person supplied any information regarding the Day Stalkers when they were debriefed by the Task Force detectives. So, it was just a waiting game for the Task Force.

IT HAPPENED AGAIN

THEY STRIKE AGAIN

However, on March 24, 1975, the worst fear finally happened to the department that could have happened, did happen. Once again, there was no treating the victim for any injuries, the reason being that the victim was dead. The victim was a male, 71 years of age, who was, like many others, alone at the time. Apparently, the Day Stalkers struck again. The police department officials, all the way up through the chain of command, from the Precinct C.O. to the Borough Commander, to Chief of Patrol, the Chief of Department, right to the Police Commissioner, were notified of this other atrocity, which was the one thing they feared might happen, and unfortunately, now it did. They were hoping an arrest would be made before this new homicide, which would stop this terrorizing crime wave. They wanted it to stop before something like this happened. But apparently it wasn't to be. Another victim was found dead. This was also in a walk-up apartment house in Remsen Village. Where the victim was apparently followed home and up the stairs and entered a neighbor's apartment. However, the Detectives were not sure if he was pushed in or if the lock on the door was compromised. In any event, they made entry to the apartment he was in. Once again, he was still fully clothed. He was discovered when the elderly person who resided in the apartment came home. She enters the apartment only to find the victim's lifeless body on the floor, all trussed up. Apparently, they had a close friendship where they shared the apartment together. She had gone out shopping, and when she came home, she tried the door and discovered that it was unlocked. Thinking he must have forgotten to lock the door. She casually walks in. As soon as she walked in, right there on the floor in the vestibule was a terrifying sight, the body of her neighbor/good friend, tied up and apparently dead. Horrified at this sight, she let out a scream and ran to her neighbor's apartment and immediately called the Police.

Once the first Uniformed Police arrived, they followed protocol, and they notified the precinct Sergeant as well as the EMS. They also asked for the precinct Detectives to respond. The Task Force Detectives are also notified to respond, as well as the Crime Scene Detectives. The EMS (Emergency Medical Service), EMT (Emergency Medical Technician), examined the body and pronounced the victim dead. (As previously stated, it is Police Department policy that no matter what condition the body is in, only an EMT (Technician) or the (M.E) Medical Examiner can make the official pronouncement of death.) Even though the victim is apparently dead, the police still need the official pronouncement from the EMT on the scene. The Crime Scene Detectives start searching and documenting the scene as soon as they arrive on the scene. Once the victim has been pronounced the body is removed. It is transported by the morgue wagon by morgue personnel. It is brought to the O.C.M.E., where the M.E. will perform a routine Autopsy to determine the exact cause of death. The Crime Scene Detectives will not leave until their work is completed. In addition to taking photos of the body and dusting the crime scene for fingerprints, they also take written notes. These notes will include not only the position and condition of the body but also the condition of the crime scene itself (apt.) The photos and notes are taken to preserve the crime scene for presentation in a court proceeding if there is ever an arrest made. They will be entered as evidence to be seen by the judge and jury. This will be done in the event of a trial. The notes noting the condition of the apartment will also be entered into evidence. However, once again, there were no fingerprints found; either they wore gloves or took the time to wipe everything down.

As previously noted, this was before the advent of DNA, which wasn't perfected until sometime in the mid-eighties, but this was 1975, so it was still on the drawing board. With DNA, any dropping of skin cells, strands of hair, any form of body liquid i.E. Blood, Urine, Sweat, may lead to an ID. This DNA evidence is put into a national DNA Database (Kodis) for future reference. If there is a filing of DNA from a previous crime where DNA was recovered, and they have a match with the current recovery, and if a person has been identified, then they will have the felon's name and previous history. But if there is no match, it will be put on file in the database. Hopefully someone will get arrested for another crime and his DNA will match the DNA on file that was left at the previous crime scene that is on file. This will help in identifying him/her and tying him/her to the previously unsolved crime. This may occur many years later, provided the DNA was preserved. The DNA can tell if it's a female or male, and usually what ethnic group it belongs to. The fact is that not one of these pieces of evidence may reveal anything to the naked eye. It would have to be developed in the lab of the M.E. office that specializes in developing and preserving DNA evidence. DNA that is recovered at a crime scene will always be sent to the

O.C.M.E. section that specializes in DNA Identification. The scientific development that has been perfected over the years will lead to a suspect sometimes with the odds as much as a billion to one. That means that the chances of having a person with the same DNA would be one in a billion. Many times, in the event of a homicide, the victim's body will yield enough evidence to tell the story of what occurred. This will be in the form of DNA from the suspect on the victim's body to identify him/her as the perpetrator of this crime. Enabling the Police to make an arrest if the suspect's DNA is in the DATABASE and has been previously identified. So, the victim of the homicide has given the Police the evidence that no other person has given them. The body tells the tale without saying a word. But during this time, as previously stated, DNA was not perfected; it was still on the drawing board, it was still a scientific dream.

The Patrol Sergeant's duty on the scene is to make out an Unusual Occurrence report (also known as a U.O.) This report through channels goes all the way through channels to the Chief of Patrol, as well as the Chief of Department, and eventually the Police Commissioner's office. The U.O. must describe as best it can what type of incident has occurred. He also must make sure the uniformed officers safeguard the scene for the detectives.

The detectives also make out their own U.O. that goes to the Detective Division, through the chain of command to the Chief of Detectives' office. The case is assigned to the Homicide Squad T.F., as homicide number three of the Push

In pattern. This homicide was in East Flatbush/Remsen Village, also the confines of the 69th precinct. The Homicide T.F. Detective catches the case, or in police jargon (the squeal), The Task Force will work on this, along with the other two Push Ins cases, because of the similarities. Back in the day, as the Detectives in the Brooklyn North Homicide Squad would say, "We Speak for the Dead". Or the Twelfth Division Homicide detectives would also have the saying "Our Day Begins When Your Life Ends". Whichever you choose, it means one thing: we have a job to do. The Task Force (T.F.) has no time restrictions as they are investigating this case exclusively, as part of the pattern. However, as history has shown, the first 48 hours are crucial to solving a homicide; the more time that goes by, the harder it is to solve. The colder the case gets, the harder it is to get that needed break. Just that one break, to open the door for them to bring the case to a successful conclusion.

If this were a normal homicide, the detective would have 3 sets of tours to work on it. If it is not solved in this period, he would go back on his regular schedule and assist other teammates with their cases while working on his in-between. However, in this case, it's part of the push-in pattern, so the Task Force investigates this case with no time restriction. The Homicide T.F. conferred regularly with the precinct Detectives, as well as the precinct Squad boss, be it a Lieutenant (Lt.) or a Sergeant (Sgt.), to inform them of the progress of the case. They also let the precinct Commanding Officer know the progression of how the case is going. The reason is that it lets them know what is going on in their precinct. This is done so that the Commanding Officer (C.O.) doesn't get blindsided at a meeting with members of the community, or a member of the media, or a higher-up in the Police Department. If the question arises, he will have the proper information for them.

As protocol, each time any detective did any work on the case, they would prepare a DD 5 (Detective Division 5), which was a follow-up report to document what work was performed. Whether it was a visit back to the scene or an interview with a witness or locating witnesses, the DD5 had to be prepared. These forms would be added to the original case folder. This was done so that each T.F. Detective knew what steps were taken when any other detectives did any work on this case. So, this would avoid a duplication of work. Even though the detectives were all highly trained and seasoned detectives, the case was still basically at a standstill. This was because there were no witnesses and no physical evidence to tie anyone to the scene.

Another part of the investigation was to also interview other victims of similar types of crimes. Even though they were previously interviewed, they would be re-interviewed in hopes that something might jog their memory. But these interviews yielded no additional information, as most of the victims could not add anything that would be considered useful. As always, they would also interview people arrested for any serious crime, hoping to come up with some kind of information to aid in this case; they are called de-briefings. After many de-briefings, they were no closer than they were on day one. They were hoping to "catch a break," as the saying goes. However, they also kept the case out of the news as much as possible to prevent fear from taking over in the Jewish as well as the local community. But as previously stated, no matter how hard they tried to keep it out of the news, nothing was able to stop the word of mouth from the neighbors. You can't keep a homicide in a large apartment house quiet with all the uniform police, detectives, crime scene detectives, as well as EMS units coming and going on to the scene all day long. Also, the mere fact that the detectives were doing a door-to-door canvas of the building, trying to locate any witnesses, made it impossible to keep it quiet.

THE M.E. DIAGNOSIS

Victim: Abraham Rosencrantz M/W/71

Cause of Death: Asphyxiation

Manner of Death: Homicide

The Crime Scene Detectives made note that there was a garment lodged in the victim's mouth. As previously stated, no matter how obvious the cause of death appears to be, the M.E. makes the final determination as to the cause of death. The M.E. diagnosis will be the official cause of death.

The M.E. disclosed that the garment that was lodged in the victim's throat was his own Yarmulke. A yarmulke is a religious article that some people may call a skull cap. It is worn by a religious Jewish person to show his devotion to GOD. But in this case, the Yarmulke was the religious article that was the instrument that caused his death. So, even though some people call it a skull cap while others call it a Yarmulke, no matter which you choose, it was the instrument of his death.

The M.E., as previously stated, can also give the Detectives a timeline on approximately how long ago the crime was committed. Again, this is done by the body; if the body were going into a Rigor Mortis State, the body usually stiffens up. This happens when the heart stops, and the muscle cells are deprived of O2; the body then starts to stiffen. Rigor Mortis sets in usually about 12 hours after death and will remain stiff. This will be for 36 hours. So, they can basically get a general timeline when the Homicide was committed. If the body was not stiff yet, then presumably the Homicide happened less than 12 hours ago. If it were stiff, it would be more than 12 hours; it would remain stiff until 36 hours have passed. Once the 36 hours passed, as previously stated, the body would then soften up and go into a relaxed state, so to speak. The body would then start to deteriorate and decay, and give off a noxious odor.

It is now established that Asphyxiation In this case was due to the victim being gagged. Apparently, the culprits stuffed his own Yarmulke in the victim's mouth. This caused him not to be able to breathe, thereby causing the victim to expire. Did they not see him struggling, wiggling, trying to breathe? All one had to do was pull the gag out of his mouth, and he may have lived, if he didn't die of fright. But obviously, they were too cruel and calloused to pull it out. To them, apparently, it made no difference if the victim lived or died; it looked more like they wanted him to die. The Detectives also noted that in many other cases, the victims were gagged in one manner or another.

However, if the gag was stuffed in his/her mouth, and apparently if it was not far enough down the victim's throat, the victim was able to spit it out. This occurred after the culprits left the scene. Which led to the fact that, in some cases, they didn't care if the victim lived or died. In this case, they left with the victim still gagged, which could have been removed as they were leaving. But more than likely, the victim died while they were doing their marauding, as it would only take 3-4, possibly 5 minutes to go without air for the victim to die. So, pulling the gag out wouldn't have saved his life at this point. There were some Detectives who speculated that possibly drugs played a part, maybe some days they were more strung out, or maybe higher than on other days. This may be the reason why some were viciously attacked, and others weren't. That theory was never proven or disproven. So, the similarities were there in all three Homicides the victims were tied and gagged, in one manner or another. They were all still fully clothed, which included their outer garments. This led to the fact that they had just entered their apartment and obviously pushed in as they entered. It happened before they even had a chance to take off their outer garments. The gagging is what caused them to choke and eventually die by not being able to breathe. This was another life lost, for no reason. It was not possible that in all three Homicides they did not notice the victim's body movements, wiggling, struggling, trying to breathe. Did they not hear him gasping for air, possibly, but not probably. All they had to do was clear the victim's air passage by removing the gag, and the victim might have lived. But either way, they apparently did not care; they continued with the Robbery/Burglary, apparently ignoring the gasping victim. All the while, he is lying on the floor with his life slipping away. The possibility that the victim choked to death after they left is highly unlikely, given the fact that they were there for a while. It was more than likely that he died while they were committing their heinous act. It probably would only take a few minutes, 5 tops, for the victim to choke to death. But no matter how long the time was, with all their greed and callousness, they continued with the Robbery/Burglary. Most likely never even checking on the victim, and more than likely did not even care that the victim could die. This was even true because usually there was someone standing guard over the victim. Was it an intentional Homicide or was it just an accidental death? When you stuff something down a person's throat to the point where they can't breathe or spit it out, it's no accident. But obviously, they did not care either way that the victim's life was slipping away. There was also the fact that they knew the previous victim passed away; it was more than likely an intentional homicide. Because any reasonable person seeing the victim gasping would have pulled the gag from his mouth. This shows just how callous and cruel they were.

Eventually, when they were done with their marauding, they casually strolled out of the apartment with their illegal goods, which were nothing more in this case than a cheap, small jewelry box. Their total haul was less than fifty dollars. Their mission was completed for the day.

Leaving behind a helpless, innocent victim, not caring if he was alive or dead. A victim who just started the day like any normal day, but ended up dead in the most heinous way. Because of the greed of some ruthless skells who were looking for some easy money. Not by going out and working for it as any normal person would do. But by their actions, they showed they weren't normal, by any stretch of the imagination. They showed that they were just vicious thugs with no regard for the elderly or human life.

CHAPTER SEVEN

THE FOLLOW-UP HOMICIDE #3

So now, with the cause of death officially established, even though it was already being handled as a Homicide once again, the Police Department had an official cause of death. The T.F. Homicide Detective, who caught the case along with his team, does a canvas of the building. The usual, knocking on all the apartments in the building, hoping to find someone who saw something or maybe heard something. Looking for any bit of information that could help. Did anyone hear anything? Did anyone see any suspicious person hanging around, entering, or leaving the building? They also canvassed outside the building, asking people who lived nearby, who may be walking by, coming or going to work or shopping. Also asking, does anyone know a kid named Ben from the area? Unfortunately, all of this was met with negative results. As previously noted, these marauders worked extremely quietly not to arouse anyone. Knowing that any noise being made, like a victim screaming or furniture being knocked over, may lead a neighbor to dial 911. This also included leaving the crime scene, where they casually strolled out the door extremely quietly, not alerting anyone to the monstrous act they had just committed.

Once again, as part of their investigation, the Detectives started checking with other Detective squads for similar type crimes. If so, was there any arrest or any other information that would aid in this case? As usual, they would also interview people arrested for any serious type of felony, hoping to get some kind of lead or information regarding this crime. They would also reach out to the streets, meaning informants. They also kept the Anti - Crime-Cops informed as to what was going on. Hoping that they would come up with some information as to who the suspects may be. Yet the tips kept coming in from the local neighborhood people, but still anonymous. Still nothing solid, just the usual bad kids live here, hang out here, always causing trouble. Still searching for the mysterious Ben, but still with no luck. He and his crew were always causing trouble, putting fear into the local people, people who lived there most of their adult lives. But again, it is not enough to make an arrest, but it does point the detectives in the right direction. Even though this may sound repetitious these are the steps that must be followed, especially when you have nothing else to go on. Hoping to come up with something solid. All they have now are no witnesses, no evidence, just a dead body.

INFORMANTS

As far as the informants, some were paid by the NYPD. These informants were known as a C.I., Confidential Informant. The amount they got paid varies; it was usually a set amount as agreed upon between the Police and the informant. They were given a confidential number and registered with the NYPD. Some informants tried to milk the Police Department by giving little bits of information. But if it proved to be of no value and the informant didn't come up with any good, solid information, he /she was determined to be unreliable and let go. Other informants were people arrested and were facing jail time. These individuals were trying to work their case off. Meaning they were looking for leniency towards their sentencing if they supplied useful information. Their payoff would be a reduction in their sentencing, or even an outright dismissal. But up until this point, they received no helpful information from anyone.

Also, among some of the investigative steps the detectives used were checking pawn shops. When the thief/thief's made a score, they would have to get rid of it if it was jewelry or gold/silver. Cash was never a problem because they would just split it up amongst themselves. But gold, silver, diamonds, any kind of jewelry, necklaces, and bracelets had to be dispersed carefully. There were always shady underworld street characters around to buy such items on the street. But there were also Pawnshops where they would pawn/hock their items. Pawnshops would usually pay more money than a street person would, plus it was instant cash, whereas a street person would want to buy it on an installment plan, which, in some cases, you had to hunt them down for the rest of your money.

Pawnshops, by law, were supposed to record whatever items they bought. The entry that was made described when and who it was bought from. How much they paid for it and what the description was. They also had to include what the due date was, meaning how long it would be held.

Back then, in the 70s, it was before the age of computers; everything was supposed to be recorded in a ledger by hand. The Police Department's Burglary Squad would make regular visits to these Pawn Shops and check their property against the entries in the ledger to make sure everything was properly recorded in their books. However, whatever the unscrupulous pawn shop owner bought that they knew or felt was illegal would never be entered in the book. Especially if it was gold, it would rarely be entered; it was immediately melted down. For they knew when they bought it from their miscreant (skells) customers, they weren't coming back to buy it back, so their names were never entered into the ledger. If it were diamonds, they would be removed from the bracelet, necklace, or ring and sold to an unscrupulous fence, a diamond dealer who was part of their illegal operation. He, in turn, would immediately fence them out to the underworld market. Or reset them in another ring or bracelet and sell them to some unsuspecting buyer. However, in some cases, the Pawn Shop dealer himself would cheat the cheaters. If it were a big score, certain pieces of jewelry, he would term junk and throw them in the garbage. The thieves had to rely on him, as they were no experts on what was real or not real. So, he paid them for what he termed good, as soon as they left out of the garbage came the ones he said were bad, because they weren't bad after all. It was like the old saying, "No Honor Among Thieves." Not all the pawn shop owners were unscrupulous; some were strictly legitimate. The miscreants, through trial and error, knew which ones they could deal with without having to worry that they would have to identify themselves. So, when the Detectives checked the books of these receivers of stolen goods, these items were never recorded, and the Pawn Shop book was always clean.

Although in most of these cases the victims had very little, these skells would take anything they thought was of value. However, they never took anything larger than they could fit in their pockets or hide underneath a coat or jacket. They were smart enough not to be walking through the streets carrying a TV or a large radio/stereo. On occasion, the miscreants (skells) would get lucky and find some heirloom or old piece of gold or jewelry that was saved from a lifetime ago, maybe generations ago. It would be pawned just like any other piece of jewelry, to them it was just another item to make money on, or as they called it," coins or bread. So, the case dragged on with many days of canvassing the streets around the area of occurrence. Hoping to come up with some information from some source they may have missed somewhere along the line. As usual, they had their eyes and ears out there looking to come up with any info; they were the Anti-Crime cops. The detectives were always interviewing people arrested for serious crimes, robberies, burglaries, and assaults. Many times, precinct uniform cops or Anti-Crime cops would arrest someone for a serious crime. They would almost always bring them right to the Homicide office for questioning regarding any info on one of the Homicides. Or Detectives from the Homicide Squad would go to where the arrest was made to interview the prisoner.

Hoping they would come up with someone willing to work a case off. Hoping to find someone with information that would break the case wide open. Many days were spent canvassing and re-interviewing people. Most of the time, it was very frustrating; as hard as they tried, they did not come up with anything.

Always with the thought in mind, as written in the textbook "Information is the Lifeblood of an Investigation". Sometimes the work was repetitive and monotonous, but it had to be done; it was the only way a case like this could ever be solved. Every tip was followed up on; most didn't lead to anything. Even if the tip sounded outlandish, it would still be followed up on. Other than someone who wanted to work off his/her pending case by giving the needed information to at least point them in the right direction, they really had nothing. Until they got that break, they had absolutely nothing else to go on. Most of these types of cases were real mysteries, real "Who Dun It" as these cases were called. However, it was people from the neighborhood who gave the Detectives most of the information, as previously stated, but it was always anonymous. They were just too afraid to come forward for fear of being hurt by these little terrors (skells).

Some detectives had the tenacity of a pit bull, meaning that once they grabbed hold of a case, they would never let up. Some cops would say about a certain detective, "If a member of my family ever got murdered, I would want him/her on my case." I know that I would get justice. As well as my family, would get closure.

CHAPTER EIGHT

THE BIG BREAK

Finally, they get a break.

On one of their daily strolls, the Day Stalkers, while passing by an apartment house, notice an elderly gentleman leaving his first-floor apartment. (They knew this building all too well.) Once again, the opportunist actions in them came out. They watched him walk slowly down the block and turn the corner. Once he was out of sight, they made their move. They knocked on the door, and when his wife answered the door, they immediately pushed her in. Then immediately sprang into action, locking the door, tying her up, and commencing with their marauding. Everything was going as it normally would with the search through drawers on the night table, dresser, and all the closets. All the while, the victim is lying helpless on the floor. With someone standing guard over her. However, within a short period of time, they heard keys in the lock. Not realizing it was the husband and fearing it may be the Police they immediately climbed out the window. Due to the fact that it was on the first floor, they were able to make a quick getaway out the window. As it turned out, the husband had just gone around the corner to buy a couple of items and the newspaper from the local grocery store. He immediately returned home as he normally would. He enters just as the last one was leaving. He sees his wife on the floor, tied up. Even though he was unaware of what was happening, he quickly realized that something terrifying had just occurred. He unties her and immediately calls the police. When the police arrive to take a report, they also call for the Patrol Sergeant as well as the Detectives. The precinct Detectives also notify Detectives from the Push In (T.F.) Task Force (Homicide Squad). Even though it was not a Homicide it fit the pattern of the push-ins where the victims were murdered. Also, maybe it was just a coincidence, but this building was the building of the last homicide, only a short while ago. The Detectives interview the victim, and although she said she couldn't identify them or the clothes they were wearing, she did provide them with a vital clue. A clue that at first seemed like not much at first, but it eventually was a clue that would help break the case wide open. The suspects were wearing "hats covered by clear plastic." It was raining lightly earlier that day, and they had clear plastic bags on their hats, apparently to protect the Felt. So, a note was made of that by investigating Detectives and documented on a DD5. Even though it was not a Homicide, because of the similarities, it would be entered into the Pattern of push-in Homicide case.

It was also noted in their report to the Chief that this is the building where Homicide number three was committed just a short time ago. So now the detectives were thinking, could it be possible that they came back to the same building after committing a homicide here? Which was just a couple of weeks ago. Or is it just a coincidence that there is another group of street urchins also doing burglaries and home invasions in the same neighborhood? The similarities were too close to dismiss the thought, Push In, tie up, blindfold, gag, ransack, all too familiar to the detectives. The detectives are thinking, are they that brazen enough to come back to the same building where they committed a homicide? Or are they just that stupid and carefree not to even think that they should stay far away from it? But more than likely, it was the attitude that the Police have no idea we committed the homicide, so we have nothing to worry about. When, in all actuality, this is a building, they should have worried about and stayed away from it.

Once again, as part of the investigation, the Detectives call for the Crime Scene Unit, hoping they will come up with anything to aid in this investigation. The Crime Scene Unit Detectives, as previously noted, are the experts in searching crime scenes for anything that may be of value that would help in building a case and solving a crime.

They did the usual documenting of the scene with photos and searched for fingerprints. When advised of their escape through the window, they concentrated on the window by dusting the inside with fingerprint powder. With their expertise in dusting, they have a eureka moment, and they pick up a latent print.

NOTE: A Latent Print cannot be seen by the naked eye; it would have to be brought up with the use of dusting powder or a chemical agent. Whereas a Patent Print would be visible to the naked eye if it was touched with grease or a liquid which had dried, like in the case of blood.

They then print anyone in the apartment who had access to the window, including the police officers, if they touched it. This is done to eliminate the possibility that the print may just belong to someone who legitimately has access to the window and is not a suspect. Now that the comparison prints are sent to the Latent Print section, they patiently wait for the results. Once the results come back and there is no match with anyone who lives in the apartment or any of the Police Officers, they are sure it must belong to one of the marauders. However, the system back then wasn't as advanced as it is nowadays. Locating a person based on one print was really time-consuming, and next to impossible back in those days with the many, many prints on file. Unless you have a name to match it against. This would only be possible if the subject had a previous fingerprint arrest. There were millions of prints to go through. So, as the print search continued, the stalkers roamed the streets free. The suspects, unaware that a print was left behind, continued with their crime spree, looking for victims and robbing them. The detectives kept digging, as part of their normal procedure, they checked with the pattern unit and the surrounding precincts, letting them know of their latest Push In Robbery.

It was then that they were notified by the Anti-Crime Sergeant in the adjoining 73 precinct that his Anti-Crime team stopped four suspicious-looking youths who were known to the officers. This was in the confines of the 73precint. This was in the afternoon on the day of the incident in the 69 precinct Push In Robbery Burglary where they tied the woman up, and her husband interrupted their marauding.

He states the facts as follows.

The Sergeant stated that his Anti-Crime officers had observed four males who were local skells hanging around the street. One of the officers recognizes one of them as a person he arrested for a Burglary a couple of weeks ago. He also recognized one of the others, who also had a previous Burglary arrest. But now they are hanging around looking like they are up to some mischief near a commercial building. So, knowing their background, and thinking they were about to commit a burglary, or maybe just did one, they did a Stop/Question/ Frisk on them. They patted them down for any weapons, but they had none. They checked the building for any sign of a break-in, with no break-in on any private property or any other crime in the immediate area, and they were forced to let them go. However, they did a detailed UF250 on them, including names and addresses, and clothing, including clear plastic covering their hats.

NOTE: The (UF250) report is used when a person stopped has committed a crime, or is about to commit, or fits a description of a person who has committed a crime.) When used right, it was a great investigative tool for the Police Department.

At this point, the 73 Anti-Crime officers did not know of the push-in within the 69 precinct (the 73 is in Brooklyn North, and the 69 is in Brooklyn South). Their department radios are on a different frequency, so they never heard of the job of a past robbery/burglary in the 69th precinct. So, after a field interrogation and ascertaining their information, it is documented on a UF 250 form, as there is not enough to hold them on anything. The miscreants who were stopped apparently have been cleared, so they are free to go. When the Anti-Crime team hears about the push-in at the 69, and the suspects had clear plastic on their hats, they immediately notify their Sergeant of their stop. The Sergeant immediately called the Task Force and relayed the info to them regarding his team's stop. The Anti-Crime Cops in this situation did an excellent job of documenting a description. Not only did they give a description of their clothing, but the Detectives noted that when interviewing the officers about their stop, they gave them more detailed information. They noted not only that they gave them a physical description as well as their names and addresses, but meticulously described their clothing. Part of the description of their clothing was the fact that they were wearing clear plastic bags over their hats. It was a light, drizzly, rainy day, so it would be a reason to have the plastic on their hats. This was to protect the Felt material from staining. Now armed with this information, the Detectives did a name check on the names that were on the UF 250s. A check with BCI (Bureau of Criminal Investigation), they found that three of these individuals had been previously arrested and were previously fingerprinted (the fourth is a juvenile, with no fingerprint record). They submitted their names for a fingerprint comparison to the print that was on the inside of the window of the last Push In. They then patiently waited for the results, hoping they would get a positive hit. Hopefully, as one of the detectives stated, we were" waiting for that bingo," that notification that we struck gold.

EDITOR'S NOTE: The 73 Anti-Crime Cop who recognized the suspects from a previous arrest and documented the clear plastic on their hats, on a UF 250 several years later, went on to be a First Grade Detective in Brooklyn North Homicide. Det. PETER VARVARO, a promotion to a well-deserved sharp cop.

CHAPTER NINE

THE FIRST ARREST

Sure enough, they got their wish, they got that "ah ha moment" within a day or two, and they were notified by the Latent Print section that they had a match. It turns out that one of the subjects who had been stopped by the 73 A/C cops had a previous arrest for burglary. His fingerprint was a perfect match to the print that was lifted off the inside of the window. That is the window where the suspects made their escape. His name is William Gadscon; his information states that he lives in Brownsville. So now, with a suspect identified, they have positive proof; it's time to make their move. Could he be part of the group that was doing these push-ins? Or was this a by chance Robbery/Burglary, a crime of opportunity? If he is one of the group of marauders who have been doing their misdeeds and leaving no evidence behind. Either they weren't wearing gloves this time, or with the quick arrival home of the husband, they just didn't have time to wipe down the apartment. They do an investigation to find out if he is still at the address of his last arrest. Once they find out he is still at the same address its time to make their move. They go to his house and set up surveillance, and within a short period of time, when he comes out, he is apprehended without incident. At this point, he is unaware that his fingerprint has been found at the last push-in robbery. Once he is under arrest, he must be given his Rights (Miranda Warnings), which are mandated by the Supreme Court of the United States. This usually occurs as soon as the handcuffs are put on, and they are given their rights on the scene if conditions allow. Or in the back seat of the RMP (Police Car) on the way to the station house. These are commonly known as Constitutional Rights. Among these rights is the right to Remain Silent and the right to Retain Counsel (Lawyer). Also, he is told that anything he says can and will be used against him in a court of law. He is asked if he is willing to talk without an attorney present. If he agrees, questioning can begin. If he does not agree, then there is no questioning, and any statement he makes after that cannot be used against him in any criminal proceeding. However, there are times when a suspect, before he/she is given his or her rights, blurts out some incriminating statement. This is known as a "Spontaneous Utterance" and in most cases can be used against him/her in a court proceeding.

NOTE: It should be noted that every person who is arrested, no matter what the crime, no matter how serious or minor, no matter who the victim is, no matter how much evidence the police have, the suspect must be given due process, which includes his/her Constitutional Rights. This is especially true when the subject is to be questioned.)

He is taken to the precinct, more specifically, the homicide office. At this point, the Detectives must be extremely careful in questioning the suspect. They can't say anything that would suggest how the crime was committed. They would have to hear this from him. This would be considered putting words in the suspect's mouth. Any statements he makes must be made voluntarily and of his own free will. He is also not told of the details of the crime, so if he makes a statement about something that was never disclosed, they know they have the right person. Most of the suspects who make statements think they can outsmart the detective/police officer and can lie their way out of it.

Note: (There are those in civilian life who will say, "Oh, the cops can do anything they want; everyone will believe them." People think that the cop is the Buck and as the old saying goes, "the buck stops here".

However, the cop is not the last word as there are Internal Affairs, District Attorneys, Attorney General's office, as well as the US Attorney's office, all of whom oversee the officers of the Police Department. Especially when it comes to a coerced or forced confession. Those days are a thing of the past. The days of a back-room beating a confession out of a suspect are long gone.

When the Detectives brought him in, they said, "Let's put him in the box."

What is the "box?" The box is an ordinary room where people are questioned.

The person could be a witness, a complainant, a suspect, or an arrested person. But sometimes, to a person who is hiding behind a guilty conscience, the word "box" can be a terrifying word. Knowing you are guilty of something and hearing one Detective say to another, "Put him in the box". This must have a chilling effect on a person who, even if he is of the hardest of caliber, may fold like, as the saying goes, "A Cheap Suit."

So now the suspect is in the box, which is usually just 4 plain walls with a two-way mirror, where all you see is your face, but people on the other side can see inside without the suspect seeing them. This room is carefully monitored by a detective if there are two suspects. The feeling is that they may make incriminating statements as they talk to each other. This room is also used by Detectives to conduct lineups.

If he is under 16, he must be placed in a special room designated for juveniles who are placed when arrested. They cannot be questioned unless a parent or guardian, or an attorney, is present. This is mandated by the courts. In this case, they have no problem, because of his previous arrest, he was fingerprinted, so they know he is over 16 years old.

If there is a lineup, the lineup procedure is as follows:

These lineups are known as Corporeal Lineups, where the victim sees the suspect in real time. As opposed to seeing him in a photo lineup. The suspect is usually placed in a lineup with people who are of similar height, weight, facial hair, complexion, and ethnic background. There are usually 6 people in the lineup, 5 plus the suspect. The five others are called fillers.

The fillers are usually people off the street who are given a couple of bucks by the Police Department to stand in the lineup. Some people, when asked to stand in a lineup, are reluctant to stand in for fear of getting picked out. But they are assured that the suspect is known to the police, so getting picked out would cause them no problem, and they would walk out the way they came in. The lineup is usually conducted with everyone seated. They are all given a number. The reason why they are seated is that some may be a little taller than others, so being seated makes them look about the same height. The suspect picks the position he wants to sit in as well as the number he wants. Lineups are usually conducted to get a positive I.D. on the suspect after he/she was picked out from a photo array or has been ID through a fingerprint. Or the Detectives may have gotten some kind of confidential info on the suspect who may have committed a particular crime.

However, in this case, the Detectives know he committed this crime because they have positive, ironclad proof that he has. Due to the fact that he left one important clue behind, a fingerprint which is as good as him leaving his name and address, and a birth certificate. Because it has been scientifically proven that no two fingerprints are alike. There is absolutely no way to dispute the identification through a fingerprint arrest. Although at times it has been tried, no attorney could ever defeat the revelation of the scientific discovery of fingerprint identification.

In many cases, even though the victim states he/she can't ID the suspect, the ADA demands a lineup. So, the detectives must comply with his demand. The lineup is conducted, and as stated, the victim cannot identify anyone. The ADA's reasoning for the lineup is that there is the possibility of seeing him in person, as she/he may be able to identify him, and the case will be stronger for the prosecution. However, as usual, this lineup is met with negative results.

CHAPTER TEN

THE STATEMENT

Now it's time for the detective to begin to question him seriously. He is immediately in denial, refusing to admit to the Robbery/Burglary/Push-in. He is vehemently denying it to the point where he is almost convinced that the detectives have nothing on him, and no one can ID him. He is to the point where he believes that he has fooled them and that he has done nothing wrong. That they don't have anything on him to tie him to the crime, and he is going to walk out the door. But deep down inside, he knows he is lying, he knows what they did, and he knows that he was part of it. Now that he is at his high point, it's time to bust his bubble. The suspect is told about his fingerprint that has been found inside the apartment window, and is told, "fingerprints don't lie." He is told, "You are in," you are going down, and you are not leaving here today. "But you're lucky we got you first". This is your lucky day; there is nothing you can do to get out of it. But you can help yourself if you tell us what you know about this and other push-in robberies. What you tell us that helps us may help you in the long run. Because we will tell the ADA that you cooperated.

This is sometimes true; in some cases, the first one that gets caught, confesses, and gives up his partners usually gets the best deal, but it's not written in stone. They proceed to tell him we know who the others are, and they are going down too. They then tell him their names; although they had absolutely nothing on the others, he doesn't know that. He has no idea they got the names from the 250 form. They never tell him how they acquired their names. They just tell him their names to show him they aren't bluffing; they really do know who the others are. They tell him once we bring them in and they start talking, they are going to give you up, and you are going down the tubes. They will throw you under the bus in a minute. So, to help yourself, you had better start talking, because this is the only way you can help yourself. They also remind him that they will tell the DA that he is cooperating. And if the DA feels that he has given information that is beneficial to the case, he may get consideration when he is sentenced. Now the suspect knows they have enough evidence on him; he remembers that he wasn't wearing any gloves. He knows that he really screwed up this time. So now his whole demeanor has changed. What the Detectives are telling him is penetrating; he is thinking about what they are saying, that maybe he could get consideration on his case. Which is possible, but either way, the ADA is notified whether he makes a statement or not. The detectives are playing good guy, bad guy. One detective is telling him that you are going to jail for a long time. While the other is telling him, "Man, this is some mess you got yourself into." But if you cooperate, it may be to your advantage. He tells the other Detective in front of the suspect, "Leave the kid alone, he is a good kid," he just made a mistake. This is your chance to help yourself. While once again the other detective comes back in the room and says what are you being nice to this guy for? Let him go to jail and rot." Feeling the pressure from the detectives must have a psychological effect on the suspect. Especially when you know you are guilty of the crime. He must be thinking this may be my chance to help myself and get out of this mess, but even if I don't get out of it, maybe they will go light on me when I am sentenced. He then starts talking. He tells the Detectives of there by chance Robbery/Burglary where they saw the old man leaving his first-floor apartment. Not knowing if he lived alone or not, they decided to give it a try. When the elderly woman opened the door, the opportunity was too good to pass up. They immediately sprang into action and pushed her in, tied her up, and started their ransacking. However, after a short period of time, they were taken by surprise when they heard keys jiggling in the lock. Not knowing if it was the Police, they immediately fled out the front window, as it was a first-floor apartment. They didn't realize it was the old gent returning home; he had just gone to the store right around the corner to buy some groceries. He stated that if they had known it was the old gent who came back so quickly, they would have overpowered him, tied him up, and continued with their marauding. The detectives ask him who else was with you when you did this push-in. He reluctantly states Benjamin Bradshaw, Ronald Watson, and a 13-year-old (who shall remain anonymous because of his age). He states Bradshaw lives in Brownsville, right near him, as the 13-year-old does. Ronald Watson lives in East New York. Now that the Detectives have him on a roll, they start questioning him about other push-ins. They tell him it's time to get these other Robberies off your chest. They tell him because we know there are more, and we are going to find out about them, and any deals, if any are made with you, are off the table, and you will be in deep trouble. They are bluffing because they have no other info, but that is something at this point he doesn't know. He then tells the detectives of their daily routine; he tells them of their M.O. and how it works. How would they meet and look for a victim? How they would follow the victim, and one guy would ride the elevator up with him/her, get off the floor before. Then join the others in the stairwell who would all run up the stairs and proceed with the push-in plan. Or if it was a walkup, they would follow the victim up the stairs, not far behind, until he got to his/her floor. Then once he/she opens the door to his apartment, they rush him/her and push him/her in and proceed with the robbery. He had a wealth of information; they did many senior citizen push-ins. Some of which were never even reported. The reason why they were never reported is that most likely, the people were too scared. Or the attitude was why report it? You're not going to get my property back, so why should I report it? He then tells them that once they did their first one, the rest was easy. Once they saw how easy it was to get away with it, they knew this was the safest way of doing a robbery. It became a matter of routine. Each one would have their own assignment, but they would alternate who would get on the elevator with the victim.

They did this so that if there was a description given of the one on the elevator, it wasn't always the same one; the description would vary. Most of the time, it was the same three others, but occasionally, other kids from the neighborhood would join in; there were anywhere from three to six miscreants (skells). Whoever showed up that day would be part of the marauders.

CHAPTER ELEVEN

SOLVING HOMICIDE NUMBER #3

When asked by the Detectives if he had done a push-in previously in this building, the building where he left his fingerprint at the Robbery/Burglary, he says yes. They ask him to tell us about it. He then proceeds to tell them how they followed the old man up the stairs, and as soon as he opened the door, they had to push their way in just as the door was closing. The old man got in quicker than most do. So, they forced the door open, as soon as the door opened, they rushed the old man, knocked him down, and immediately tied him up. Then one of them stuffed something in the old man's mouth to keep him from yelling. They asked him what was stuffed in his mouth, "he said his Skull Cap." Once he states they put the skull cap in his mouth, they know they have one of the right culprits. This was a fact that was never released to the public; only the police and the EMT/M.E. would know. That it was his skull cap that was lodged in the victim's throat. The skull cap was the victim's own Yarmulke. They ask him who was with him, and he names the same three who were stopped with him by the 73 A/C cops. They were Ben Bradshaw, Ronald Watson, and the 13-year-old. Now they have the names of his three accomplices (skells). So now they know that there were four skells involved with this homicide. Now that ask him to continue with the story of this invasion. He states that once the old man is secure, they search him and take a couple of dollars off him. They then immediately searched for anything of value in the apartment.

They now asked him the big question: who put the (skull cap) Yarmulke in the old man's mouth? After some prodding, he reluctantly stated, Ben did it. When asked what Ben's last name was, he said Bradshaw. They asked him if he was with him when he was stopped by the 73 A/C. They do this to make sure he is not just throwing a name out just to satisfy them. (Ben is the one who was recognized from a previous arrest for a burglary by the 73 A/C cop.) They asked him what they got from the victim. He states that all they got was a few dollars, and one of them took a little music box. He liked it so much that he had to take it, even though they never took anything that was large. This was a small box that fitted under his coat. Now they asked him the bigger question: did he know the victim was dead? If he knew the victim was dead, he showed no emotion. His answer was that he was not sure whether the victim died because he never looked at him. (Obviously a self-serving statement) The detectives tell him you were in that apartment for a long time, and you did not notice him struggling, gasping for air. He answered that he was not sure if he had taken notice that the victim was not moving, he was too busy searching the apartment.

So now they have the answer to who committed Homicide number three.

It was time to work on Homicide number one. They asked him if he knew where the other buildings were where they did Push Ins, and he would say that he wasn't sure where some of the buildings were by the addresses. But he would possibly be able to identify some of the buildings if he saw them. So, the Detectives take him around the area where the incidents occurred. He said they did so many that he wasn't sure where each one was, but he did remember some locations. Apparently, they did more than was reported. This was possibly because some victims were too scared to report them. They then took him specifically to the area of the building where the First Homicide occurred, which was not far from Homicide # 3; it was just a couple of blocks.

He says he knows this building; it's a walkup and it's within blocks of Homicide number three. He then tells his story. He names the other three suspects who were with him, one of whom was thirteen years old. He stated they saw the old man walking down the street by himself, and he looked like an easy vic (victim), so they decided to follow him. When the victim entered his building (it was a walk-up), once again, they executed their plan. They followed him upstairs in their usual manner, trailing not far behind. Once the victim reached his floor, they set up, ready to pounce, watching from the doorway of the stairwell. Once he opened the door, they made their move. They immediately ran up, pushed him down, and one jumped on him while the other closed and locked the door. He was immediately tied up and gagged. They also searched for him for any valuables, as well as searching his apartment to look for anything of value. The Detectives asked him what he was gagged with, even though they already knew they wanted to hear it from him. He answered that it was his scarf, which was apparently his Pray Shawl. (A Pray Shawl is a religious garment Jewish men wear over their shoulders when they go to the Schul/ synagogue to pray.)

The theory was that he had just come from the Schul from praying, and unfortunately winds up being the victim of a monstrous act. The instrument of his death was his religious Pray Shawl. They then asked him who wrapped the Pray Shawl around the victim. Again, after some prodding, he reluctantly states it was Ben. They ask what Ben's last name is, and he states Bradshaw. They also asked him for the names of the others involved, and he immediately supplied them with the names of Ronald Watson and the thirteen-year-old. Like the other Push Ins, they rarely found anything of value, just a couple of dollars. As previously stated, they were mostly poor people who were barely surviving on Social Security. So now Homicide number one was solved, it was time to work on number two.

SOLVING HOMICIDE # 2

Once again, the Detectives take him around the area where the second Homicide occurred, which is a city housing project. The detectives feel that he must know this victim is dead because of his cohort's statement to the younger kids, "what we did today you will see on the news tonight". Upon arrival at the building, if he knew that the victim was dead, he acted like he didn't. When they approached the building, he was cool and calm. Never showed any fear or emotion. They asked him who he was with, and he stated Ben Bradshaw, Ronald Watson, and the thirteen-year-old. Again, this was done to make sure he wasn't lying. They ask him to describe, as best he could, this Push In. He tells the Detectives they were hanging around the building when the vic came by, again this old guy looked like an easy vic. He describes how they followed him into the building, and the victim got on the elevator. As usual, they executed their plan, and one of them (Ronald Watson) would get on the elevator with him. He would then ask the old man what floor he was going to and say out loud, you are going to five, I am going to four. Thereby sending a signal to which floor his cohorts should go. When the elevator reaches four, he immediately gets off. He runs upstairs and meets his accomplices on the stairwell of the fifth floor. When the victim gets off the elevator, they watch him slowly walk to his apartment. As soon as he opens the door, they immediately run up to him and knock him down. One of them immediately closes and locks the door while the others are tying him up. Then one of them stops him from screaming. The Detectives ask him how he did this. He states one of them took a pillow and covered his face with it; by doing this, he not only could not see or scream, but he was also unable to breathe, thereby causing his death. When asked who put the pillow on his face, once again, he reluctantly answers Ben. Again, when he is asked what Ben's last name was, he states, Bradshaw. He then goes on to describe how they searched him and the apartment. In this search, once again, all they got was a few dollars. Again, it's not worth taking a life for. Apparently, they didn't find anything else of value, other than the few dollars. Like the others, he is just a poor old man living on Social Security, and as usual, has nothing else of value.

They then go back to asking him who put the pillow on his face, again after some prodding, again he reluctantly says, Ben. They asked him again to make sure he wasn't just giving them a name to placate them. Again, they ask him for Ben's last name, and he states his name was Bradshaw. Once again, they do this to make sure he is not lying to them. They go over the story to see if he changes it in any way. They ask him to describe the events of the day the way they happened. He states they started out the day as usual, looking for a victim. They walked around the East Flatbush/Remsen Village section but had no luck.

So, they headed back to Brownsville. On the way back, they passed the Senior Citizen building. Since they didn't make a score for the day, they decided to try their luck at this building. Even though it was a little close to home, it was just far enough away. They apparently were desperate, or maybe they were just blood thirsty. They had to complete their day by getting another victim; this one may be a jackpot. So, they hung around the building hoping for a victim. After a short while, their Vic comes home, he goes into the lobby and waits for the elevator. Once the elevator comes down, and he gets on, they put their plan into action.

He describes how one of them (Ronald) got on the elevator, and the others ran up the stairs to his floor by a signal given from their point man on the elevator. The point man gets off the floor before, then immediately runs upstairs to meet his fellow marauders. He stated that when the old man gets off the elevator and walks to his apartment, as soon as he opens the door, he is immediately pushed in. He is then tied and silenced. He searched for any valuables, as the other culprits were searching his apartment for any valuables. When asked again how he was silenced, he states that a pillow was put on his face. Now they ask him if he just lay the pillow on his face, or if he physically held it on his face. After some hesitation and some prodding, he stated Ben held it down.

The reason they ask him to repeat all the info, even though he had previously confessed. They did this because they wanted to see if he had changed his story in any way. Also, his statements will be recorded on a DD5, which will be presented to the ADA upon his/her arrival. The ADA will perusue them, then he (the ADA) will question the suspect.

The fact that the pillow was being used to gag him was never disclosed to anyone. Only the Detectives involved, which included the Crime Scene Detectives as well as the EMT and the M.E., would know this. It was never disclosed to the media. It would only be known to someone who was present at the crime scene or who was involved with the committing of the burglary/robbery.

Now the detectives knew they hit a jackpot with number two and were on the right track. They knew that with this suspect, they struck gold. Now it's back to the office to concentrate on all three Push In homicides. They show him pictures of the crime scene and the victim lying on the floor, tied up. They ask him if he remembers the scene, and he answers that he does. They ask him to describe what they did, which he does; they are doing this to lock him into that apartment on that day. He states all he did was search the apartment (a self-serving statement), but it still puts him on the scene of the homicide. Now that they have locked him into that apartment on that day, it's time to confront him. It's time to tell him that the victim died, and it is now a "Murder committed during the commission of a Felony." If he didn't know this before, he knew it now. Even though he most likely knew the victims were dead, the detectives told him so to reinforce the fact to him that it was more than a burglary. It's a Homicide committed during a Felony. When he is told of the victim's death, he shows no emotion. Which is why the detectives knew that he already knew the victim was dead. The Detectives are also sure he knew the victim was dead, just by his partner bragging to the neighborhood kids. He states that he didn't do anything except search the apartment; this is obviously another self-serving statement. As stated prior to this, it was never disclosed to the public that this death was part of the pattern of this Push In Robbery/Burglary ring. Whatever people knew in the building where it happened couldn't be helped. But they were mostly older people who didn't get around much and more than likely talked about it in their own circle of friends. This did cause a great deal of fear among them, but it was something they had to live with. But apparently, they did not know of the other two homicides, or of any other push-ins that were done in the area.

Their thought in mind was always, will I be next, or who will be next, when will it happen? Some were so afraid that they would not leave their apartment to go shopping for groceries, and relied on their neighbors or relatives to shop for them.

At this stage in life, as scared as they were, some were just too old or too poor to move away. They were trapped in their own environment, forced to live in fear. They had no idea that this was part of a pattern, because if something happened two or three blocks or a mile away, given the fact that they were elderly and didn't get around that much, it may just as well have been fifty miles away. They never found out about it. Even if the story did hit the newspaper or TV at the time, it got very little coverage. Because the police tried to let out as little information as possible to downplay it to avoid panic in the community. So now, once again, the Detectives zero in on this incident, which led to the death. They go over his whole story all over again, and they ask him once more to go over it. Again, they are doing this to make sure he is telling the truth and not just giving them names so they will get off his back. Because of what he is telling them, they will relay to the ADA. He was questioned again as to who placed the pillow on his face, again he had to be prodded. Was he reluctant to tell them it was Ben Bradshaw because of his loyalty to Ben? Or was he that afraid of Ben that he had to be asked repeatedly who put the pillow on the vic's face? Did he have a sense of loyalty to his partner in crime, or just a fear of him, or maybe retaliation from a family member? He apparently knew Ben had an older brother. He signs a confession describing the crimes and makes a full admission to the Robberies/Burglaries, which were part of the Homicides. Although some parts of the statement were self-serving, like admitting he was there but didn't always take part in the crime, like tying the victims up, but maybe just did some searching of the apartment. He still put himself at the crime scene, but apparently didn't realize that he was part of the conspiracy, and that was enough for him to be charged as an accomplice to Murder.

Note: The Detectives, as well as the ADAs, know that even though a person confesses, sometimes they will try to minimize or justify the reason for their action, which may or may not have contributed to the homicide. The suspect's feeling is that they know I was there, so I'll tell them so, but at the same time, I am minimizing my part in what I did. They do this by telling half-truths.

THE ADA ARRIVES

The District Attorney's office is notified and informed of the arrest. A riding Assistant District Attorney (ADA) is sent to the station house, specifically the Homicide Squad. The ADA is called the riding DA because he/she is on standby for cases such as this, where he/she is needed to take statements. Meaning they had to go out to the field to take a statement. However, sometimes even if there is no statement to be made by the suspect, who, although he may have given a statement to the detective, refuses to give one to the ADA. This is sometimes because the ADA may come on too strongly to the suspect, causing the suspect to fear giving the ADA a statement. Whereas the detective may have a more friendly approach and created more of a cohesive atmosphere where the suspect was at ease talking. However, the ADA is still there to make sure everything is done properly, so an arrest can be authorized. With an arrest for a Homicide the ADA will have to take a statement from the arresting detective or any witnesses. The ADA will come to the station house and record all the facts, especially if there is a witness to be interviewed. The statements will be typed by the ADA's stenographer, as well as videotaped by his videographer. Also, the ADA must authorize the arrest. He/she, as previously stated, may want a lineup. They may have to confer with the District Attorney (DA, the boss) and inform him/her of all the facts. If the DA feels there isn't enough to have a Prima Facia case, he/she will tell the ADA that the arrest is not authorized. However, in the case where the suspect is willing to make a statement, the ADA will advise him of his constitutional rights and question the suspect while the suspect is recorded and videotaped. If the suspect does not want to make a statement, then the ADA will also record this.   In other rare cases where the suspect is willing to make a statement, the ADA may want the suspect to be brought to the DA's office. This is done for the purpose of administering a Polygraph Test by their Polygraph expert.

The test is commonly known as a Lie Detector test, even though the Lie Detector Test is not admissible in court (because there is the possibility it may be faulty and is not always accurate). The test is sometimes given if the ADA feels that the suspect is giving a false confession. The test will give the ADA a good barometer on whether the confession is a true one. For some strange reason, sometimes, people confess to a crime they didn't commit. This is done sometimes for notoriety or to gain fame, which has been done many times in the past. A good example of this is the case where a suspect confessed to killing in recent times was the 1996 Murder of a six-year-old child in a Midwest state. The case went unsolved for a couple of years, and out of nowhere, this guy confesses. But once he is brought in and questioned and most likely given a polygraph, it will be obvious he fabricated his whole confession. This situation, where he is giving a false confession, illustrates what a person may do just to gain fame and notoriety. He only knew what he had heard on TV and read news accounts, so he was not arrested. Apparently, he was mentally unstable.

So, a polygraph will give the DA a good barometer of whether the suspect is being truthful or not. This would include any serious crime, such as murder, rape, robbery, kidnapping, or burglary, or serious Assault. No matter what the crime is, the DA will not prosecute or authorize an arrest if they feel the Police did not proceed properly and according to the law. The DA may not usually prosecute if the person fails the polygraph. Even though a polygraph is not admissible in a court proceeding, the ADA will have to disclose the fact that the suspect was polygraphed and whether the suspect passed or failed. It is mandatory with NYPD procedure to call the DA when an arrest is made for a Homicide or any other serious crime. This could also be for any of the serious crimes previously mentioned, or if the victim is seriously injured or likely to die.

REGARDING THEIR RIGHTS

The ADA will advise the suspect of his/her rights. The same rights that were administered by the detectives are given by the ADA to ensure that the rights were given properly. Once again, part of the rights that are given to protect an individual against self-incrimination. As provided in the Fifth Amendment to the Constitution, the "Right Against Self Incrimination." In that he was not forced or threatened by anyone, specifically the detectives. As previously stated, it is all being recorded by the ADA's stenographer. The Detective who is making the arrest is present, as well as any other police official who is present, while the statement is made, and must be recorded as present during the ADA's questioning.

The suspect in this case gives a complete statement to the ADA on all three homicides. He describes how they would follow the victim into his/her building. How would one then ride the elevator up with the victim and get off the floor before? Or if it was a walkup, how they followed the victim upstairs by staying a safe distance behind, which wasn't hard, since the victim was climbing the stairs very slowly. He then describes how they attack the victim from behind and push them in. He also tells the ADA of tying them up and gagging them, which was done regularly. He admits everything, including the push-ins where the homicides occurred, but added that he was not sure the victims had expired. (which is more than likely a lie) He then gives the names of his cohorts and how they participated in one way or another. Now, with all the facts known, he has named the others. It was time to round up the others.

They are as follows.

Ben Bradshaw, Brownsville, Brooklyn, William Gadscon, Brownsville, Brooklyn, (First Arrested left (fingerprint) Ronald Watson of East New York, Brooklyn, Carl Harrison, Canarsie, Brooklyn, Unindicted Conspirator; Canarsie.

13-year-old Juvenile Record Sealed

CHAPTER TWELVE

ARREST OF THE OTHERS ON HOMICIDE #3

Now that he has given a statement on all three Homicides and who his conspirators were its time to round them up. The next day, the Detectives go out and round up the others. When each one is brought in, they are given their Miranda warnings. One is a juvenile who is thirteen years old; he must be given his rights separately and questioned in front of his parents, or counsel (a lawyer). They are the same constitutional rights that are mandated to be given as per the Supreme Court ruling against self-incrimination, even though he is a juvenile. Even though their cohort had given the information on them, they just couldn't arrest them based on the co- conspirator statement. But they are brought in for investigation. They still need admissions from them or some kind of physical evidence. So, they are still afforded the same rights. Including that their statements that if any were to be given were made voluntarily after being advised of their rights.

Each one is questioned separately, so neither one knows what the other is saying. This is the norm. They start by asking them if they know of any push-in robberies/burglaries in the area. Each one is in denial, stating that they have no knowledge of any push-ins. So, after an hour of questioning regarding the Push Ins, and not get anywhere. The detectives feel it's time to play hardball.

They break the news to them that their partner has been arrested based on his leaving his fingerprint at the scene of a push-in. When he got arrested, he gave you guys up as being involved with him on the last Push In. This changes their attitude; now the feeling is that the detectives must know. That's why we are here. They don't know exactly what he told the detectives; they just know he gave them up. They admit to being part of the burglary team on that day. Now that they have admitted to the failed push-in, it's time to question them regarding homicide three. They ask them if they remember if they did a push-in a couple of weeks before, in the same building. More specifically, on March 24, 1975, they stuffed the Yarmulke down the victim's throat. Again, they are being questioned separately, so each one didn't know what the other was saying. In the questioning of each one, there were a lot of fingers pointing, meaning each one was quick to give up what another conspirator had done. Each one was being asked separately how the robberies were committed, reminding them they already had information from their cohort. This put the thought in their heads that the detectives know what happened, so lying to them would not be a good idea. They were then told that the victims died because of the robbery. Knowing that a victim died because of their push-in, put added pressure on each suspect. So, each suspect felt that the detectives knew everything about their crimes. This made it easier to get a statement from each one. This was easy because each one did not know what the other said. But as usual, even though they admitted to being part of the marauding, they tried to give a self-serving statement. Like putting themselves on the scene but not really doing anything else, or just searching the apartment. Each one pointed their finger at the other; this was done by all four. The detectives never actually put them on the scene; this was done by themselves.

This put the thought in their heads that the game was over; these detectives knew everything. Once again, the detectives played good guy, bad guy. They specifically zero in on Homicide Three, the one where they shove the Yarmulke down the victim's throat. They put one suspect against the other by telling them we talked to your partners, and they gave you up. Each one, not knowing what the others said, started giving their partners up and admitting to their part. Especially when it came to the thirteen-year-old, no one had a clue about how much he told the detectives. It was at this point that each one had admitted to taking part in the Homicide, Robbery/Burglary. Also, again at the same time, each tried to give a self-serving statement by minimizing what he had done. They did this without realizing that they were still part of this conspiracy. They still were putting themselves at the scene but denying taking any action or very little action to cause the death. Apparently, not realizing that no matter what they say, they are still part of the conspiracy and are accomplices to the death. However, when questioned about who stuffed the Yarmulke down the victim's throat, they all seemed to indicate that Ben Bradshaw did it. Basically, they all agreed that Ben was their leader, they all followed Ben's lead, and it seemed like Ben liked playing that part. When Ben was questioned, he was confronted with the fact that his cohorts gave him up as stuffing the Yarmulke down the victim's throat, but he denied doing so. He said he didn't remember that he did, or he didn't. But at this point, they had all four of them locked into the apartment where the homicide took place. This was more than enough to get a Grand Jury Indictment. There was no way they would be able to wiggle out of this. Whatever crimes they had committed in their lives, this was the big time, this was a serious matter, Murder. There was no taking a plea at arraignment, where a Felony was reduced to a Misdemeanor. Not this time, this is going all the way to the top. Murder, Robbery, Burglary, amongst other charges.

The juvenile's case, because of his age, was severed right from the beginning. He was questioned separately in front of his parents. His case was immediately sent to the Family Court (Children's Court). No matter what the outcome of the case is, the records are sealed, closed to the public, as well as Law Enforcement

CHAPTER THIRTEEN

ARREST ON HOMICIDE ONE/TWO

Now that they have enough to arrest them on Homicide number three, it's time to work on the first and second murders. They advised them of their rights (Miranda Warnings), and each agreed to waive their rights in that they did not need or want a lawyer and were questioned without council/lawyer.

So now the questioning starts all over. They remind them of the first Homicide that occurred on January 9, 1975, the one where the victim was suffocated by his own Pray Shawl. But they never tell them that he was suffocated with his own Pary Shawl. They would have to hear from one of them. They are questioning them separately, again using the same tactic, "your partner gave you up". Soon they start admitting to being involved in the crime, but again give a self-serving statement that they were on the scene but didn't do anything, but maybe searched the apartment. Again, they all seem to indicate that Ben Bradshaw was their leader; they followed him. Also saying that it was Ben who put the (scarf) Pray Shawl on the victim's face and in his mouth. So now, with the questioning of the remaining suspects, number two and three (the fourth was the 13-year-old whose arrest has been severed) Based on their own admissions, after being read their Miranda Warnings, the detectives have enough now to arrest them on Homicide number one.

ARREST ON HOMICIDE NUMBER TWO

Now they start questioning them on Homicide number two, the one committed on February 4, 1975, the one in the City Housing Project. They question them on how they entered the victim's apartment. They stated how they used the elevator procedure, where one would ride the elevator and get off the floor before. During this questioning, the Detectives confirmed that it was Ben who made the statement, "What We Did Today You Will See On The News Tonight". So, without a single witness, the detectives built a case based on bits and pieces they received from the community, and admissions from the suspects themselves. As well as the plastic bags covering their hats, and of course, the fingerprint lifted during the Robbery/Burglary. All these bits and pieces, when put together they were able to solve these three homicides. By putting one piece at a time together.

So now the detectives have cleared up all three homicides by arresting these four marauders.

During the questioning of them regarding the Homicides, two more names pop up as possible accomplices. So now they must go out and round up the other two suspects. There are two sixteen-year-olds who don't live that close to the suspects but live in nearby Canarsie. Whereas the others live in Brownsville and East New York.

Once they bring the other two in for questioning after giving them their Miranda warnings, these two suspects aren't as cooperative as the other suspects. Apparently, through word on the street, they know that the others were brought in for the murders in Remsen Village/Brownsville. So, when they were brought in, they apparently knew why they were being brought in. Meaning they aren't admitting to the murders as the others did. However, the ADA felt there was enough for an arrest. Even though at this point the case against them is apparently a circumstantial case, it's enough to get the case to the Grand Jury. Eventually, with the five suspects arrested (the 6th is the juvenile) after statements were taken, they were arraigned in Brooklyn Criminal Court on Murder, Robbery, Burglary charges as well as other charges. Within three days, a hearing was held, as per 180/80 of the Criminal Procedure Law.

(Which states that when a suspect is held on bail and is in custody, a hearing must be held within 72 hours of arrest, or the suspect must be released.)

However, if there are extenuating circumstances, the Judge may grant the DA extra time to keep the defendant in beyond 72 hours. But it is not necessary in this case; they need no extra time.

In the case where he/she is not in jail, there is no rush for 180/80, because the suspect is not incarcerated. But in this case, they are incarcerated, so there was a need for a hearing within 72 hours. Once the hearing was held, the judge hearing the case decided there was enough evidence to send the case to the Grand Jury, where all felonies go. Sometimes, a defense attorney and an ADA will agree to waive the hearing and send the case directly to the Grand Jury. This is sometimes done by the defense attorney to possibly see if the Grand Jury does not indict.

Grand Juries are made up of a body of 16 to 23 people; they are made up of normal, everyday people, who are people of your peers. The Grand Jury is held in private/secret; the ADA presents the facts and witnesses to the Jurors. The Jurors, after hearing all the facts, witnesses, and evidence, confer amongst themselves and then vote whether to indict or not. This is done behind closed doors. As always, Grand Jury hearings are secretive, and the results are not made public until the findings are unsealed. The Jurors will vote on a True Bill, which means there is an indictment, or a no true bill, which obviously means there is no indictment. With regards to the matter of this session, the Grand Jury, after being presented with overwhelming evidence, came down with a vote of a True Bill on four of the suspects. This means they voted yes to indict four of them on all charges. One of the five is not indicted, for lack of evidence. The case of a 13-year-old has already been severed and sent to the Family/Children's Court.

Now that the Grand Jury has handed down an indictment, it can be unsealed. They are charged with Murder/Manslaughter during the commission of a felony, as well as several counts of First-Degree Robbery, First-Degree Burglary, and First- and Second-Degree Assault, as well as Larceny. In theory, these charges, when added up collectively, could add up to over 100 years in jail if they go to trial and are convicted. But assuming there is a conviction, it will be up to the sentencing judge to mete out the punishment. When an indictment is handed down, the person must be arraigned on the felony charges, where in this case, the top charge is Murder. Bail must be set, and usually in Murder Cases, it is set very high or no bail at all. This apparently was the case in this situation: NO BAIL. However, the defendants are also guaranteed under the Sixth Amendment of the Constitution the right to a fair and speedy trial by an impartial jury.

Eventually, there is a Conference meeting held. The purpose of this meeting is to see if any resolution can be obtained for the case, usually a plea of some kind. If no resolution is reached, the case is marked for trial.

There was no resolution on this case, so it goes on the calendar, and it's marked for trial. Before trial, there are usually motions made by the defense attorney, as well as the ADA. There is usually a discovery hearing, where the defense attorney will try to uncover some facts that may lead to certain evidence being excluded. They would also request a suppression hearing, which is to suppress their statements. In this case, it is whether the Miranda warnings were given properly or whether they were given at all. Miranda warnings, which are set forth as the Fifth Amendment of the Constitution, are given to ensure the defendants' rights against self –incrimination. (Meaning he/she shall not be a witness against himself/herself.) If the court finds that the rights were not given properly or not given at all, or that force or coercion was used to obtain a confession, then the court will suppress the statements. When the statements are suppressed, they cannot be used against the suspect in a trial, no matter what the charges are. In a case such as this, where there were no actual witnesses to the crime, this would be detrimental to the District Attorney's case.

The Detective who initially gave them their rights would have to testify, as well as the ADA who also gave them their rights. If the court ruled that the rights were given improperly and the statements were suppressed, more than likely the charges would be dropped and the defendants released. If this were the case, then the DA would, in all probability, go to the next higher court to try to get the statements reinstated back into the case, and the reinstatement of the charges. There was no need for that in this case because the courts upheld the admissions.

CHAPTER FOURTEEN

THE PROSECUTION

The suspects are now being held on Riker's Island, where all jail case prisoners are held until their trial comes up. It is also a jail where people are sentenced to 1 year or less. If the sentence is more than a year, the prisoner is sent upstate to one of several jails in NYS. Each defendant, when indigent, is supplied with a lawyer through the Legal Aid Society. When it is a serious case, such as this one, there are lawyers who are known as 18B attorneys. 18B attorneys are private practice attorneys drawn from a pool of attorneys who are on a list that, when called upon, must defend a client when the case has been assigned to him/her Pro Bono (meaning no charge).

Sometimes they are paid a menial amount by the Court System. Usually, a set amount, no matter what the charges are. The fee paid is nowhere near what they would get if it were a private practice case. Contrary to what some people believe, they are highly competent attorneys and are some of the best. As one attorney would say, "my job is to defend the person to the best of my ability, no matter what he/she is charged with, otherwise I would not be doing my job". I never ask a client if he/she is guilty or not.

Like all good lawyers, they will use every legal tactic to try to get the charges thrown out or reduced. Looking at any technicality or loophole, they can hang their hat on where they can get some pertinent evidence of the case to be thrown out. Even though the statements were upheld, he/she sometimes will still try to get them thrown out. The ADA would state his reasons why the statements should stay in, as opposed to the defense attorney, who would try to get the statements thrown out. One such tactic is a Miranda, or Wade/ Huntley hearing.

(Miranda's right to remain silent)

(Wade/Huntley is for purposes of Identification)

In this case, there was no ID, so there was no Wade hearing. (Huntley hearing, basically, is the same as Miranda) The Detective who took the statements would have to testify as to how and when they gave the defendant his Miranda warnings.

Miranda warnings were a precedent set in Arizona in 1967, where Ernesto Miranda was arrested and convicted for committing robbery, etc. He appealed his conviction on the grounds that he was not given his Constitutionals Rights against self-incrimination. He won his appeal, and his conviction was thrown out by the US Supreme Court. This was based on the fact that his statements were given without being advised of his Constitutional Rights. However, he was retried later based on other evidence and found guilty and was convicted for a second time. But nevertheless, the precedent was set where the Constitutional Rights had to be given before statements were taken and henceforth known as "Miranda Warnings." Which is the Fifth Amendment of the Constitution.

The Constitutional Rights are, in substance, as follows. You have the "Right to Remain Silent and the Right to Counsel/Attorney," and any statements that are made can be used against you in a criminal proceeding. "Council would be supplied to him free of charge" if you can't afford an attorney. Now that I have advised you of your rights, are you willing to make any statements?

A Wade Hearing deals with identification and whether the identification was made legally.

In the case of Wade, Mr. Wade was convicted of a Bank Robbery in Texas that was committed in 1964. He was arrested, and a lineup was held; the lineup consisted of 5 other males. The lineup was viewed by two employees of the bank who picked the subject out. Based on their ID, he was tried and convicted.

He appealed his conviction based on the fact that he wasn't afforded counsel during the lineup.

Even though he had council his counsel was never notified about the lineup by the Police or the DA's office. His attorney sued, and in 1967, his conviction was overturned by the US Supreme Court, since counsel was not present. Mr. Wade was set free by the courts. Thereby setting the precedent known as a "Wade hearing for the purpose of identification."

Huntley's hearing is basically just about the same as Miranda warnings. Usually, when a Wade hearing is held, it's usually coupled with a Huntley hearing. They are usually known as Wade/Huntley hearings. These hearings are held to ensure that the defendant was given his rights properly and that the identification of the defendant was done properly, especially if a lineup was conducted. Also to affirm as well as the rights if they were given, that they were given properly, and that he/she understood them. Once the hearing is over, the judge hearing the arguments will decide on the legality of the statements. If they were taken illegally, then anything considered not taken legally would be suppressed (thrown out) Thereby taking the strength away from the ADA prosecuting the case.

The reason being this case was built on admission from the defendants themselves due to the fact that there was no other physical evidence regarding the homicides. There were no eyewitnesses, and none of the victims from previous Push Ins could ID the suspects. The only witnesses they had were victims from previous push-ins, who, although they couldn't ID the suspects, were brought in as witnesses just to establish the fact that they were victims of push-in Robberies, and it was part of a pattern. Other than the fingerprint where they escaped out the window, there was no other evidence. But the fingerprint had nothing to do with the homicides. So, in a case where there was no other evidence, everything was hinged on the judge's decision. Fortunately, the judge ruled in favor of the D.A.'s office in that the statements were taken legally, so the case could move forward and on to trial.

After all appeals were exhausted, the statements were upheld by the courts. The judge who was hearing the case ruled that the cases be severed so that one defendant's case would not prejudice the other. The judge apparently gave more consideration to them than they gave to their victims. He did this, thereby giving each defendant a fair trial. In all toll there were six arrests, five of whom were brought to justice. Apparently, the DA's office took their strongest cases and went forward with them; these were the cases where they felt the best chance of gaining a conviction. Even though they were suspected of committing many more crimes, they just didn't have enough strong evidence to go forward with those cases. After all the legal wrangling, convictions were obtained against four of the defendants.

(The fifth was a 13-year-old who was previously convicted in Juvenile Court, and because he was a juvenile, his record was sealed.)

It should be noted that at the time of their trial, there was no sentence of LIFE WITHOUT PAROLE.

So, during the month of July of 1976, the defendants were sentenced as follows.

Benjamin Bradshaw: The top charge he was convicted of was Murder 2nd degree. He was sentenced to Twenty-Five Years to Life.

William Gadscon: The top charge that he was convicted of was Murder 2nd degree. He was sentenced to twenty-six years six months to life, and was paroled after serving 24 years.

Ronald Watson: The top charge he was convicted of was Manslaughter Second Degree. He was sentenced to fifteen years but was released after serving only five years.

Carl Harrison: He was convicted of Burglary and was sentenced to three years in jail. He was released after serving one year of his sentence.

The fifth shall remain anonymous because he has not been convicted of any crime.

Even though it appeared the defendants got off easy, the ADA did the best he could with what he had, considering there were no living witnesses testifying against them and no physical evidence.

There was no one who would be able to say they saw the defendants in the apartment, or leaving the apartment, not even close to it. There were no witnesses to any one of the victims of the homicide. With regards to the Assault of the woman who lost an eye, she failed to ID anyone.

At the time of the crime, the only witnesses they had were the suspects themselves, who, although they never came right out and said yes, we killed them, did put themselves at the scene of the crime. This was done by giving their self-serving statements and pointing to Ben, who did the gagging in all three of the homicides, while they allegedly did the search for valuables.

But as the Chief of Detectives also stated, this case was built on bits and pieces, and the detectives did the best they could with what they had. As well as the ADA prosecuting the cases, which also had very little evidence to prosecute them. Considering they didn't have a single eyewitness to identify any of them, or any tangible or physical evidence. But they received lots of anonymous tips from the residents of the area, which helped them build a case and pointed them in the right direction, for which the Police were grateful.

The thirteen-year-old (because of his age, shall be unnamed) was convicted as a Juvenile Delinquent. He was convicted of Murder but because of his age, his record was sealed. Most likely, the top sentence was only three years in a home for juvenile defendants. He will be released when he is sixteen.

It is also noted that Benjamin Bradshaw died in prison of unknown cause after serving only eleven years. Some would say that it was poetic justice. While some of the detectives, most of whom are retired by now, would say it wasn't fair because he beat the system by dying. He should have lived to serve at least twenty-five years, and then died; was there a feeling that would be justice?

The reason why they were not tried on all the charges on all the victims, apparently, the DA's office went with the strongest cases, where he felt the evidence was the strongest. There was also the feeling that some of the jurors may have felt the confessions were taken illegally. Feeling that, why would they confess to every push-in on their own free will? There must be some coercion on the part of the Police or ADA. If this were the thought, they would possibly refuse to convict the defendants. Thereby, this may lead to a hung jury. Or possibly, if all agreed, it would lead to an acquittal. If it were a hung jury, that would most likely lead to a retrial, with maybe the possibility of an acquittal. So, what it amounted to was that the DA's office went forward with the strongest cases. Cases where they felt they had the strongest chance of gaining a conviction, not only to convict the bad guys, but to keep their batting average up (as the police would say). So, even though there was the possibility that there may be more suspects involved, the DA's office had no choice but to go with the cases where they had the strongest evidence against the persons who were arrested. There just wasn't enough strong evidence to arrest any others or even charge the suspects that were already in custody for some of the other Push Ins where the victims survived, because they couldn't ID the suspects anyway.

Note: after the arrest and conviction of the Push Ins Robbers, the Push Ins during that period had stopped in the Brooklyn South Area.

As an ADA once said, sometimes to reach a successful conclusion, "you have to reach into the gutter and make a deal with the devil". This translates into the fact that, sometimes, as guilty as the person is, you must make a deal with them. Especially if there is a chance that, on some technicality or juror nullification, the defendants could win an acquittal. To prevent this, the DA sometimes must make a deal with one of the defendants. A deal with him (and his attorney) that he will get a reduction in his sentence when he is sentenced in return for his cooperation. But at the same time, he is still pleading to a felony, but by doing so, he is aiding the DA's office in convicting someone they didn't have a strong case against. The old time Detectives would call this "Trading little ones for big ones".

CHAPTER FIFTEEN

THE TABLES ARE TURNED

Now that the defendants are serving their sentences, the case of the push-in robbers was closed and done with, or so it appeared. But it was not to be. Several months later, two Federal agents appeared at the 12th Division Homicide office, and no, they weren't there for a friendly visit. They were there to serve subpoenas on the Detectives that were involved in the arrest of the Push In Murderers, also known as The Day Stalkers. Now the detectives were on the defensive; it was they who needed attorneys. Apparently, the defendants' attorneys had made an allegation to the US Attorney's Office of the Federal Government that the Civil Rights of their clients were violated. They stated that their confessions were obtained illegally. They stated that their rights were not administered properly, and the confessions were forced and coerced. Therefore, the confessions should be thrown out, and their convictions should be vacated. So now the Detectives had to obtain legal counsel, meaning they had to hire lawyers. This was done through the Detectives Union, who supplied them with lawyers, not by the Police Department, as you would think. The City Corporation Council monitored the case and acted as Co Council for the Detectives. The reason being, if the allegation was substantiated and the confessions were tossed, the city would more than likely be hit with a huge lawsuit. This would be against the NYPD, as well as the detectives involved in the arrest. The Corporation Council handles all lawsuits against the city; in this case, it would be specifically against the Detectives. If it was found that the statements were taken by force, the officers involved could be brought up on administrative PD charges. However, there was the possibility that the DA's office could bring Perjury charges as well as Assault charges if the confessions were gained illegally or by using force. Or there was also the possibility that they could be charged by the US Attorney's Office for Violation of their Civil Rights. Because the days of forced confessions were long gone.

The Detectives involved had to appear at the US Attorney's Office. They would have to be given their rights and would be asked to waive immunity. Waiving immunity would mean that anything they say can be used against them in a criminal proceeding. Each Detective would have to give their statement regarding whether the rights were given properly and legally. The ADA who took the statements was also questioned as to his involvement in the taking of the statements. Besides his verbal statement advising the defendants of their rights. He also offered as proof the videotaped confessions that were taken at the time of arrest, showing that their Miranda Warnings were given to each one before being questioned. This showed they willingly and knowingly gave their statements after being given their rights, and there was no coercion involved.

Now, with all the information at hand, the US Attorney's office conducts a full investigation regarding the taking of statements. After a thorough investigation by the US

Attorney's office, it was determined that the confessions were obtained legally there was no need to pursue the matter any further. With this finding, their convictions and sentences are upheld, and the case is officially closed, with their sentences remaining intact.

DEFENSE LAWYER TACTICS

It should be noted; at most trials, the defense attorneys sometimes would try to put in the minds of the jurors or the judge that there was a possibility that force was used in gaining a statement. This is done by asking certain questions of the Detective/Officer. Like asking the Detective/Officer, "You say the defendant made these admissions voluntarily." You said, "You never used force? Remember, Detective/Officer, you are under oath (a scare tactic to put fear into the Detective/Officer, hoping that the Detective/Officer will break down and drop his guard). There is also the possibility that this may put the thought in a juror's mind that the confessions were taken by force. But again, it was a tactic that didn't always work, but the defense strategy was to try as hard as he/she could to put that thought into the mind of the jurors. No matter what the crime was or what the defendant was charged with. Hoping that the jury might feel the Detective/Officer was lying and possibly vote for an acquittal. Or even getting at least one juror to believe them, which would lead to a hung jury. This has happened on occasion in the past. Because in a Criminal trial, it must be unanimous, all 12 jurors must vote to convict or acquit; if there is one holdout either way, it would end in a hung jury. Then it would be up to the ADA if he/she wanted to retry the case or just drop the prosecution. Usually, the ADA will poll the jury, and if he/she sees that a majority was voting for acquittal, more likely the case would be dropped. But if the poll showed the majority voted to convict, then the ADA would more than likely choose to retry the case. When this happens, the defense usually sees the odds were against the defendant, and after conferring with the defendant, may look to make a deal. This usually leads to the defendant taking a plea to a reduced charge, which usually comes with a reduced sentence.

It should be noted in a Civil Trial that a unanimous decision is not needed (meaning all jurors must agree . Whereas all you need in a Civil Trial is a Preponderance of Evidence to reach a successful conclusion either way.

It is also to be noted that no matter what the crime is, no matter who the victim was, if the courts found that the confession was obtained illegally, then the statements would be thrown out. Which may in some cases lead to a mistrial or an outright dismissal? Unfortunately, this has happened in the past, where even though there was overwhelming evidence against a defendant's guilt, due to an oversight or technicality, a guilty person was able to walk free. However, it has also happened numerous times after a person has been convicted and has served several years of his/her sentence. Many years later, defense attorneys or the courts suddenly find some technicality or some newly discovered evidence. Evidence that had been overlooked or possibly withheld by the DA's office or the Police. Where the defense accuses the Prosecutor of Prosecutorial Misconduct for withholding crucial evidence from the trial, and a decision by the courts will overturn the conviction and set him/her free. Which usually comes with a large lawsuit against the officer and the city.

AS THE SAYING GOES

"JUSTICE IS BLIND"

The fact remains that even though they were suspected of several push-ins, in which the victims were brutally assaulted and robbed. There just wasn't enough strong evidence to bring them to trial on those cases. The D.A. took the strongest cases, which were the three Homicides, went forward with them, and was able to gain a conviction. There may have been some additional charges that they were not convicted of, but the Murder convictions were substantial. Even though with two of the defendants the sentence was substantial, while three of the others really got off very easily. Considering the damage they caused both physically and mentally, they all should have spent their entire lives in jail. As previously stated, their sentences were just not enough to justify all the crimes they committed. The only justice, some would say, is Ben Bradshaw dying after serving only eleven years. But as some others would say, he beat the system; he should have served 25 years, then died, that would be real justice.

CHAPTER SIXTEEN

SUMMATION OF THE DAY STALKERS

LUCK PLAYED A BIG PART WITH THE STALKERS

In looking back at the Day Stalkers, good luck played a significant part in this case. Since the way they treated these elderly people, they were lucky many more didn't die. Especially given the fact that they were not just killers but serial killers.

Just slamming them to the floor, tying them up, and torturing them just enough to frighten them was enough to kill them. It was sheer luck that only three victims died because of all the brutalizing they did to the victims. Considering the age was somewhere between 65 and 86 years old. Any type of physical force used against them could have been fatal. In that respect, they were extremely lucky. They were also lucky that more of their victims didn't have a heart attack or go into convulsions from being gagged and tied, which they did to just about all their victims.

But it was obvious they never even thought or cared that the way they treated them could have led to murder. In fact, in the cases of the three murder victims, it appears that it looks like it was intentional. The reason being that by gagging them and seeing them struggling and squirming to try and get air, it was obvious that the victims could die. They could have easily prevented them from dying by simply pulling the gag from them. But they chose not to. The question is, why did they murder some victims and not others? In the case where they assaulted the uncle and nephew, why didn't they murder them instead of just violently assaulting them, causing them to seek hospital treatment? The same goes for the woman who was blinded in one eye. Why not finish the job and murder her? Was it just the callous attitude that whoever died as a result of the way they were treated was just the misfortune of the victim? Because obviously, they could have murdered more than just the three victims. As far as their motive, it was greed, looking to hit that jackpot, hoping to find that pot of gold. Why did they just pick on "any old person?" Was it because of what they had learned in jail, "all those old people have money?" If that was the case, they were stalking in the wrong neighborhood, because it was really a poor neighborhood. Why didn't they stalk them after cashing their check at a bank or a check-cashing store? This way, they were sure they had money on them. But apparently, even though it was known that it was part of their M.O., that was not the case in these three Homicides. None of these three victims was coming from a bank or a check-cashing establishment where they had just cashed a check. So was it just the fact that their leader, Ben, hated old people that much that he stalked any old person he saw? Or did he believe as he was told, "they all have money?" Because most people they stalked had very little money and were living just above or below the poverty level. There is the possibility in some cases that their miscreants (skells) own families had more money than the victims they were stalking/robbing.

In all three Homicides in no way did any of the defendants say outright yes, I helped kill them, or yes, we knew they died. But basically, using the self-serving statement, I was there and maybe helped tie him up. Or maybe they stated, I was there, but I just searched the apartment, never outright admitting to the murder. But by their statements, it was enough to put them on the scene and get a murder indictment against them. Being they admitted they were there and were part of the conspiracy. Each one that was convicted really didn't get enough of a sentence to justify the amount of damage they caused emotionally to the victims that survived, or to the murder victim's family.

NOTE: It was also noted that although the M.E. gave a timeline of the death, he could only say it was in the last twelve/thirty-six hours. He could never give an exact time. There is the possibility that these homicides occured between the hours of nine and ten thirty am. The Anti-Crime officers didn't start until nine thirty Am. At the time between 9:30 and 10:00 am, it was role call time, as well as training regarding any new laws, any recent patterns, or any new felony arrests. They would leave the office at 10 am, and maybe had to gas the car up, which was another 15 minutes or so before they got into the zone. It is possible that the stalkers had already completed their dirty deal and were already out of the area. Judging by the one victim who was found with his groceries under his body, he was out early shopping, before 9:30 am, which the detectives found out on their canvas. Was it possible the stalkers knew the hours of the Anti-Crime cops, and this is why they roamed the streets early, or was it just dumb luck? Given the fact that when 73 Anti-Crime stopped them and did a UF250, it was in the afternoon, after they did the early morning push-in, where they left the fingerprint behind. If it were realized that the stalkers were doing early morning push-ins, the Anti-Crime boss would have adjusted their hours to start earlier. There was also the possibility that if the officers saw them go into a building and stopped them from going in, this would be before they committed a crime. It would be extremely hard to follow them into a building and observe them doing a push-in. By the same token, if they stopped them from coming out of a building, they would have to justify stopping them. Then detain them and do a canvas of the whole building to see if any crime was committed. Which would be extremely time-consuming, considering all these buildings where the homicides occurred were large apartment houses with many apartments on each floor.

LUCK PLAYED A BIG PART IN THE

POLICE DEPARTMENT

The Police Department was also lucky, lucky that only three people were killed due to the fact that they did so many push-ins where the victims were violently attacked. The detectives were also lucky that the suspects eventually made their mistake and left a fingerprint behind, coupled with the fact that the Anti-Crime cops from the 73 precinct did an excellent job of reporting on their stop, as far as filing a 250 form (Stop Question Frisk). This then led to good detective work in breaking the case wide open. Whereby they made several arrests. This was also good luck that they were arrested before they had a chance to continue their spree and possibly cause another death or two. This would have put significantly more pressure on the Police Department and generated more fear amongst the seniors. Had they not made the mistake of leaving the fingerprint behind, who knows how many other push-ins they may have done before they killed someone else? Before the Police were able to put an end to this reign of terror.

The police were also lucky, given the fact that the community helped by giving them tips. Tips from people who were living in this neighborhood all their lives and saw or knew of some of the serious crimes that had taken place prior. They also knew many of the kids from the neighborhood, some of whom were grandkids of their friends. But these kids (the stalkers) were different; they appeared more frightening to them. So much so that they were afraid to walk the streets because of them. So, they informed the Police of them, but did it in a covert manner, anonymously. Even though they were anonymous tips it pointed the detectives in the right direction. It gave them an insight into who the suspects may be and where they may have lived or come from before they were arrested. The detectives were also lucky that their leader (Ben) had brazenly bragged to some younger kids "What We Did Today You Will See On The News Tonight" So in the end it was their bad luck by leaving the fingerprint behind, and wearing the plastic on their hats but good luck as well as good investigative work by the detectives that caused the end of their reign of terror by the,

SERIAL KILLERS

who were known as the

THE DAY STALKERS

But the question among some detectives remained: why were some victims brutalized, like the woman who lost an eye, or the uncle and his nephew, who were also beaten. As opposed to the woman who was in bed, or other victims who were just threatened, but not harmed. Could it be possible that on certain days, they were in a drug-induced rage that led them to act so violently? It was a question for which there was never a credible answer.

THE DAY STALKERS

CONTENTS: SENIOR CITIZEN ROBBERY UNIT

CHAPTER I

BIRTH OF A NEW UNIT

CHAPTER II

MORE THAN INVESTIGATORS

CHAPTER III

INVESTIGATIONS

CHAPTER IV

DECOY UNIT

CHAPTER V

I AM A MEMBER OF SCRU

CHAPTER VI

THE BEGINNING OF ATI CRIME

CHAPTER VII

NEAR THE END OF MY TIME IN SCRU

CHAPTER VIII

THE PUERTO RICO CONNECTION

CHAPTER IX
SUSPECT IS IN CUSTODY

CHAPTER X

A NEW PATTERN

CHAPTER XI

A GAME XHANGER

CHAPTER XI

ANTHONY GOES UNDERGROUND

CHAPTER X111

THE TRIAL

CHAPTER X1V

SUMMATION OF THE DAY STALKERS

CHAPTER ONE

BIRTH OF A NEW UNIT

SENIOR CITIZEN ROBBERY UNIT

(SCRU)

Now that the push-in pattern is closed, regarding the homicides. NYPD still had a problem with Senior Citizen Robberies. The problem was not only in Brooklyn South/Brooklyn North but also in other parts of the city. Apparently, the Bronx, as well as Queens, had their own problems with Senior Citizen Robberies. After much consideration, the department decided to create a unit that would only handle Senior Citizen robberies. They obviously realized that the precinct Detective Squads didn't have the time to handle the older, delicate complainants. Complainants who were sometimes hard of hearing, had bad eyesight, and had problems walking. It would be time-consuming for Squad Detectives to handle these cases, time that they didn't have. This is the first time in the history of the NYPD that a unit was created just to handle Senior Citizen Robberies exclusively. This was created exclusively for robberies, not assaults or larcenies. So sometime in mid 1976, the Senior Citizen Robbery Unit of Brooklyn South was born. It was also opened in the other Boroughs around the same time. The unit was made up of young active cops, male and female, who were both eager and aggressive.

Each precinct in Brooklyn South was scoured searching for its best officers. Once a list was established, each officer was given an interview by the Lieutenant/Sergeants who oversaw the unit. They only wanted the best officers for the unit. Officer's that would be considered best suited to do the job. In Brooklyn South, the unit was made up of investigators as well as a decoy team. The units were under the Borough Task Force, which was under the Uniformed Patrol Bureau. The Decoy Team would usually concentrate in an area where there were many senior robberies. In some cases, some would be part of a pattern. So, no matter where there was a robbery of a Senior Citizen in Brooklyn South, they would have to address it first if it was part of a pattern.

It would be addressed in the following manner.

One of the members would dress as an elderly person and walk the streets in hopes of getting mugged (robbed). The decoy, most of the time would be a woman, but also at times, if the pattern called for it, one of the males would dress as an elderly male, and he would be the decoy. The decoys were closely monitored by the backup team. It was successful some days, but on other days, as hard as they tried, they had no luck. It was like a day going fishing, one day you catch a large Stripper or Blue Fish, other days you can't even catch a Minnow. The Brooklyn South Senior Citizen unit also had four Gold Shield Detective investigators that were assigned to it. They were drawn from various Detective squads in Brooklyn South. These Detectives were assigned to the Detective Bureau but were on temporary assignment to the SCRU unit, which was under the Patrol Bureau. They were brought into the unit as an incentive for the cops who were called White Shield investigators. These White Shields were doing the same work as a Detective did. The incentive being, hopefully, one day the White Shield will one day get the Gold Shield. The cops were known as White Shield investigators, even though their shields were Silver. That was the term used for them, as opposed to the Detectives who had the Gold Shield. The unit was commanded by the Lieutenant, who also had the uniform Task Force Cops under his wing. The Brooklyn South SCRU also had two Sergeants assigned to it. They supervised the unit every day, as opposed to the Lieutenant who only appeared on occasion but oversaw the unit on a regular basis.

The Sergeants would tell the officers that someday the unit would probably be absorbed into the Detective Bureau. When that happened, everyone assigned would get the Gold Shield. That was wishful thinking on the Sergeant's part. Even though they meant well and believed it to be so. It was a hollow statement that wasn't to be. It really wasn't fair to the cops who were doing the same exact work as the Detective sitting next to him. They did investigations exactly the way a Detective would do. Everything that a Gold Shield would do, they did, following every step of the investigation. The only difference was that the Detective made much more money, and their title was considered much more prestigious. So basically, it boiled down to the Police Department was expecting the White Shields to do what the Detectives did for less money, and without the prestige that a Detective had. As the cops would say, the department was "dangling a carrot in front of your face" by letting you believe you were eventually getting the Gold Shield. But nevertheless, these officers gave it their all. Never letting the conditions they were working under stop them from being dedicated and working as hard as they could.

Eventually, there came a time when a lawsuit was initiated. This involved Police Officers from all over the city working in several different units, I.E, Detective Squads, Organized Crime Control Bureau (OCCB), which covered Public Morals Division, Narcotics Division, and Auto Crime Division. The officers in these units were like the SCRU unit in that the officers were working side by side with the Detectives but getting no recognition or compensation for it. The name of the lawsuit was, as the cops called it, "The White Shield Suit." As it wangled its way through the court system, each time the Cops won in one court, the city would go to a higher court and appeal, only to have the Cops' victory denied. However, their loss never deterred the White Shield cops from their dedication to performing their job diligently.

CHAPTER TWO

MORE THAN INVESTIGATORS

The officers in the SCRU were not only law enforcement officers, but also investigators. In some cases, they were almost like community affairs officers or social workers. The reason being they would also help the victims.

Some of the ways that they would help the victims are as follows.

When a senior citizen got robbed of his/her Social Security money, when they had no family to help them, the officers would help them to try to get reimbursed from the Social Security Dept. If need be, they would take them to the Social Security Office, also supplying the Social Security Department with proof they were victims of a robbery of their Social Security money. They would also get them help through the Crime Victims Compensation Board.

They would also pick them up and take them to view photos at the borough office or scour the neighborhood with them, hoping to see the thugs on the street. This was done in a case where the victim stated they could identify the suspect, which was very rare. When needed, they would also pick them up and take them to Criminal Court or the Grand Jury to testify, then bring them home.

All these things that a SCRU officer did, a precinct Squad Detective didn't have the time to do. It would take time to pick them up, bring them to where they had to go, and then take them back. In a busy Detective Squad, the cases would still be coming in, and they would be losing investigative time to work on these cases. Whereas SCRU, which was a specialized unit, allowed the time for this. Also, the investigators would only work on one type of crime, a Senior Citizen Robbery. In a precinct squad, the saying was "we catch everything," from Dis Con (Disorderly Conduct) to Homicide.

CHAPTER THREE

INVESTIGATIONS

However, every borough had its own criteria for how cases were handled. During that period, the Bronx was a single borough, as was Queens. Queens became two: North and South. Brooklyn was always two boroughs, as was Manhattan North and Manhattan South. Staten Island was always one borough, as it was always the quietest. It was the volume of work, not the size of the area, that dictated whether it would be divided into two boroughs. In the boroughs of the Bronx and Queens, any senior citizen robbery, no matter where it occurred, whether it was on the street or inside a building, the case went to the SCRU of that borough. In Brooklyn North, it was the same; wherever the robbery occurred, the case would go to the SCRU so long as it was a senior. However, in Brooklyn South, the criteria were different; it had to be inside a building only. It didn't make a difference if it was in the hallway, foyer, lobby, or elevator, or apartment, just so long as it was inside the building, and off the street, especially if it was in a residence. Which, in some cases, would be called a Home Invasion. If it were on the street, it would go to the precinct Detective Squad concerned, which sometimes led to hard feelings. Detectives and or Sergeants of Squads that didn't know any better would think that the officers of the SCRU were picking and choosing their cases. They had to be made aware of the borough order that mandated how the cases would be assigned. More than likely, the reason Brooklyn South only handled inside (off-street) robberies was because that area had a significant amount of push-ins, or hallway robberies, besides the ones that eventually led to the Homicides. The borough commander wanted more concentration on the push-in to hopefully make an arrest and avoid any other push-in Homicides, as in the past pattern. Because it was obvious there were also many other indoor robberies in the area, other than the homicides. In the Brooklyn South SCRU, the borough was broken down into zones. Each zone had a team of investigators assigned to it. If a case came in within your zone and you were off another team, would be assigned that team would do a preliminary investigation for you. This way, the case was given immediate attention; instead of waiting for. the proper team to come in. When you return to work, the case will be officially assigned to you. You would then start your own investigation and do a follow-up by reinterviewing the victim or witnesses. This would be done even if they said they can't ID or didn't want to pursue the matter. However, the difference was in a Detective Squad when a Detective caught a case where the victim said he/she could not ID the suspects, and there were no witnesses, the case would be closed with Negative Results. In a case where the victim/complainant did not want to press charges, the Detective would close the case as Un Co Operative Complainant. However, in the SCRU, the investigator could not close out a case in such a manner. They had to be investigated regardless of what the victim stated.

This would be done by doing a canvas of the area/building where the robbery occurred. This meant several trips back to the area to speak to people whom you may have missed on the first or second time around. It would be time-consuming, but it was something that had to be done. The feeling was that you had to give it your all in hopes that you could build a case, make an arrest, and bring the case to a successful conclusion. Whereas the precinct Detective did not have the time, the case load was too heavy, and didn't allow it. The case had to be closed as soon as possible. This was also at a time when there was no DNA to help with an investigation. There were also no cameras, videos, or still photos to aid in the investigations. This had to be done by the good old pounding of the bricks. This meant doing canvases on foot, seeking information.

Nowadays, with the aid of modern science, DNA evidence sometimes tells the whole story. Especially if it is recovered from the body in the case of a Homicide. The body sometimes actually tells the story, without saying a word. This makes the investigation a lot easier. But to reiterate, this was before DNA/Cameras, just good old-fashioned pounding of the bricks.

CHAPTER FOUR

THE DECOY UNIT

In Brooklyn South, the Decoy Unit specialized in addressing street robberies. This unit was created even though the precincts had Anti-Crime Units; the Anti-Crime cops did not do any investigations. Also, they rarely wore any disguises; in fact, there was a department order at one time forbidding them to wear disguises as working people. Or represent themselves as Utility or Phone Co. workers, or delivery people like UPS. This was because a subversive group allegedly pulled over a telephone company. employee and searched him at gunpoint, thinking he was a decoy cop. This was during the period when certain police hating subversive groups were ambushing cops. So, for the safety of these civilian workers, decoy cops could not pretend to be them. Especially since their unions complained to the Police Department. So, the Police Department ordered it to be terminated. Although many still did this on their own, even though it was unauthorized by the department, if something went wrong, they would have a serious problem with the department. Also, the fact that the Anti-Crime units were confined to the confines of their precinct. Whereas the decoy unit would work a given area where there was a high volume of Senior Citizen robberies anywhere in the borough, and were encouraged to blend in, disguise-wise. They would look at the statistics for the Borough and ascertain information as to where and when these robberies were occurring. They would then target that area with a plan as to what the pattern was dictating. They would be dressed as the elderly and walk around the area being monitored by the backup team. Where a civilian would be hoping and praying that they wouldn't be mugged and would get home safely. It would be just the opposite with a decoy; he/she would be praying to get mugged.

When the unit first started, the decoy team went to a professional makeup artist for help. He made them up to fit the part they were playing; he gave them advice and tips on how they could apply the tricks to make themselves up. So, once they learned they were on their own. Considering they were not made up by professional makeup artists anymore, they did a pretty good job of disguising themselves. Using a gray wig and a kerchief with Aunt Maggie's dress and Grandma Mary's coat off, they went, hoping to get mugged. Sometimes they would walk with a cane, another time just with a little slow shuffle. Trying as hard as they could to blend in and duplicate what an elderly person would look like to a perpetrator. Hoping to attract someone who was out there just waiting for a victim to stalk and attack. Hoping to reel in some miscreant who was up to no good. Swooping down on him/her as soon as they committed their attack on the victim.

The male decoys also made themselves up as elderly gentleman, walking along slowly with a cane, barely moving along. The part was played extremely well by both the male and the female decoy. You would think they had some professional acting or training, the way they performed. Both male and female decoys and their backup team did an excellent job, a job that sometimes was not given enough recognition by the higher-ups in the department. The officers made many arrests for street crimes, of which many were usually purse snatches. Where the perpetrator would sneak up behind the victim and snatch the purse/pocketbook before the victim even knew what happened. If taken from a victim, the charge would be Grand Larceny from the person. If there wasn't an on-the-spot arrest of a crime against a civilian, there probably would never be an arrest. Because if the case went to a Detective Squad, the victim's statement usually would be, "I was robbed from behind, so I can't identify anyone." The case would then immediately be closed. However, the decoy team made many observation arrests that were executed against ordinary civilians, as well as from the decoys. When they saw a person who didn't look right, they would carefully watch him. If he did a robbery/purse snatch, they would immediately swoop down on him, and before he knew what happened, he would be in cuffs. If the arrest wasn't made on the spot, there would most likely never be an arrest if the case went to a detective squad.

However, if there was any force used, for instance, if the person resisted by holding on to the purse, and any force was used to wrest it away from the victim, it would then bring it to a different level of crime. It now would become a robbery, which there were three degrees of. The NYS Penal Law definition of Robbery is "The taking of property by force or fear." The amount or type of force used would dictate what level of robbery would be charged. Depending on the amount of force used, where the victim may be injured, and depending on how serious the injury is, or if the suspect was armed with a weapon and displayed or used the weapon. If the victim was injured, it would also determine the appropriate degree of Robbery that the suspect would be charged with for the crime. The charge could be anywhere from a robbery 3rd, which is the lowest degree, to a robbery 1st, which is the highest. Which is usually applied when the victim is hurt or a weapon/firearm is used.

Eventually, they had a pattern develop on a particular block in East Flatbush where the victim was usually an elderly male. It was a bit unusual that the suspect was only attacking males. But that's what the pattern described. So, they set out to put the bait out. One of the males dressed as an elderly man, who played the part quite well. He was a great cop who was a good street cop. He was excellent for the part. He was also prematurely gray, which helped him fit right into the part. They got him a first-floor apartment on the block where most of the robberies were occurring. The backup team was also able to get an apartment on the same block across the street and directly opposite the decoys building. The backup team's apartment would be called the O.P. (observation post). The building's owners were more than happy to supply the apartments on a temporary basis. With this thought in mind, hopefully, this will make our block safer. So, with the two apartments set up, all they had to do was set out the bait and hope to catch the big one. With the decoy walking back and forth on the block and the backup team monitoring him covertly from the nearby Observation Post (O.P.) across the street, it was a waiting game. Every day, the decoy would take a stroll down the block and hope to be followed back to his building. He did this several times during the day. Several days went by with no luck. But they kept the surveillance going anyway. Now it was more than a week without a bite. The thought was that maybe the suspect moved on to a different neighborhood. Maybe he was in jail on another crime. But after giving it some deep thought, a decision was made to keep it going for another week or two. They just couldn't give up that easily. This turned out to be good thinking on their part. As luck would have it, finally, one day their ship came in. As the decoy was walking down the block as usual, the backup team noticed a male a short distance behind who appeared to be following him. The team notified the decoy through a radio that he had in an earpiece in his ear that he was being followed. So, he immediately entered his building and his apartment, which was on the first floor. The suspect immediately followed him into the building. This was not an elevator building, so the suspect must have realized that the victim disappeared so quickly; he must have gone into a first-floor apartment. Within a couple of seconds, there was a knock on the decoy's door. The decoy answered with a frail-sounding voice, asking who was there. But there was silence. He waited about a minute, and he heard nothing. He then looks out the peephole. He sees the suspect right opposite his apartment at the door on the opposite side. The door then opens, and the suspect immediately pushes the elderly male in and apparently locks the door behind him. He immediately notifies his backup team of his observation, and they come running across the street. They gently try the doorknob and realize the door is locked. So now they are all at the door waiting. Now they could hear the elderly male being battered around, begging and pleading for mercy. Then, after several minutes, there is silence. With the door being locked, there is not much they can do but wait for him to come out. If they try to break the door down, there may be a back window that leads to a courtyard where the suspect can escape through. But they couldn't get back to it because the basement door that led to the courtyard was locked. It was locked, apparently, because of burglars using it to sneak in or escape out of the building through that exit. So, they had no choice but to be patient and wait and hope and pray that he doesn't kill the old guy, or maybe with the silence, he has already done that. Apparently, during this silent period, the skell is searching the apartment for any valuables. So, there they waited with hearts pounding, adrenaline pumping, hoping that the old man was still alive and they could catch this savage, this monster who would beat and rob an elderly man. Finally, after several minutes, the door cracks open with the backup team standing on each side of it. This is the moment they have been patiently waiting for. This is the moment when all their tensions are going to be relieved. This is the moment their adrenaline, which has been built up while waiting for this monster, will be relieved as they take him into custody.

As he starts to peep out, he is faced with four angry cops; he has only two choices: peacefully surrender or try to fight his way out. He makes the mistake of trying to fight his way out. Unfortunately, he made a grave mistake because the harder you fight the cops, that's the harder the officers are going to fight you. He is pushed back in as the cops try to take him into custody. He is fighting furiously and violently. The cops are fighting just as furiously. There is a reason some perpetrators try to fight their way out of being arrested, whether it is one cop or four. The reason is that they know they are going to jail, which may be for a long time, so they try their hardest to escape. But he is no match for four angry cops, who are dead set on taking him into custody. After several minutes and a violent struggle, they have gained control and are able to handcuff the suspect. Now that he is subdued, they can attend to the elderly gentleman. The old man is on the floor, bleeding and battered but alive. He is immediately rushed to a local hospital for treatment, where he is admitted for his injuries. The suspect is also taken to the same hospital to have his wounds tended to, wounds that he sustained while violently resisting arrest. (As he was probably saying to himself as the song goes) "I fought the Law and the Law won." The suspect was charged with Attempted Murder, Robbery 1st degree, Burglary 1st degree, Assault 1st degree, as well as Resisting Arrest. Surprisingly, it was his first arrest. But more than likely, the first time he got caught. When they searched him, it was revealed that all he took was a few dollars and a cheap old wristwatch. Really not worth going to jail for or nearly beating someone to death for. A hearing was held in Criminal Court, where the judge found enough evidence to send the case to the Grand Jury. Eventually, he is indicted by the Grand Jury on all counts, including Attempted Murder as well as several other charges, which include first-degree Robbery/Burglary.   Eventually, a conference hearing between the ADA and the Defense Attorney is held. The reason is to see if any agreement can be made to resolve this case without going to trial.

There was no way a defense attorney was going to trial with four cops who were witnesses as he was committing an assault, as they were listening in helplessly right at the door of the apartment. Coupled with the fact that he was caught right in the victim's apartment.

All his defense attorney can do is work out the best plea that he can for his client with the DA's office. He then must hope the judge will agree to it at sentencing time. Eventually, a plea agreement is reached. He will plead guilty to reduced charges of robbery 2nd, burglary 2nd. Even though it was his first arrest, he was sentenced to 10 years in prison. The judge took into consideration the seriousness of the crime and the age of the victim, who was in his eighties. He also took into consideration of the fact the violent nature of the beating he had given the elderly man and the injuries the old gent sustained. The only good luck that was with him was that the old man didn't die from the beating. So, the judge saw fit to give him the maximum sentence allowed by law, according to his plea.

The sad part was that although there were several robberies with the same M.O. (Method of Operation) in the same area and the suspect fit the general description, none of the previous victims could identify him. In each of the robberies, he used force, which was his M.O., and the victim was always a male. He did this even if the victim offered no resistance. He was also smart enough not to admit to any other crimes. In each of the cases, the victim was shown a photo lineup with the suspect, but each failed to ID him. This is not unusual in Senior Citizen cases, where the victims can't ID a suspect. The officers of the decoy team knew that he was responsible for other robberies, just by the mere fact of his M.O. But with no other identification by any other senior, knowing something and proving it in court are two different things. So, there is not much they can do about it. However, it was noted that after his arrest, there were no other crimes of that type in the immediate area. This led to the closing of that pattern. It was then back to the usual routine, walking the streets, hoping to get mugged. Trying to put fear into the bad guys "be careful big brother is watching," and the next person you mug just may be a cop.

CHAPTER FIVE

I AM A MEMBER OF SCRU

In February of 1978, I was asked to join the Brooklyn South Senior Robbery Unit. I was told, like everyone else in the unit, that one day the unit would possibly be absorbed by the Detective Bureau, and we would all get the Gold Shield. Which was my goal since I came on the job. I was in the precinct Anti –Crime Unit working with all good cops. Anti-Crime, which, in my opinion, was one of the best units the Police Department ever created. But I also wanted the Detective Shield, and at that point, the department stopped with the discretionary awarding of the Detective Gold Shield. So, I decided to take my chances and go to the SCRU in hopes of getting a Det. Shield.

The Senior Citizen Robbery Unit was basically started to combat Senior Citizen Robberies throughout the city. However, all the different units in the Police Department are great. Each different unit handles its job in an extremely professional manner. Each time they bring a case to a successful conclusion, it's extremely rewarding.

THERE ARE MANY GREAT UNITS IN THE NYPD

There is the Emergency Service Unit, as well as the Harbor/Scuba unit and the Aviation Division. Along with many other units that make the NYPD the greatest department in the USA. They are the units that are called by the cops when the cops need help.

THE DETECTIVE BUREAU

The Detectives get the same satisfaction when solving a serious crime, such as homicide, robbery, or burglary. The precinct squad is probably the hardest-working detectives of all. They get all kinds of cases thrown at them in a busy squad. As soon as they close one case, they catch two more, it seems.

The Narcotics detectives get the same satisfaction when locking up a hardcore drug dealer. Especially after he just sold to an undercover or was dealing drugs near a school.

All the different units in the department, Harbor, Scuba, Aviation, Crime Scene Unit, and so many others working together is what makes this department (NYPD) one of the GREATEST DEPARTMENTS in the USA.

But the Street Crime Unit/Anti-Crime Unit was the one that made the type of arrest that kept people from walking the streets in some neighborhoods. The Street Crime/Anti-Crime cops were the ones who made that on-the-spot observation arrest. They were the ones who got that Robber as he was robbing a victim on the street. Or they were the ones who grabbed that Burglar right in the act of burglarizing a house or an apartment. If it wasn't for the on-the-spot observation arrest most times the patrol officers would get there after the fact. The suspects are usually long gone, and the crime is just another statistic.

THE UNIFORMED PATROL OFFICERS

With regards to the Patrol Force, these men and women are probably the hardest working and most underappreciated unit in the department. They are the first line of defense; they are the ones who hold the lid down on the boiling pot of NYC. They also get probably the most scrutiny, be it the Internal Affairs Bureau (IAB)or the Civilian Complaint Review Board (CCRB). So, as they tell you, in the academy, "the Patrol Force is the Backbone of the Department," but they get the least amount of recognition. Yet they are the guardians of the city.

CHAPTER SIX

THE BEGINNING OF ANTI-CRIME

Sometime in late 1971 and early 1972, the precinct Anti-Crime Unit was formed. Some boroughs authorized it later than others on a precinct level; prior to that, it was on a Borough level only. It was made up of almost all young active cops. I was assigned to the 69 precinct Anti-Crime unit and considered myself lucky to be chosen. There were very few females on patrol back then, maybe two in the whole city who were part of a pilot program. (The females weren't put on Patrol until sometime in 1973). When they became equals to their male counterparts after they won a Lawsuit in court. So, there were no females in the Anti-Crime unit at the beginning. Prior to the Anti-Crime unit being formed, when there was a precinct condition, the Commanding Officer would have to call in a specialized unit to address the situation. Sometimes this would cause other problems; the reason being that sometimes a local resident would get arrested or summoned by one of these outside officers. Where a cop assigned to the precinct would maybe just give the person a warning and tell them not to do it again, and overlook it if it was something minor. This made better relations with the local community, the people who then had more respect for the precinct cop.

The Anti-Crime unit was created to address local street crimes, crimes that affected the everyday lives of people. Crimes such as Robbery, Grand Larceny (from the person), Burglary, or Grand Larceny Auto. However, the department frowned on a Grand Larceny Auto arrest. The reason being Anti-Crime worked in plain clothes and unmarked cars. Many times, when the Anti-Crime Officers tried to stop a stolen car, the driver of the stolen car would flee. Or as the cops would say, he was "BOOKING." This sometimes leads to a high-speed chase through residential neighborhoods. This can create dangerous conditions for the officers as well as innocent civilians, or even the suspects (skells).

I LEFT ANTI-CRIME FOR THE

SENIOR CITIZEN ROBBERY UNIT

Even though I loved doing what I was doing and working with the cops I was working with, who were all good street cops, the lure of the Gold Shield encouraged me to agree to accept the offer and become a member of the Brooklyn South SCRU.   I went there with the thought of going into the Decoy Unit, but when I got there, I was told that I would be an investigator. Being an Anti-Crime cop for several years, I was used to making on-the-spot street observation arrests for crimes as previously described. These were the type of crimes that made people afraid to walk the streets, afraid of getting robbed and maybe beaten or maybe even killed. Also, having their homes broken into or their cars stolen, the things that some people worked for all their lives, only to be taken away from them in a couple of minutes. Most of the time, these crimes were committed by someone who was strung out and needed money to buy drugs.

But with car thefts, it was sometimes organized crime people who were stealing for profit, not just joyriding or drug money. The way they would profit would be, the car would be stripped and the parts sold off mostly to collision shops out of junk yards and sold as used parts. This would be very profitable, with the profits being over 100%, considering the car was attained for nothing. If you hadn't gotten caught the profit was too great to pass up. Getting caught would be costly, because then you had to raise bail money, if bail was set, which in most cases wasn't. You then would have to hire a lawyer to represent you, which can be costly, especially if you didn't qualify for a legal aid lawyer.

The other method of making money with stolen vehicles would be changing the VIN (Vehicle Identification Number). This is known as tagging the car; it would then be sold with phony papers locally or maybe even shipped out of the country. This was also very profitable. Those were the type of arrests I was used to making as an Anti-Crime Cop.

So, with my background, I thought I would be better suited for the Decoy unit, but the bosses thought otherwise, and I was assigned as an investigator. I was partnered up with a good cop, a cop who was also there in hopes of getting his Gold Shield. As the cases came in, I found out it wasn't as easy as being on the street as a street cop as far as making an arrest. Most of the time, the victims could not ID their perpetrators or, as in many cases, were too afraid to ID them. Most of the arrests I made in the SCRU were after developing information on suspects, where we would usually get a confession out of them. We usually did that in this manner.

If there were two of them, we would turn one against the other by telling one that his partner had confessed and laid the whole blame on him. Which, in many cases, was true. This would usually infuriate the other, and he would thereby make a self-serving statement, usually like most do, putting himself there but not taking any part in it. Then we would go back to the other and tell him that his partner gave him up as the aggressor. This would usually enrage him, and he would lay all the blame on his partner. But in doing so, he put himself more deeply involved.

But in the case of a lone suspect, it was a little harder. I usually would tell him I have a witness who gave him up and identified him. If he was inexperienced, he would sometimes fall for it. But the hard-core ones who had the street smarts, the experienced ones, especially the ones who had a previous arrest, would usually not take the bait and would have to be cut loose. Only if we had additional evidence could we arrest him. Most of these robberies were either in a hallway, vestibule, or entrance way to a building, or sometimes on an elevator. The ones that were the Push Ins into the apartments were the hardest; they usually never saw or got a good look at the face or faces of the suspect. My partner and I caught several push-ins, but an arrest was rarely made.

Eventually, we catch a push-in case in the Pink Houses in East New York, where a woman was robbed in her apartment after getting off the elevator. There were a couple of skells on the elevator with her, but they got off the floor before hers. My partner is up, so it's his case. We already know the M.O. by talking to the uniform cop who took the report. She was assaulted during the robbery and had to be hospitalized. We went to the hospital to interview her. We see she is battered, and on the left side of her face/cheek, she has the pattern of a sneaker footprint. My partner had a picture taken of it, entering it as part of the case. He interviews her, and basically, she states what the old people usually say, "I was hit from behind, I never saw their faces". They pushed me in as I was opening the door. She stated she wasn't sure if it was three or four skells. When she went down, one of them stomped on her face, leaving a foot/shoe print. We do the usual canvas and interview the people on her floor, as well as several people in her building. But as is normally the case, no one saw or heard anything. So, at this point, after an exhaustive canvas, the case must eventually be closed with N/R Negative Results.

With regards to the sneaker print, at the time, there was no one local unit/person who would be able to ID the manufacturer by the pattern of the shoe/sneaker print. Even if there was back then every kid in Brooklyn wore the most common brands of sneakers. So, more than likely, there would be many who had the same pattern. Without any other substantial evidence, there would be no arrest, especially since the victim couldn't identify.

During this period, we caught many robbery cases, and most ended with negative results since most of the time the elderly could not identify the suspect.

Eventually, there was a pattern in the Flatbush section of Brooklyn, the confines of the 63 precinct. The pattern was that the suspects (Skells) were coming down Kings Highway (a major roadway in Brooklyn). They usually operated out of a stolen car. From witness accounts, there were usually three of them in the car. Their M.O. was to cruise up and down Kings Highway, and if they saw a woman walking alone, one would jump out of the car and snatch her bag. Over a two-week period, there were several like this, where they would jump out of the car and snatch the bag. As the protocol was written by the Borough Commander, if it were on the street, it would be a precinct squad detectives' case. If it were inside a building, it would be a Senior Citizen case.

On one of their journeys, one of the women (victim) made it into the vestibule of her apartment house. Undeterred by this, the skell runs into the vestibule wrest her bag from her, and makes off with it. Even though it's in the vestibule, its our case, as it is off the street, the case is assigned to the Senior Citizen Robbery Unit. My partner is up, so it's his case. We interview the woman, and as usual, she can't ID. A couple of days later, we are in East New York on one of our cases. We hear on the police radio that the 63 uniformed cops ran a plate that came back.

stolen. They say holding three. (meaning 3 suspects) So, my partner and I think these could be our guys. So, we drove down to the 63, and by the time we got to the scene, they went to the station house with the prisoners. We go to the station house, and we talk to the cops and tell them we have a case of a robbery out of a car. We tell them we want to talk to them regarding our case, and they say no problem. There were three arrested for the stolen car. We give each one their rights separately and interview them on our robbery, eventually we use a little trickery in that we say we have a witness who picks the one out who was in the vestibule. The plan works on one of them; he folds and admits that he was the one who snatched the bag. We couldn't get the other two to confess, they never got out of the car, but at this point, we didn't care. We had our guy for our case, and the uniform had him with the other two for the stolen car. It would be up to the precinct detective who had the pattern of street robberies to follow up on them. So now we take him upstairs to the detective unit to process him for our case. We ID ourselves and tell the detective what we have, and within a minute, he runs into the Sergeants' office. Next thing you know, the Sergeant comes over to us and berates us that we stole the collar (arrest) off his detective. He states this is part of a pattern and the arrest should be his detectives'. We tried to tell him we followed protocol, that it was off the street, and we arrested him only on our case, and all others would be up to his detective to follow up on. The problem was that his detective wasn't doing his job. It was right in his precinct, so he should have come down and interviewed the prisoners, but he didn't. He should have been down even before we got there and started questioning them. But he didn't come down, but now that he sees we made an arrest, he feels we have taken his arrest from him. But by not coming down one flight, he feels we stole the arrest. We tried explaining the protocol to his Sergeant, that when it's a robbery of a senior inside a building, the case is assigned to us, win or lose. But he was adamant that we stole the arrest. He stated that by us making the arrest, we interfered with his pattern and any arrest that would have been made. The possibility existed that when we proved that the case was ours, he wanted to save face with his detective and that he was defending him. There was no way we would give up that arrest. So now that we are finished with our paperwork, we are ready to leave to go to the ADA's office to draw up our case. The Sergeant states that he is coming to the ADA's office with us, we think, why? But he is a Sgt. So, we don't ask why. When we got there, we laid out our case to the ADA, and he had no problem with it. Now the Sgt brings out all the 61's (complaint reports) of all the past robberies out of a car that the other two/three suspects were involved in (there were about 8 or 9 cases), he shows them to the ADA. He stated that this is the pattern that this suspect was involved in with the other two. The ADA asks him, "Do you have his ID for any of these others?" He answers no, the ADA tells him to come back when you get his ID or any of the others' IDs. With that, he leaves.

The reason why we didn't have a lineup with him is not only that the victim couldn't ID him, but the uniformed cops still have him for the stolen car, which he was arrested in. So, the ADA was satisfied that he would probably plead to the lesser charge of Grand Larceny, which would cover all charges, as he is only sixteen and it's his first arrest (think batting average).

ANOTHER PUSH IN

About a month goes by with the normal catching of cases where we cannot get anyone to ID a suspect. I then caught a push-in case that happened in the Boulevard Houses, in East New York, Brooklyn. The Boulevard Houses are a City Housing Project at the time in the tough neighborhood of

East New York. They were only blocks from another tough project, Pink Houses. These are the types of projects where cops would sometimes go to take a report or even make an arrest. They would have to watch out for Air Mails (a cop's description of something thrown off the roof at them), a brick, a bottle, or any other type of missile meant to hurt the cop.

NOTE: There was a case in Manhattan where a cop was walking into the courtyard of one of these tall buildings, and an Air Mail was thrown down from the rooftop at him. It turned out to be a 30LB can of Joint Compound. The cop was struck in the head and killed. Fortunately, an arrest was made.

So, when you entered the grounds, walking to a building, you made sure you watched the rooftops for any flying objects. It didn't make a difference what you were there for; caution had to be taken. You could have been there to help someone, somebody who was injured or ill. It could have been an elderly person or a baby who needed help. Or maybe to interview the victim of a crime. To the miscreants (skells) who were throwing the missiles, you were the natural enemy. You were entering their territory, even though you were invited there, it didn't make any difference to them. To some of them, you were just the enemy encroaching on their territory, apparently always thinking you were there to arrest someone. So, with this in mind, we were always careful whenever we entered the grounds. Always looking up at the top of the building.

INTERVIEW OF THE VICTIM

The victim, an elderly black female, basically stated the facts of a typical push-in case to the uniformed officers who took the report.

She entered her building, to be specific, 804 Ashford St., and eventually got on the elevator. When she did, a young male entered with her. She thought nothing of it; it was just a normal event. She was a resident of that building for many years and rode the elevator for what seemed like a million times without anything ever happening. He was a young male, which was not unusual; there were many youths living in the projects. So, most of the residents of the building were used to teenagers hanging around the building or riding the elevator. She, being an elderly female, thought nothing of it, as most of the youths were respectful to the elderly people in the building. This one was no different. When he got on the elevator with her, he asked what floor she was going to and pressed the button for her floor, which was five. He then got off at four. She thought nothing of it; it was just another good kid who lived or was visiting someone in the building. But then it happens, she becomes the victim of a push-in robber.

HER STORY WAS AS FOLLOWS

She went to the check-cashing store to cash her Social Security Check. She then went to a local Bodega to buy a few grocery items with her food stamp card. She then walked home, which was not far from the Bodega. When she got to her building, she got on the elevator, as did a young male teenager. She paid no mind to him, as previously stated, many young males lived in the projects. She had ridden the elevator many times with teenagers and never had a problem; they were all good kids. He was also a gentleman and asked what floor she was going to and pushed the button for her floor, which was five; he said he was going to four. So, she basically paid no mind to him, again thinking he was just a normal kid from the area. Just one of the kids who has ridden the elevator many times in the past without any incident. He is standing close to the elevator doors, facing the front. She is behind him towards the back of the elevator. When the elevator reached four, he immediately exited. (He was staying close to the doors, more than likely, so she couldn't get a good look at his face.) She went up to the next floor, five, and exited. She walks to her apartment slowly, as seniors usually do; little did she know he was stalking her from the doorway of the stairwell. She puts her package down as she fumbles for her keys. Eventually, she unlocks her apartment door, which has two locks on it. He is apparently waiting patiently for her to open the door; she picks up her package and starts to enter. Once she opens the door and enters, he immediately springs into action. As soon as she opens the door and steps inside the apartment, he immediately runs up to her, knocks her down to the floor, and grabs her pocketbook. In doing so, she is slightly injured, and she lets out a scream. He then hears a male voice call out. "Ma, you ok?" So, he immediately runs out of the apartment back to the elevator. The male, it turns out, was her son, who was in his bedroom and came running out when he heard her scream. The son, who is in his mid-thirties, heard her scream and, not knowing what happened, ran out to help his mother. He sees her on the floor, and she yells at him that she was just robbed of her pocketbook. The son then runs out to the hall and to the elevator just as the doors close and go down. He runs down the stairs as fast as he can. He beats the elevator down to the first floor and stands in front of it. His heart is pounding; both his fists are clenched, waiting to inflict as much serious pain on this skell as the skell did to his mother. When the door opens, he is shocked to find the elevator is empty. The victim, in the meantime, calls the police. When the Police come, the uniformed officer takes a report. Through channels, the case is sent to the Senior Citizen unit.

The case is now assigned to the Senior Citizen Robbery Unit; I am up so it is my case. The next day, we went to the victim's apartment to interview her. She relays the story as it happened. She states she doesn't know where this suspect came from. She was alone on the elevator when she got to her floor. As she was entering her apartment, she was knocked down from behind and was slightly injured. However, she never saw the suspect's face. She is quizzed about being alone on the elevator and asked if she is sure she was alone. However, in rethinking, she does remember a nice young man was on the elevator with her, but he got off the floor before. She paid no attention to him; to her, he was just another kid who lived or was visiting someone in the building.

My partner and I realized this is the usual M.O. (Method of Operation) of the Push In Robbers, who get off the floor before. So, we zero in on this person who was on the elevator with her.

However, she states she never paid attention to his face and never saw the face of the suspect who robbed her. So, identifying him would be impossible. We asked her if she could remember anything about the clothes he was wearing. All she remembered was that he was wearing some kind of red garment. (This would later become a key factor in identifying him). Now we are interviewing her son. He basically repeats the story of how, after hearing his mother's screams and finding out what happened, seeing her on the floor, he immediately ran to the elevator. As he got there, it was just going down. He further states that he ran all the way down to the first floor before the elevator got there. Only to find an empty elevator when the doors opened. So, he goes back up the stairs to see if maybe he is hiding in the stairwell or on the stairs. As he does so, he opens the door to each floor and looks at every hallway to see if he is hiding on one of the floors. This was met with negative results, but he is sure he is still in the building.

He then goes on to say that there are a couple of bad kids who live in an apartment on the second floor (the victim lives on the fifth floor). He knows they are the local troublemakers of the building. Although he cannot prove it, he feels that they had some part in it. Because he knows they are always in some kind of trouble. He also knows the suspect never made it out of the building. He was asked if he told the uniformed officers who took the report of his thoughts. He said he didn't think about telling the uniformed officers at the time because he was too upset about his mother. So, he never gave those kids a thought. Overnight, giving it some deep thought, he remembered about these two individuals. He realized that they were troublemakers and figures. Since the suspect never got out of the building, it had to be one of them. So, he wanted to relay this information to us, as he wanted this miscreant arrested as badly as we wanted to arrest him.

So, we then formulated a plan and responded to the apartment where the kids live to interview these possible perpetrators.   We knock on the door, as soon as it opens, we push our way in, shouting, "You're under arrest for robbery." You robbed that woman upstairs. We tell them we have a witness who saw you run away. They immediately make a spontaneous utterance (an outburst statement) and blurt out we didn't do it. James did it." Immediately, our antennas went up, and we went into investigative mode. Ok, tell us who James is, and you better not be lying because if you are, we will make it harder on you in court. Of course, the whole thing was a bluff, but in the eyes of the law, you are allowed to lie/bluff a defendant if you don't use any physical force or make any false promises. They then went on to say they were in their apartment when suddenly there was a hard knock at their door. When they opened it, it was James. He was sweating and appeared to be nervous when he asked them if he could stay in the apartment for a while. They stated that they didn't know what he did, but as a courtesy to the street, they let him in. They said James stayed for a couple of hours until it got dark and then left. During this time, he never said what he did, but they knew whatever it was, it wasn't good. We asked them where James lived and what his last name was. They said they didn't know; they only knew him from the street by the name James. When asked for a physical description, they gave a basic general description; they did say he was wearing a one-piece Red Snowmobile suit. They then stated that once it got dark, James left the apartment, which was after several hours. However, when they mentioned the Red Snowmobile suit, this immediately struck a chord with us, remembering that the victim said he was wearing something Red. Although they said they didn't know where James lived, they did tell us where he hung out. They further went on to say that he hung out in the vicinity of New Lots Ave and Cleveland Street near a butcher shop. They begged us not to give them up in exchange for giving us the information. Because if word got out to the street, their names would be mud, as the saying goes in the street, "Stitches for Snitches who wind up in Ditches ". That is the creed of the street. If it got out, they would never be able to walk the neighborhood anymore. We assured them that if they were telling the truth, we would keep it our little secret. So now we have started looking for James, so we go to the vicinity of New Lots and Cleveland Street several times that day. Finally, a day later, we get lucky, sure enough, we see a kid with a Red Snowmobile Suit hanging out in front of the butcher shop.

When he turns his back, we yell out, "James." He immediately turns around, and we know we have our man. We then jumped out of the car and bum rushed him, immediately cuffing him and throwing him in the back of our unmarked before he even realized what happened. Now we started telling him how he was under arrest for robbing that woman, and how her son saw him get on the elevator and recognized him from the neighborhood. Another lie/bluff, but a necessary one to protect our informants, because we gave our word we would. Protecting them benefited us in two ways: number one, they gave us info on James, and number two, maybe in the future, they would have information about another crime, and again help the police. Knowing the police didn't expose them previously. Convinced that we had an eyewitness, James starts to unload. So, we immediately give him his rights (Miranda warnings), and he goes on to state how he saw her cash her Social Security check at the check-cashing store. He then stated how he followed her to the Bodega and eventually to her home. He stated as she walked through the projects, he paralleled her on the sidewalk outside the project. He did this until he saw her turn into her building. He admits getting on the elevator with her and getting off the floor before. He describes running up the stairs, the one flight to her floor. Then, as soon as she opened the door, he pushed her in, and she fell. As he grabs her bag, she screams for her son. He hears a male voice answer. So, he runs to the elevator and makes his escape. However, James was true to the code of the street; he never gave up the fact that he hid in the apartment of his friends.

Apparently, not realized they had given him up. We kept our word to them and never told him that the kids in the apartment that he hid in gave him up. His confession was a perfect one; he filled in all the boxes for us. There was only one more question, what happened to the pocketbook? He then went on to tell us where he threw the pocketbook. He threw it over a fence of a vacant lot on Linden Blvd and the vicinity of Elton St.

We go to the location and look for a lot, and sure enough, there is the pocketbook in the middle of the lot. My partner (who was much more agile than I climb the fence) and retrieved the pocketbook. Inside we find the victim's ID minus the money and minus her Welfare and Food Stamp card. When asked about the cards, he stated he tried to use the food stamp card, but the bodega owner was suspicious and didn't accept them, so he got nervous and threw them down a sewer.

In actuality, we could have arrested the kids in the apartment for harboring a felon. This would come under Hindering Prosecution in the NYS Penal Law. There is no way James stood in that apartment all that time with that Red Quilted Snowmobile suit zipped up with the pocketbook underneath. If so, they would have seen the bulge under the suit. So, in all probability, even though they had no part in the Robbery, they knew what he did. They were knowingly shielding him from the police. However, we didn't arrest them because we went along with the code of the street and kept our word to them. As previously stated, they may help Law enforcement in the future. So, it was what the old time Detectives used to call "Trading Little Ones for Big Ones." Meaning they gave us the big one, a Push In Robber, where we had absolutely nothing to go on. But with their information, we were able to make an arrest. This is why we gave them a pass for Hindering Prosecution.

Now he is under arrest, and we must do the paperwork and fingerprinting. The incident happened in the 75th precinct; however, the Senior Citizen Unit only worked until midnight. This was 1979, and the fiscal crisis was still looming over the city; overtime was extremely hard to come by, especially when you were in a specialty unit. They wouldn't allow your partner to stay with you to assist with the paperwork and transport you to court with your prisoner. I would have to depend on the precinct to have my prisoner, and I would be transported to the court/ADA's office, which some precinct cops resented and weren't happy to do. Some felt like they were Taxi Drivers. So, when I heard on the police radio the 69 Anti-Crime team (my old team) made an arrest for robbery with multiple suspects, I figured I would do all the paperwork and fingerprinting at the 69 precinct and get a ride to court with them. So, I proceed to go to the 69 precinct. Once there, among other notifications, I notify the District Attorney's Office of the arrest. In most cases of an arrest of a suspect over 16 for a Senior Citizen Robbery, an ADA (usually, who they call the riding ADA) must respond to enhance the case. This was mandated in the Senior Citizen Unit. (except in extenuating circumstances) One of the ways he would enhance it is to have a lineup, and he would supervise it; another way would be to take a statement if the prisoner was willing to make one. He also had to take a statement from the victim, as well as the arresting officer. In this case, the suspect agreed to make a statement. This was partly because I treated him right.

One of the things I learned is that sometimes, if you have a suspect who wasn't a hardcore felon, if you treat them right, they will cooperate. I basically used to tell them we could go either way with this; it's up to you. I then would tell him, "You are the bad guy, I am the good guy, your job is to commit a crime, my job is to try and catch you". You committed a crime the other day, but you got caught today, so I won, and you lost. But think about how many times you committed a crime and didn't get caught, and the Police lost, and you won. Because you know this isn't the first crime you committed. I would also add that I'm sure you are way ahead of the game. This strategy worked with many prisoners, and the arrest went smoothly. Also, if the prisoner was cooperative, I would buy them something to eat, which they really loved, a nice hot Italian Hero and a Cola was better than a bologna sandwich or Peanut Butter and Kool Aid, which is what they would get at Central Booking or court if they didn't make bail. He says he is hungry, and he knows he is going to Central Booking and what garbage he will have to eat. So, when one of the cops goes out for sandwiches, I buy a sandwich for him and myself. When the sandwiches came in, I uncuffed him, and we sat there and ate like buddies instead of adversaries. We also discussed things in general; he basically said he didn't have a good home life. Even though he was not homeless, he spent a good deal of his time on the street and had no real family supervision. That was one of the reasons he had the snowmobile suit on; it was good for the cold weather, since he spent most of the time on the street. He went on to say he hung out by that Butcher Shop because that is where he hustled, as people would come out of the store, he would ask for their change. Although he didn't threaten them, some people felt intimidated, so they gave him some change. While others felt sorry for him and gave him some change out of sympathy. But the others who were street-wise would tell him to screw off and get a job, and gave him nothing. After we ate, I cuffed him up again to the metal chair with one arm. I had him in the interview room (the box), as this is where the ADA would question him. The ADA finally arrives, and now he wants a lineup. I told him she was hit from behind and never saw his face. But he was adamant about a lineup. I said to the ADA that he was going to give you a statement regarding the robbery, and she can't identify him anyway. So what good is a lineup? The ADA says that if, on some technicality, the statement gets thrown out? We have nothing. I say we still have nothing because she can't ID him, he says, at least we can show the court we tried. So, one of the Anti-Crime cops and I set out to look for fillers for the lineup. We would pick guys up off the street and pay them $5.00 to stand in the lineup. We had to convince them that even if they got picked out, it meant nothing because we know who the bad guy is, and absolutely nothing would happen to them if they were picked out. The problem was that it was February, and it was a single-digit temperature, and very few people were hanging out on the street. So, we must hunt high and low to find fillers. Eventually, after about an hour, we rounded up 5 fillers. We returned to the precinct to hold the lineup.

The son of the victim brings his mother down to the precinct, and she views the lineup for less than two minutes, and of course, neither she nor the son can ID him. The ADA takes a statement from her and her son about how he chased him to the elevator and never saw his face. So, they finished and were on the way home. Now it's the suspects' turn. The ADA advises him of his rights, to which he says he understands them. He states that he does not want a lawyer. The ADA questions him about the crime, and he willingly admits to it and tells him exactly how he did it. He is being videotaped, and his statements are being recorded by the ADA's stenographer. He also throws a sort of self-serving statement in by saying he didn't want to hurt her; he just wanted her pocketbook. But she probably fell because when he pulled her pocketbook, she was heavy-set and lost her balance. Which could be true, or maybe not, depending on how hard he pulled on the pocketbook. He did this because he was hungry and had no money for food. He knew she had money because he saw her cash in her Social Security Check. He also admitted stalking her from the check-cashing store to the bodega and eventually to her home. When asked if he had done any other robbery of any kind, he denied doing any others. (Probably a lie, he wasn't that stupid.) He said this was the first time he had done a

Push In; it was possible but not probable because he had too much experience in executing it. When asked how he knew about the Push In Robbery trick, he said he heard about it on the streets in the hood, and how safe it was. How you rarely get caught. He was asked if he had committed the other robbery in the Pink Houses, my partner's case. He denied ever being in the Pink Houses ever. More than likely, he wasn't lying about that one. As far as doing the push-in, he was somewhat right; most of the push-ins there rarely are any arrests made. He just picked the wrong victim, who had a son residing with her, while most live alone.

I also gave a statement regarding my arresting him and his statements to me. My statement was recorded as well by the ADA's stenographer and video recorded by his videographer. My arrest is done, all I have to do is wait for the Anti-Crime cop to finish up so I can go down to Central Booking with them. The ADA never asked how we developed the information on James. So, I never volunteered it because I knew if I did, he would want to put the two brothers who gave us the info in front of the video under oath. This would expose them, and how we got the info, as we gave them our word, I never told the ADA. If I was put on the witness stand and asked under oath about how we developed our information, I would have to give them up or possibly face a perjury rap if I lied. Fortunately, it never came to that. Experience told us that with an ADA, nothing is off record. So, if we told him off the record, he would still most likely subpoena these two youths. Thereby blowing their cover and breaking our word to them. So, you could forget about them ever cooperating with the Police again. They would also have to fear the streets and be labelled as Snitches. So, I did my best to protect them as I said I would.

The ADA is taking statements from the Anti-Crime cops and their complainants (they had a commercial robbery), as their prisoners are in the cell and refused to make any statements. My prisoner, who is still handcuffed to the chair in the interview room (the box), is getting impatient; he keeps telling me he wants to get it over with by going to court. I explained to him that we must wait for transportation, so please be patient. I kept him handcuffed to the metal wrought iron chair with one arm to the chair, instead of both his arms behind his back. That would be quite uncomfortable to be in that position for a long period of time. I also kept him in the interview room by himself for a reason. The reason being I was afraid that if I put him in the cell with the other prisoners, they would tell him not to make any statements. Being they were streetwise and hard-nosed and refused to make any statements. Even after he made his statement to the ADA, I kept him there. For fear that the other prisoners may put peer pressure on him, and for him to tell the ADA he wants to recant his statement. Even though it was too late for that, it may add confusion to the confession later if it went to a Miranda hearing; it may become an issue (right to remain silent and self-incrimination). The way it was, he was willing of his own free will to make a statement, while the other sources may have influenced him not to do so.

HE MAKES A BREAK

So, he is sitting cuffed in the interview room with one arm to the chair. I am about ten feet away, around the corner in the squad room. I am talking with the Detectives and the Anti-Crime cops; every so often, I would stick my head in the room and assure him we were leaving soon. We had to wait for the other cops for transportation. He would say that he was tired and wanted to go to court to get it over with. So, an hour or so goes by, and one of the Detectives who came back from an interview on one of his cases says to me, "Who had the prisoner with the red jumpsuit?" I said I do. He says what did you do give him a D.A.T. (Desk Appearance Ticket), which can be given out for a Misdemeanor arrest only, meaning the person would go home and go to court at a prearranged date. I say (jokingly) yeah for a 2nd degree Robbery, I gave him a DAT, he says I'm not joking, he just walked out the front door downstairs. I ran to the interview room, where there was an empty chair with a handcuff hanging from it. The Detective says he walked West on Foster Ave. So, one of the Anti-Crime guys jumps into my car, we go west on Foster about 4 or 5 blocks down, and we see him walking down one of the side blocks (thanks to his red snowmobile suit). We immediately drove down the block. We jumped out of the car, and I grabbed him and gave him a slap on the back of the head. I said, what the hell did you leave for? I treated you right, he said, "I got tired of waiting for you". When we got back, I asked how did you get the cuffs open. He shows me a bent-up paper clip on the floor. He said he picked the paper clip up, bent it up, and stuck it in the keyhole of the handcuff, and kept playing around with it, and presto, the cuff popped open. So, he decided to walk out. Here is the ironic part: the ADA's videographer is sitting right there, outside the room, and he said good night to him. The videographer, only a short while earlier, had videoed him, making a confession to a 2nd degree robbery. As he admitted this to the ADA under oath while being videotaped. This videographer was no stranger to taking statements for felonies, as he has been on several cases with the ADAs that I have previously witnessed. You would think the videographer would have the brains to say, "Hey officer, your suspect just walked out the door," but no, he stupidly stood there and watched him walk out. Talking about someone not wanting to get involved, this guy gets first prize. When I thought about it later, he, being the ADA's videographer, knew the guy committed a 2nd degree robbery sees him walk away, and didn't even tell the ADA. The DA's office should fire him, but I let it go because the ADA never realized what happened; if so, he would have charged him with escape, and I would have been charged by the department for losing a prisoner. So, it's like the old saying, "some words should be left unspoken." Why open a can of worms? So now it's no longer Mr. Nice Guy; he gets rear cuffed and stays that way until we leave for Central Booking. In all honesty, I have to say they were a cheap set of cuffs. I sometimes carried 2 sets, one was a good Smith and Wesson, the other was the cheap set. I used the cheap set on him, for something like that, because we were at the station house. Never thinking he would pick the lock on the cuffs like that, and he would walk right out of the Station House. That was my bad; you learn from your mistakes. Besides learning about not using the cheap set, I learned another lesson: never trust a prisoner. By doing so, I could have lost him that night without getting him back; luckily, I got him back before anyone higher up in the Police Department noticed. If so, it would cause me to be charged by the Police Department for losing a prisoner. In doing so, two things would have happened.

The first i would have been extremely embarrassed.

The second, more important, would be that I would probably be suspended for a couple of days because of losing a prisoner, and it would be a mark on my permanent record.

THE PROSECUTION

He is arraigned on second degree Robbery, as well as Burglary and Assault. When his fingerprint report came back, surprisingly he had just a couple of minor arrests. He is represented by Legal Aid. We have a hearing, and his attorney requested a Wade Huntley hearing. However, there was no Wade hearing because the victim could not identify him, his whole case hinged on the statements he made. So, we have a Miranda hearing regarding his statements that he made to me as well as the ADA. At the hearing, the attorney is trying to get the statements he made to me thrown out on a technicality. Stating that his rights (Miranda Warnings) were not given properly. I stated I gave him his rights right at the scene of arrest, while he was in the back seat of the unmarked.

He asked me to repeat the rights that I gave him. The judge tells me I can read them from a copy I have in my memo book if I want to refresh my memory. Which I did, the ADA also must testify regarding the giving of the rights as well. After testifying at the hearing regarding the statements he made to me, as well as the statements he made to the ADA while being videoed, the judge ruled his statements as being taken legally. The case is then sent to the Grand Jury. Eventually, after the victim and I testify at the Grand Jury, he is indicted on the previously stated charges. Soon after, he takes a plea and is given three to five years in jail. This is basically because of the victim's age, as well as the minor injury she received when he knocked her down. He could be eligible for Parole after serving one-third of his sentence, which means he can be out in less than two years. But at least he is off the street and hopefully learned a lesson.

OF COURSE I CHECKED HIS SNEAKER PATTERN!

CHAPTER SEVEN

NEAR THE END OF SCRU FOR ME

I have been in the unit for about a year and a half, and I am getting bored by the day. I still can't adjust to dealing with senior citizens. I still can't get used to the fact that it was frustrating dealing with elderly people, people who couldn't identify or didn't want to identify out of fear. It's not that I didn't like seniors, I just couldn't get used to not being able to make arrests the way I was used to making them. Also, I didn't like sitting in the office waiting for a case to come in. I was used to prowling the streets all day seeking the bad guys, waiting to pounce on the skells the instant they committed a crime. As far as the Senior victims, some did try to ID, but they couldn't really identify even if they wanted to. I remember bringing one person down to the Detective Bureau in Brooklyn South because he was adamant that he could ID. So, I brought him to view photos at a place they called Mirra Quik. It was where they had all the pictures of people who were arrested in Brooklyn. I had my hopes that he might be the one to make an identification, he assured me he could. I tell the detective in charge of the unit the facts of the case with a general description of the suspect. This way, he has an idea of what type of crime and the type of pictures to show the victim. When we got there, I told the victim take your time, look at all the photos. If you find one that looks good to you, just put it on the side, and I will investigate further. I'm doing some follow-up work on the phone on another case, a few desks away. After a while, I walk back to where he is viewing the photos. I ask him, "See anyone that looks familiar?" Who may have robbed you? He points to a stack of about 20 photos, he says, these guys." My hopes went out of the window. Looking at the back of each photo gave a physical description of the suspect. Not only were they different in age, but they were also different in height and weight, as well as skin complexion. So here was another letdown, another case closed with Negative Results.

However, the cases kept coming in, there was always something to investigate. There was always another senior getting robbed in Brooklyn South. If a case came in another zone, and that team were off, some other team in the office would do the preliminary. When the catching team came in, they would be given the case. This way, no time would be lost in starting the investigation. If there was an immediate arrest to be made, the team that was covering would have to make the arrest. But most of the time we got there after the fact that it didn't happen too often that an arrest was made. As far as any patterns on the street, the Decoy Team would concentrate on that pattern.

THE BEGINNING OF THE END

I have been in the unit for almost 18 months, and I still can't get used to dealing with the elderly. As hard as I try, I just can't accept the fact that an arrest doesn't come as easily as an observation arrest made on the street, where I got instant satisfaction of arresting a skell. Or an arrest that is made when a job is broadcast over the police radio of a crime in progress, and you get the guy right there, or get him based on a description. Most of these arrests usually wind up being pled out to after a hearing in Criminal Court or after a Grand Jury indictment. Usually, the charges are reduced by the ADA, so it makes a plea deal a little easier to agree to for both the D.A. and the defense attorney. A defense lawyer will see how strong a case is, and instead of taking a chance with a trial, where the sentence would be much longer if the person were convicted. He usually would make a deal with the D.A.'s office, and if it was agreeable with the judge, the case would be ended with a plea of some kind. Usually, a much lighter sentence is more than likely if he/she went to trial, possibly even probation, no jail time. That's usually an offer, the defense attorney as well as the defendant can not refuse.

I am on the way out to an interview, and I am not with my regular partner. I am driving through a commercial area; I observe a male standing in front of a doorway to a factory. He appears to be looking from left to right. I pull over about a half a block away, and I am watching him through my side view mirror. Sure enough, he opens the door and again looks from left to right, then enters. Within a minute, he emerges carrying a carton on a hand truck and strolls down the block. I immediately made a U-turn. I watch the suspect while my partner goes in and asks the owner if anyone had permission to take anything from his office. After locating the owner who was in the work area, he looked around and saw that there were a couple of cartons missing, as well as his hand truck. My partner comes out and informs me of this. We then drive around the corner and down the block. Here is the skell, and he is loading some more cartons onto the hand truck. We immediately placed him under arrest. It turns out he apparently made several trips into the unoccupied office while the boss was in the work area. With the office empty, he helped himself to several cartons which contained Cups and Saucers. Then he hid them around the corner underneath a parked truck. He then went back for the last one, as well as the hand truck. A good observation, Burglary arrest, I'm thinking. I called my boss and informed him of the arrest. He immediately tells me it's not a Senior Citizen arrest, so give it to Patrol. I explained to him that I was the one who observed everything. And I would have to be the one who had to testify to it at court and the Grand Jury. The owner never saw him, so I would have to ID him if there were a Wade hearing held. If I gave it to a uniformed cop, either way, I would be the one to do all the testifying at court. We went back and forth, with him demanding that I give the arrest to a Patrol Officer. But I held my ground because I was the only witness, so I would be the one who would be testifying in court. Also, I would make a couple of hours O.T. on the arrest, which, at the time, O.T. was very scarce in the unit. Eventually, he reluctantly allowed me to take the arrest. It turns out that the person I arrested was involved in a murder case, where he flipped on his associates. So, this is another wedge the DA's office could hold against him to testify against the others in the Murder case. So, it was another bad guy off the streets, even though it wasn't a Senior Citizen case.

Instead of being applauded for a keen observation burglary arrest, I was reprimanded. I assume the reason behind it was because they didn't want me to spend time with a non-Senior Citizen arrest and make a little O.T. But I looked at it in a different way. I took a bad guy off the street. A person who was possibly a serial burglar who would have gotten away with another burglary hadn't I made that observation. He is indicted by the Grand Jury, so this gives the DA more leverage to have him testify against his buddies in the murder case.

The owner of the firm was ever so thankful to me, because that was a special order and they were in his office waiting for the trucking company to pick them up.

If I hadn't made that observation, the owner, when he found them missing, would have called the police to make a report. When the case went upstairs to the Detectives, it more than likely would be closed with Negative Results being there was no witness to the theft. So, it would have been another crime recorded with negative results against the precinct's crime statistics.

Or it may have been reduced to lost property, which is not a crime. This would be one less statistic on their Index Crimes. If it was recorded as a Burglary, then it would be another statistic being recorded as an Indexed Crime.

Index Crimes are as follows: Murder, Rape, Robbery, Serious Assault, Burglary, Grand Larceny, and Grand Larceny Auto.

These are the crimes that all Police Departments base their crime stats on. These stats are sent to the FBI to classify how well the department is managing crime in their respective departments. In the NYPD, the Precinct Commanding Officer does not want to submit stats that show crime in his/her precinct is rising. So anytime they can downgrade a crime to a non-crime, it's done. Sometimes it's done rightfully, other times the rules may be stretched, especially if it is a borderline crime/non-crime.

CHAPTER EIGHT

THE PUERTO RICO CONNECTION

I am assigned a case where it was an early morning Home Invasion Burglary/Robbery. Sometime between four and five a.m., two young thugs enter the second-floor apartment of these two Senior Citizens. This was in the East New York section of Brooklyn. They are both wearing black woolen hats, which are makeshift ski masks covering their faces with eye holes cut out in them. The victims are all sleeping. They go to the bedrooms and roust the victims out of bed at gunpoint. They then have them sit on the couch in the living room. However, that night, the grandson and his younger sister were sleeping over. The grandson was about 17 years old, and his sister was about 13 years old. They, too, had been awakened at gunpoint and were also seated on the couch. Now, with the four victims seated on the couch, the suspect with the gun fires a shot over their heads and into the wall. He does this to show them the gun was real and to put fear into them. With that, he tells the other culprit to go downstairs and let their third conspirator (Skell) in. A few minutes later, he comes up with the third partner, who is much older (in his twenties) and well over six feet, he is not wearing a mask. The suspects then tie the victims up with some chord they had with them. Then, while the suspect with the gun holds them at gunpoint, the other two ransack the apartment. After a while with their dirty deed done, the suspects leave the apartment, taking whatever meager property they could find with them. Once the victims feel safe, they untie themselves. The victims then immediately call the police. When the Police arrive, they take a report. The report is eventually sent to the SCRU through channels. I am assigned the case. When I interview the elderly victims, they say they can't ID the suspects, as the suspects were wearing a ski mask, which was previously described as woolen knit caps with eye holes cut out in them. But they can ID the one without the mask, the bigger, older one who came up last. When I interviewed the grandson, he went on to say he knew who one of the suspects was. He states that even though he is wearing a makeshift ski mask, he recognizes him by his voice and his eyes. He knows his name and where he hangs out. He proceeds to tell us that he hangs out in a park nearby and gives us the location. He gives us a description as well as the suspect's name. Armed with this information, my partner and I scoured the area where he hung out. We see a suspect that fits the description of the suspect's physical appearance and clothing based on the info that was supplied to us by the grandson. We approach him and ask him if he is Julio Costa, the name that was given to us by the grandson. He readily admits that it is his name; we immediately placed him under arrest. In questioning him, we find out he is 14, a juvenile, so we must have a parent or guardian present when questioning him. We take him to the station house, while my partner guards him, I pick up his mother. I explained to her what we arrested her son for. I told her this is a serious crime, and although he is a juvenile, he was still facing serious charges. We also used a little "Scared Straight" on her, telling her if he kept doing things like this (home invasion) at this age, what would he do when he is older. He can wind up in jail for many years, maybe even for life. So, this is his chance for redemption. The mother is very concerned, and you can tell she is a decent, law-abiding person. We also told her that it would be more favorable to him if he cooperated with the investigation in the eyes of the court. After giving him his rights in his mother's presence, with his mother urging him to tell the truth, he gives us a full confession. He also gives up his conspirators, their names, and where they live. The kid with the gun is also 14 years old, and the bigger, older one is in his twenties. When questioned about how they made entry to the victim's second-floor apartment. His answer amazed us. They shimmied up the outside phone wires and the conduit housing other wires to the 2nd floor. Since it was on the second floor, the window was unlocked, so they pushed it up. After they were both in the apartment, they proceeded to wake everyone to get them up and out of bed. They then sat them all on the couch. Then one of them went downstairs to get the older, larger suspect, while the other held them at gunpoint. Apparently, the older one, who was in his twenties, was too large and not as agile as his two younger cohorts to climb up on the wires. He was also much heavier, so in all probability, the wires most likely wouldn't have supported his weight. So, he waited downstairs for one of them to let him in. Now, with the names of the other suspects, it was time to round them up. We went to suspect number two's house. His name is Manual Rameriz, he is home, so we place him under arrest in front of his mother. He is much more of a hard-nose and is uncooperative, denying everything. His mother is on his side, obviously believing her son is innocent (he is the one with the gun.) When we got to the station house, I gave him his rights in front of his mother. I then took her into a separate room away from her son. I explained everything to her about how I got the information. I again use the Scared Straight act on her, also told her that this arrest may be a blessing, telling her if he is doing a home invasion at 14, what will he do at 18-20 years old. If he gets caught at that age, he will be facing hard time in jail. Once I convinced her that we just didn't just arbitrarily arrest her son and that the information had been given to us by his cohort, her whole attitude changed. When we brought her back to the juvenile room where juveniles are processed, she immediately berates her son. She does this to the point where she had to be restrained from physically serving him, a good old-fashioned mother's beating. With that, she urges him to tell the truth. Then, in her presence, a full confession is given. He also gives us the name and address of the third suspect, the one without the mask. They are under 16, so they are processed in Family Court, which is much more lenient than Criminal Court. Sometimes the punishment in Family Court for certain offenses amounts to a little more than detention after class in High school. This really doesn't put much fear into them. Unless they get some kind of real detention, like being put in a Juvenile Home or a juvenile training camp, there is no real fear. That's why there was no fear of going to the Children's Court. In most cases, their records are sealed by the court, so you don't even have access to them. You may never find out the disposition of the case, whether the juvenile was convicted or the case was adjudicated by other means. To the juvenile, it is sometimes like a badge of honor to tell their friends I was arrested, and nothing happened to me. In some cases, all that does is encourage them or others to commit crimes. There was no fear of punishment if you got caught. With regards to our juvenile skells we (I) never found out what their punishment was. The records were sealed, which more than likely was some kind of probation. As far as the gun goes, we never recovered it. He gave the gun to another kid from the park by the name of Hector (last name unknown). We were never able to find the mysterious Hector, probably a lie, so the gun was never recovered.

NOTE: As an Anti-Crime cop, I once made an arrest of a 15-year-old for a stolen car. Prior to arresting the juvenile, I spoke to the owner of the car. He was quite upset and angry that his car had been stolen. I had to calm him down for fear that he might get in trouble if he caught the culprit. Eventually, I arrested the kid with the car. When we went to the Children's Court for some reason, we had a hearing. But it's not like in Criminal Court, we sat around a large table, with the youth, his mother, and his representative (an attorney, legal aide) on one side. On the other side, there is the complainant, and I, the Corporation Council Attorney who represents the city. It was more like an informal meeting when we discussed the case. Next thing you know, the complainant is basically saying he didn't want the kid arrested, he just wanted his car back, as far as he was concerned, he was only a kid that didn't realize he was doing something wrong. Everybody agrees with this; it now looks like I am the bad guy for making the arrest. So, I am upset and say my piece, I ask how they all forgot that he stole a car, that he, the complainant, was angry to the point where he wanted to harm the youth if he caught him. Also when I arrested him, he was driving wildly through the streets at a high rate of speed. If he hit someone, he may have killed them. No matter how you look at it, no matter what his age was, it was a dangerous act.

The result, the Corporation Council attorney tells me, and the complainant, is that we can leave; we are no longer needed at the proceedings. Which more than likely meant he didn't want me to see him tell the kid, go home and be a nice boy, and try not to steal a car again. Your RECORD is SEALED.

TIME TO LOOK FOR SUSPECT # 3

So now, after they are processed in family court, it's time to look for the third suspect, whose name is Antonio Vargas; his name and address were given to us by the younger ones. We go to his address, which was supplied to us by the juveniles, which is on Sutter Ave. We interview the landlord, who basically tells us that the suspect rented a room for a short time but moved out a couple of weeks ago. He tells us he moved to Logan St, which is only a couple of blocks away. He is not sure of the address but tells us the cross streets. So, we go to Logan St. and do a house-to-house canvas (search). We interviewed several people on the block, but we have had no luck. We do the whole block and are coming up with nothing. Finally, we get to the next-to-the-last house on the block, and we get lucky. We talk to the owner and ask her if Antonio Vargas (the name supplied to us) lives here.

She tells us yes; he did rent a room here for a little while, but moved out rather quickly with no forwarding address. But the information had to be dragged out of her as she was reluctant to talk to the Police. She really was not freely giving us any help as to how long he was here, and how long ago he left. While we were talking to her, we noticed a young girl who was pregnant walking by in the background. We ask her who the girl is, and she states it's her daughter. So, we use a little strategy, we ask her, isn't he coming back when the baby is born? She says, "Why do you say that? We told her he is telling everybody that he made her pregnant. With that, she gets furious, "That's not his baby." He only rented a room here; he had nothing to do with my daughter. It's the Sergeant in the precincts, baby." So now it's OK, we will drop this line of questioning immediately. The reason being back in those days, many a cop who was born and raised in suburban L.I. never had any dealings in an inner-city neighborhood. The closest they came to NYC was going to a stadium for a game. Or went to Madison Square Garden for a concert. So, when they came to the PD, it was a whole different culture. Being assigned to an inner-city precinct was a new experience. So, meeting a cute little Latino girl took on a new life. He found himself a new girlfriend, or maybe two, in the precinct where he worked in Brooklyn. In some cases, he even left his family (wife) for his newfound love. So, some things are better off left unsaid; there is a possibility that this Sergeant may or may not be a married man. This really has no bearing on the case either way. But at least we made our point with her. The point being that this guy is bad-mouthing her daughter, like she is a loose woman, so he is not a nice guy. Hopefully, if she does get any info on him, she will give him up to get revenge on him for slandering her daughter. I leave her my business card just in case she comes up with any additional information. In the meantime, we are at a standstill, and we have nothing else to go on. But then we get lucky.

About two weeks went by when I got a call from the woman we interviewed, where he last lived the one with the pregnant daughter. She tells us to come by as she has some info for us. We respond to the house, and she hands us a wallet. She states that the postman delivered the wallet to her house because it had an identification card in it with her address. Apparently, the suspect lost his wallet, and a good Samaritan found it and threw it in the mailbox. The Postal authorities treated it as mail and deliver to the address with postage due. I take possession of the wallet and go through some miscellaneous junk papers. However, I struck gold; I found a Puerto Rican driver's license with a picture of the suspect on it. It also had an address on it in Ponce, Puerto Rico. I then took the picture and put it in a photo lineup for viewing by the victims. I immediately then showed the photo lineup to the grandson as well as the grandparents. Both the grandfather and the grandson pick him out, without hesitation. The grandmother and the granddaughter couldn't, but I had two ID's, and that was good enough. So, I play a hunch, being his landlord, said he left kind of quick, I thought maybe he fled to Puerto Rico. So, I contacted the authorities in the town where he lives. I inform them that he is wanted for a Home Invasion. I ask them if they could make an indiscrete inquiry if he lives at the address that is on the license, and if he is currently residing there. After several days, they answered that he was there. But they will not take any action unless I send paper down (meaning an Arrest Warrant). They also said, "Are you sure you have the right guy?" When I ask the officer why? He states this guy comes from a prominent, well-to-do family, and his mother is the president of the local bank. I am taken back but I inform him we have two positive IDs, so I know it's not a mistake. So, I tell him it's understood, and I will get an Arrest Warrant for him. I then respond to the Brooklyn D.A, s office extradition/rendition unit to obtain a warrant. (Rendition is between 2 states) (Extradition is out of the country). "But everything out of the city is commonly known as extradition." We drew up a warrant, I swore to it before a judge, a copy is filed with the court another copy is filed with the DA's office. I have our (NYPD) copy that I bring to our Correspondence Unit, to transmit the warrant to Puerto Rico (Correspondence Unit is responsible for all in and out of the city notifications from and to NYPD). Within a few days, I was notified by the authorities in Puerto Rico that, based on my warrant, they would attempt to arrest the suspect. When they do, I will have to go down to pick him up and bring him back to NY. However, their court will not hold him for more than 48 hours. I notify my bosses and notify the Borough office that the Chief of the borough must approve the trip out of the country to bring the prisoner back. In talking with the authorities in Puerto Rico, they further say he has no previous arrest record in Puerto Rico. They reiterate the fact that he comes from a well-to-do family, and his mother is president of a local bank. They say when they informed his mother, she was in total shock and couldn't believe he would be involved in anything like that. Apparently, he was in NY visiting relatives, and somehow, he got involved with these two miscreants (skells). Who may have been members of a tough street gang in East New York that went by the name of the SEX BOYS. The name was derived from the name of a street in East New York, Essex St. If you drove around the area, you would look at the street signs, and the ES would be blacked out, leaving just the name Sex. It was like what the animals do to mark their territory. They were a bunch of tough kids, so something like this was not surprising. These gang members were mostly Hispanic, but did have some Black kids as members as well.

A LITTLE BROOKLYN HISTORY

However, not to be outdone, at one time, East New York had many Italians and Irish who had a gang; they too had taken their gang's name from a street in East New York. They were called the NEW LOTS BOYS, with the name taken from the street, New Lots Ave. At the corner of Ashford St and Livonia Ave, where the Livonia Ave Elevator train crosses Ashford St, in the concrete sidewalk was the name in Octagon-shaped tiles, "New Lots Boys." This was maybe seventy feet from New Lots Ave. This was there from the forties until the area was renovated in the last couple of years. With Ashford St being cut off and the street replaced with a small mall, underneath the EL train.

NOTE: Going back to the 60'S there were many race wars between the whites, who were mostly Italians and Irish, against the Blacks and Hispanics that were moving into the area. The whites, feeling they were being pushed out, started a group within the New Lots boys. It was called SPONGE (SOCIETY PREVENTION OF NEGROES GETTING EVERYTHING).

It was a loosely fit gang of about twenty who showed up at events held by blacks to protest them. Which usually led to large fights where the Police had to call in extra Police to quell the disturbances. It was territorial race wars for territory rights. Eventually, most of the Italians and Irish moved on. However, there were some Italians/Irish who refused to leave; they remained and lived in harmony with the blacks. However, going even further back, there was a Jewish Gang of gangsters that ruled the streets of East New York and Brownsville. They were known as Murder Incorporated and were responsible for many homicides. So, the gangs in East New York and Brownsville flourished many years back as far as the early 1920's. Just with different ethnic groups.

CHAPTER NINE

SUSPECT IN CUSTODY

I am notified by the authorities in Puerto Rico that they have the suspect in custody. So now, with the suspect in custody in Puerto Rico, I notify my immediate Sergeants of the arrest based on my warrant and the fact that the suspect is now in custody. I would have to go to Puerto Rico to pick up my prisoner. Arrangements would then have to be made through channels with the Police Commissioner's office to grant me the time and expense money, plane fare, hotel, and meals. So, the first step would be to go through the Commanding Officer (Chief) of Brooklyn South. Of course, I am excited, as are several other officers in the unit, as I am the first officer to get a trip out of the country based on a case in the SCRU. I am getting prepared for my trip when I get a call from the Lieutenant in the Borough office. He tells me the Borough Commander is not authorizing you to go. I ask why not? He states the Chief states it must be a Detective, not a Police Officer, to go. I explained to him that there was no Detective assigned to the case, I am the investigating officer, and this was my case (I am doing detective work). He stated he would get back to me. Several hours later, he calls me back. He states he spoke to the Borough Commander (Chief), and he again states it must be a Detective, as a Police Officer would be on O.T. after 8 hours, and a detective would not, which is totally false. I explained it wasn't for the O.T. and that I was willing to waive it, but it was the principal of the matter. All the work my partner and I put into getting this suspect identified. (It should have been my partner and me going to P.R.) He said he understood, but the Borough Commander was not sending a Police Officer out of the country. I tell my bosses about this, and they are very sympathetic about it, but basically, they say he is the boss, and there is nothing they can do about it. They never made an attempt to talk to him.

The Chief, who had most likely well over 30 years on the job, had the attitude, it's my way or the highway. He ruled the borough with an iron fist. So, no one would dare speak to him on my behalf, for fear he would send them packing out the door. You would think he appreciated the fact that I put so much work into the case, getting the third skell identified, he would authorize at least me to go with the Detective or with the Detective from the D.A.'s office. This was just another way the Police Department was taking advantage of the officers in the SCRU, not affording them the same privileges as a Detective. As others would say about the SCRU officers, the department is dangling that carrot in front of your face, never giving it to you. But at the same time expected you to perform like a Detective. More than likely, the Borough Commander didn't have any idea who was going to Puerto Rico from the D.A.'s office. Because whoever it was wasn't directly working in the Brooklyn South area, and apparently, he didn't care who went from the D.A.s. So, he authorizes a Detective from my unit who didn't put two minutes' work into the case, and knew absolutely nothing about it, to go. As well as someone from the D.A.s to go along with him. Prior to their departure, Det. Datellio (from the SCRU) apologizes to me and explains how he was just ordered to go to Puerto Rico. He had no say in the matter. I accept his apology, because I know he is telling the truth. My anger was not directed at him.

They left on a Friday afternoon and didn't come back until Monday morning. They stayed the whole weekend in Puerto Rico on the city's dime. Just coincidentally, the officer from the D.A.'s office was Puerto Rican, so he was able to visit his relatives while he was on his stay over, a free mini vacation. So now that I know I didn't get the trip to P.R., I go home feeling dejected. I am thinking the whole weekend that after all the work my partner and I put into the investigation, two strangers who knew nothing about the case get a free trip to P.R. It's Friday, I have the weekend off. (while they are in P.R.) I go home feeling very dejected and unappreciated for all the work we put into the case. I have two days off, but I'm thinking for the whole two days, where another Detective may have said who cares about the 3rd guy I got two bodies, the third is in the wind somewhere, and I can close my case out with two arrests. Never even trying to find out who the 3rd perpetrator is or where he was. Or, since he had the name, he may put a wanted card on him and file it in the system. If he ever got arrested in NYC for anything, the wanted card would pop up that he is wanted, and the officer who filed it would get notified that he is in the system as just being arrested. It would then be up to the officer to rearrest him on his original case. But I went that extra mile in getting the 3rd suspect identified and where he was. It would have been much easier to close the case out with two arrests and a wanted card filled in on the third skell. But I didn't, and as it turned out, no one really cared.

NOTE: Detectives work on many cases; it's very rare that their investigation leads them out of the country. Especially to a vacation country like Puerto Rico. So, a trip to P.R. to pick up a prisoner on a case you investigated would be a memory to last a lifetime. It would be the envy of many Detectives. So, for Detectives who didn't put two minutes into the case, it would be even more of a conversation piece. And a gift from the Police Department, an all-expenses-paid weekend in Puerto Rico.

I RETURN TO WORK AFTER MY DAYS OFF

So, when I come back to work after my two days off, I come in for a four to twelve tour. On my desk, I find a copy of an arrest report. It reads as follows.

Det. DATELLIO of the Brooklyn South SCRU, along with POLICE OFFICER RIVERA of the Brooklyn D.A.'s office, responded to Puerto Rico to pick up prisoner Antonio Vargas on warrant number BK123456, Kings County, New York.

I read the arrest report, and my blood is boiling. I am absorbing this and reading the arrest report over and over. The reason why I am reading it so many times, realization has just sunk in. I knew someone from the D.A.'s office was going, but I had no idea it was a Police Officer. I thought it would be another Detective from the DA's squad. So, P.O. Rivera got a trip to Puerto Rico, but I couldn't go; he, too, had nothing to do with the investigation. A Detective from my office who didn't put two minutes' work into the case went along with him. They left on a Friday and didn't come back until Monday morning. That's all that was going through my head as I must have read it a hundred times in those few minutes. It should have been my partner and me who went to Puerto Rico to pick up the prisoner. Afterall my partner was with me every step of the way in arresting the first two skells and searching for skell number three. As I am absorbing this, my boss calls me into the office, and he immediately jumps all over me, "Why didn't you go to court this morning? You were supposed to be there." You had to arraign your prisoner. I throw the arrest report on his desk and say with an expletive, "How the @#$$# did I know, no one ever notified me." I was home all day. Why didn't one of them go to court to arraign him? They brought the prisoner back. Did they get the trip? Was it because they knew absolutely nothing about the case and absolutely nothing about his arrest? If the judge or the ADA were to ask them for any details regarding the case, they couldn't even begin to give them an answer. It would have to be something to the effect: I don't know anything about the case, I just was told to respond to P.R. to pick up a prisoner, who was wanted on a warrant.

Another thing, why didn't one of them at least notify me? That they were back, and the prisoner was lodged, and needed to be arraigned. Now realizing he is wrong, first he tries to put me on the defensive, he tells me to "stop brooding over this." Which just upset me more. He tells me the Borough Commander not only screwed you but screwed everyone in this office. In depriving you of going, he took the incentive to work from everybody in this office. But by this time, I had enough. I was at my breaking point. I shot back I don't care, he didn't screw anyone else; it was I who got screwed, it was me who put all this work into this case, I want out. I don't want to work here anymore. I walked out of the office and was so upset and disgusted that I put a slip in to take time off and go home. One of the female decoys tells me come on, come with us, we are going out to eat before we start working. Come and relax, cool off. So, I went with them and unloaded, and of course, they were all very understanding and agreeable. However, after unloading, even though I did feel better, I still wanted out. I am thinking of how petty the boss was when I made the on-duty observation burglary arrest. How they tried to make me give up the arrest. Telling me it was not a Senior Citizen case, never giving me credit for a keen observation arrest that would have never been made without an on-the-scene observation arrest, and recovering a couple of hundred dollars' worth of merchandise. The case would have gone to the Detective Squad and would have been closed out, with no arrest, especially with no witnesses. Or maybe even like I said, downgraded to Lost Property, which is not a crime. (Just another way to downgrade their crime statistics). As previously stated, they sometimes did in precincts to keep their index crimes down. There were several other minor incidents that I overlooked, but now everything has become part of the big package. So, the next day when I went back to work, I walked into the office and stated I meant what I said, I still wanted out. This went over their heads. They really didn't want to hear that I wanted out, but I was determined to leave. I just had enough, and you could thank the Borough Commander for putting the icing on the cake to make me feel that way.

They then try to justify the sending of a Detective from my office and a Police Officer from the DA's office because the trip was funded by the DA'S office. Even so, neither one of the officers knew anything about the case nor put in two minutes' work investigating it. But my point was I was told I couldn't go because I was only a Police Officer, but the officer from the DA's office was the same rank, the same union as me, yet he could go. This is another way the department was using Police Officers in the SCRU. We were doing detective work, but were not afforded the same privileges and status as a detective. I am saying to myself that the Borough Commander was not fair; he, as a Chief, had the power to let me go, and no one would have said a word to him; he was the Chief of the Borough, he was the last word in the borough, he was the buck, and the buck stops here.

So, as I am rehashing the whole situation over and over. I remember what the old-time Sergeant said to me when I was a rookie, "whoever told you the job was fair, is either a liar or just doesn't know what he's talking about." Once again, how true those words turned out to be.

In the meantime, I still must finish what I started. I go to the Grand Jury along with the victims of the crime. The suspect is indicted for the home invasion, Robbery/Burglary. Somewhere down the line, the suspect pleaded guilty. It was a case that was strange, in that I never ever saw the suspect in real time, never put my handcuffs on him, never had any contact with him at all. Never even had a chance to ask why, how could he get involved in such a serious crime, with his upbringing? What was he doing with these two kids who were several years apart in age? Where/how did he meet them? How did he get involved in the Home Invasion? How did he get involved with these two possible gang members? Those were questions I never got to ask or get the answer to. He is indicted, and somewhere down the line, he pleads out.

I was never contacted by the D.A.'s Office regarding his plea or his sentence. That was another unanswered part of the puzzle. Also, as far as identifying him, other than a photo lineup, there was never a lineup held. Where the victims would view it, and make a positive ID. Because that was standard operating procedure (S.O.P.) where the ADA wants a Corporeal lineup, especially because his ID was based on a photo ID only. If he made any statement/confession, he didn't make it to the officers who brought him back. If the ADA questioned him, I would have to be present, but it never happened.

With his mother being a prominent person who most likely was wealthy, I'm sure she hired the best NYC lawyer to represent   him. I always felt that the DA's office never notified me or spoke to me about this case, because there was the possibility they worked a deal, and maybe he got to serve his time in Puerto Rico? Or maybe he served no jail time at all? All I was told was that he pleaded guilty as charged. At this point, I had the wind taken out of my sail, so as long as I got a guilty plea out of it, I was satisfied. I really didn't care that much, as far as I was concerned, I did the best I could, and apparently, no one in the NYPD cared. But I thought about another thing I was told when I first came on by another old hair bag, it's a thankless job, "what did you do for me today?" It would be up to the DA's Office and the judge to complete the job as far as sentencing, whether it be probation or if there would be any incarceration.

So, with the case concluded, I still wanted out. At this point, I had enough, but I would continue giving it my all until I left. I just couldn't find it in myself to be a slacker.

CHAPTER TEN

A NEW PATTERN

There were always new cases coming into the Senior Citizen office, so there was never a shortage of work to be done. At the time, Brooklyn South had many senior citizen robberies. If they were on the street, the case would go to the Detective squad concerned. As previously stated, we only handled robberies that were committed off the street. The Decoy Unit was out every day, hoping to be mugged, which the cops would then say to the perpetrator as they were arresting him, "You made my day". But the Borough (pattern unit) and the SCRU kept an eye out for any new pattern. Eventually, a new pattern was noticed. They noticed one area where there were several push-ins in the same area. Basically, it was the area of East Flatbush with the same type of victim, elderly and frail. With the usual M.O. of being pushed in after getting off the elevator and walking to their apartment. Or if they walked up the stairs, they didn't realize they were being followed upstairs. As the cases came in, the investigators were analyzing each one and putting a pattern together. They noticed that after interviewing all the victims, the statements were just about the same. "I got off the elevator and walked to my apartment. As soon as I opened up my door, I was pushed in." Usually, when asked if there was anybody on the elevator with them, they would say no. But when their memories were refreshed by the investigators, if anyone was on but got off, they would think back and say yes. They would then say but he got off the floor below mine, so I was alone. He was really a nice young man; he even pushed the floor button for me. This was basically repeated by just about all the victims. When describing what took place, they stated the following.

I was pushed in, then dragged to a chair, then I was tied to the chair blind folded and told not to scream or make any noise, or he would hurt me. The statements were almost the same with all the victims. They would go on to say there were two of them because they would converse with each other. One would say to the other, "Hurry up, we left the Buick double-parked outside," and we don't want to get a ticket. The other would acknowledge him with a short answer. Like Yes or Ok. They -he would also open the refrigerator and whatever drinks were in there, soda, milk, juice, two glasses would be left on the table with leftover liquid. In each of the cases, the glasses were dusted for prints but came back negative. It was obvious that gloves were worn or glasses were thoroughly wiped down. There was also no DNA back in those days, so there was no help there. With each victim that was interviewed, more information was gleaned from them. Some of the ones who were a bit more alert said they really heard only one person moving around. Others said the voices sounded similar, as if they were really one person. It didn't take long for the investigators to figure out that more than likely it was only one person. It was just one person trying to make it appear that it was a two-man team. Also, more than likely, there was no Buick. This was probably done to throw the cops off so they would be looking for two suspects driving a Buick for a getaway car. Basically, the ruse was to make it look like there were two robbers who came by car. When there probably wasn't any car at all, and most likely one robber. With the investigation continuing, it seemed like they were hitting a stone wall. They also checked with other boroughs to see if they had any similar types of crimes. They found that Queens SCRU had a similar pattern, so a decision was made to bring the investigator who had similar cases over to Brooklyn to work with our unit. There was the possibility that the suspect was working in two boroughs. But with all the resources, the case was still going nowhere. The investigator from Queens was eventually sent back when there was a robbery in Queens about the same time as one in Brooklyn. So, more than likely, it was not the same person, so that theory was blown out. So, it was back to square one again. There were several push-ins basically with the same M.O., so it seemed obvious it was one skell trying to make it appear like two. They were trying hard and hoping to break this case, but it seemed to be going nowhere. They were looking for just that one break, something that would at least give them a possible clue to who was perpetrating these heinous crimes against the elderly. Some of whom were well into their eighties.

THEY CATCH A BREAK

Eventually, they develop information on a suspect who may be involved in these cases. Each person who gets arrested for a serious crime in Brooklyn, the investigators debrief the suspect. They are asked if they know of anyone who is committing any serious crimes, like Robberies or Home Invasions. Each time a name is given, the investigators do a check on the individuals, and each time they clear the suspect. Eventually, they come up with the name of Anthony Bradshaw, a record check on him reveals he has a conviction for robbery and has served time. He is currently out of jail. Further check leads to the fact that he doesn't live that far from where the Push Ins are being perpetrated. Now things are starting to look up. So, they look further into his background. One day, after doing some investigative work regarding him, it hit them like a bomb. They realize that he has the same last name as a person who, with a group of other kids, was convicted of push-in robberies that were turned into Murders of a couple of senior citizens. They were also not far from where this new pattern was. These victims were killed during a push-in robbery a couple of years earlier in East Flatbush/Remsen Village, which is not far from where these current robberies were being committed. These were the homicides where the elderly victim choked on his Yarmulke or the one where the victim was suffocated with a Prayer Shawl, while another was smothered with a pillow. Further investigation hits them like a bomb; it is discovered that he is the older brother of the convicted murderer, Ben Bradshaw. Ben is the young man who put the gag (Yarmulke) in the victim's mouth. That eventually caused his demise. So now it looks extremely possible that he is a good suspect. So, a decision is made to monitor him right from the minute he leaves his house. They find out where he lives. So, a plan was devised; they would stake out his house and follow him all day until he went home. If he got on a bus, they would follow the bus until he got off. Then they would follow him on foot. He never used the subway: From where he lived to where he roamed, there was no subway line in the immediate area, so it was always by bus or on foot. Every day they followed him, he would lead them to East Flatbush, not far from where he lived.

But following him was no easy task. As one officer said, he was like a tiger on the prowl, always on the alert, always looking at his surroundings. He was always walking and looking around from left to right. He would be walking East then suddenly turn and start walking West. Then he would be walking North and suddenly switch to walking South. He would then suddenly cross the street, and again he changes his direction. More than likely, he was doing this to make sure he wasn't being followed. This made it extremely hard to follow him; apparently, he was very streetwise. It was also true to use one of the officers' words, he was "prowling like a Tiger or Hyena" looking for an easy prey. Like he was looking for a wounded or weak defenseless animal. This went on for a couple of days with the officers following him as best they could. Eventually, he apparently realizes he is being followed, and now he starts playing a game with them. He would see an old person walking, and he would start walking faster, getting closer to the person. With their hearts pounding, their minds racing, saying to themselves, "We got you, go ahead, make your move." Then, just when he is within striking distance, he would harmlessly walk by the person without even looking at them. He would also walk up to a person who was about to enter an apartment house. But again, as they were entering, he would just walk by, again, without trying or even looking at them. It was at this point that the officers realized they were being played. But it was also then that they realized that this was their prime suspect in the push-in robberies. Prior to being made every day, he went to the same area and aimlessly walked around the East Flatbush section.

But catching him would be no easy task now that they were burnt by him, meaning he knew that he was being stalked. Just as he was stalking, looking for a victim. So now it was back to square one; they decided to stop doing surveillance on him, because it was just a waste of time. They would go back to their routine and hope he goes back to his routine. All they could do was wait until he somehow slips up, and somehow, he gets caught, even if it was by a uniformed officer. Or maybe they would get lucky, and a witness/victim would be able to ID him from a photo. Or maybe someone would see him on the street and recognize him from a previous robbery and alert the Police, who would then make the arrest. But that was just wishful thinking, because it never happened.

CHAPTER ELEVEN

A GAME CHANGER

Now that he knows the police are watching him, he is being more careful, he is lying low, and the push-in robberies s have stopped. Even though he is their number one suspect, there is not much they can do. He is too street smart to follow, so they just must wait until he slips up one way or another. Hopefully, he won't kill anyone in the meantime. Apparently, after a short period of time, once Anthony felt that he wasn't being followed anymore or he needed money, he was back to his old routine. He did another senior citizen robbery with the same ruse. Acting like there were two of them. Pretending he had a partner who was nothing more than a phantom. It became obvious that Anthony learned from his brother's mistake. It is better to work alone; this way there is no one who can turn against you, so he was still out there doing his thing. The only difference between Anthony and his brother Ben was that Ben apparently was more vindictive and used physical force against his victims. Whereas Anthony threatened them with physical injury but never hurt anyone. Just fear alone got them to cooperate.

However, soon enough, the Police fears are short-lived, the one thing that everyone feared and didn't want to happen, happened. The Police are notified of a DOA (Dead on Arrival) of an elderly woman in her eighties who lived alone. A neighbor of the woman went to call on her, and found the door unlocked, so after calling out and getting no response, she pushed it open. She sees a terrifying sight; her lady friend (Harriet Goldberg) is tied to a chair, she is fully clothed with outer garments, and a cloth is covering her face. She realizes that she is apparently dead. So, she immediately calls the Police. When the Police respond, they call for EMS. They also call for the Patrol Sergeant, as well as the precinct detectives, and the Homicide Squad. The Crime Scene unit is notified as well. This is standard in any Homicide or any serious crime, or where a person is likely to die or be seriously injured. The Crime Scene unit did their usual and dusted for prints as well as documenting the scene by taking pictures of the homicide/victim and surroundings. As usual, there were no prints lifted, but pictures revealed the victim was fully clothed and blindfolded by a cloth over her face and tied to a chair.

This scene almost fits Anthony perfectly; this is Anthony's signature. Tied to a chair, blindfolded. Also, the fact that this was the area Anthony was frequenting. The only thing missing was the two glasses with liquid in them. All the other facts pointed towards Anthony, especially the area where it happened. Still, they had no proof or evidence that it was Anthony who was responsible for this homicide.

The Homicide Detectives did their usual canvas looking for witnesses, but again came up empty. So, once again, knowing something is one thing, but not having enough to prove it in court is another. Even though they do an extensive canvas, they can't come up with any witnesses or any info that would aid in this case. This is not unusual because, like similar crimes, with victims being elderly, they never realized they were being stalked. Also, a person walking alone would never raise anyone's suspicion that he was stalking an elderly victim; he just blended in with the neighborhood. The Detectives from the Homicide Squad contact the officers of the SCRU. The officers from the Senior Citizen unit give all the information they have on Anthony to the Homicide squad, but also advise them how elusive Anthony is and how impossible it is to follow him. The case is assigned to the 12th division Brooklyn South Homicide Squad for investigation.

MEDICAL EXAMINERS DIAGNOSIS

Victim: Harriet Goldberg F/W 82 years old

Cause of death: Heart failure, possibly caused by fright

Manner of Death: Homicide

The M.E. put the timeline at more than 12 hours due to the condition of the body in the Rigor Mortis state. But it was less than 36 hours. In the performance of the Autopsy the M.E. noted that there were no visual marks on the body, no bruises, no welts, no cuts, no abrasions. There was no evidence of strangulation. No ligature marks were found on her neck. The binding where she was tied to the chair was very loose, so it did not cut off her ability to breathe in any manner. So, it was obvious the heart attack was brought on by fright only.

The Homicide is kept as quiet as possible, trying not to let it hit the newspapers or TV. This was done again to prevent panic in the community. So, in all probability, if Anthony did allegedly do this push-in, he probably does not know his victim has died, if in fact it was his victim.

So now Anthony is a suspect in a Homicide as well as the push-ins. But Anthony is still out there doing his thing; obviously, he doesn't realize his last victim died. Soon, the Senior Citizen unit gets another Push In in an apartment house, this time it's an elderly male. The victim is blindfolded and tied to a chair. He is interviewed and states that he was pushed in by two males, and he was immediately blindfolded and tied to a chair. He said they spoke to each other about a car being double-parked and had to get out in a hurry before they got a ticket. But he also said it sounded like only one guy moving about in the apartment. He thought maybe the other was standing guard over him. When they left, he said it seemed like it was only one man leaving by the sound of his footsteps. Once again, the Crime Scene unit is called. They do their usual dusting inside the apartment, as well as taking pictures. Again, there are two glasses on the table that are half-filled, but again, they are negative for any prints. They then do a check for fingerprints by dusting the inside and outside of the door to the apartment. The Crime Scene Unit Detective does a good job and comes up with fingerprints on the outside of the apartment door. The prints are lifted and submitted to the Latent Print section along with Anthony's name for comparison. Within a day or two, they get notified, "You have a match." The fingerprints are one hundred percent a match to Anthony's. The officers from the Senior Citizen unit are excited; they finally have some good conclusive evidence, his fingerprints. They have finally got their wish. All their hard work has paid off. So, the first thing they do is put a picture of Anthony in a photo lineup. They did this with hopes that this victim could pick him out. But once he is shown the photo array, he cannot pick anyone out. Even though he could not pick him out, it was not much of a letdown, as they are used to Seniors not being able to identify anyone. It was just wishful thinking that he could pick him out.

Now they immediately run to the DA's office and confer with one of the Bureau Chiefs. They informed him of the pattern and of all the Senior Citizen Push Ins that Anthony is suspected of. Including the possibility that he may be responsible for a Homicide. They inform him of his last push-in of an elderly man and the fact that his fingerprints were found on the outside of the victim's apartment door. They are all excited that they have finally got a hit with his fingerprints, that he has been more than likely doing all these push-ins, at least this one for sure, by leaving his prints. But they are quickly brought down from their high; their bubble is about to be busted. The DA tells them he cannot authorize an arrest; the fact that the fingerprints were found on the outside of the door is not enough. The building is an apartment house with many apartments. It's possible he was there to visit someone, and may have accidentally leaned on the door, thereby leaving his prints.

Also, the fact that the victim cannot ID him based on his previous failure to ID him in a photo lineup. The victim had stated he never got a good look at his face because he was grabbed from behind, dragged to a chair, immediately forced in, tied, and blindfolded in a matter of minutes.

The Chief tells them he understands their frustration, but there is no way he can get a conviction based on the fingerprints on the outside of the apartment door. Along with the fact that they have no other witnesses or any additional evidence. There is absolutely no way you can prove that he entered that apartment. He also repeats the fact that the victim failed to pick him out in a photo array that contained his picture.

So, the officers leave the DA's Office feeling frustrated and dejected. The feeling that his prints were left at the last push-in just assures them they were on the right track, they have the right suspect, the right predator, just not enough to arrest him. The Chief tells them that when you have additional information/evidence, come back, and we will authorize an arrest if you have enough information to prosecute.

NOTE: Most Senior Citizens victim cannot pick anyone out, especially when they are attacked from behind; this is the norm.

So, they go back to the office dejected and talk it over with the bosses. They tell them of their frustration with the DA's office. The bosses decided to have a team meeting, with each one giving suggestions on where to go from here. The fact that the DA won't prosecute based on the print on the outside of the apartment door is frustrating. But by talking it over with the bosses, they realize that with his prints on the outside of the door, they really don't have a solid case. So, realizing they had nowhere to go from here, a decision was made to bring Anthony in and throw everything at him, hoping he would break down and confess. Knowing it was a desperate move, they decided to take the chance. They go out and stake Anthony's residence. Once he comes out, they immediately grab him. They place him under arrest; they give him his Miranda Warnings in the auto and bring him to the office. Anthony says he understands them and is willing to be questioned. He is cool and calm. They bring up all the push-ins/robberies and tell him they have enough evidence to arrest him; that's why he is here. They tell him of his little charade where he pretended to be working with someone else. Anthony denies everything; apparently, Anthony learned three things from his younger brother. The first is to work alone, so no one can turn on you as they did to his brother.

The second admit to nothing and make no statements.

The third is don't stick anything in a victim's mouth, as he /she may choke to death on it.

They lay out all the cases, and Anthony denies being involved with any of them, completely denying everything. Now, as a last resort, they confront him with the fingerprints on the door. Anthony tells them those are not my prints. They tell him there is no denying it; they are your prints. Because prints don't lie, no two prints are alike. Anthony denies they are his prints, saying, "I was never in that building." So now they have him in two lies: the prints are not his, and he states he was never in that building. Again, they tell him, fingerprints don't lie; they are 100% yours. He is told you can deny it all you want, but they are your prints. They even try to give him an out at the same time to try to get an admission out of him. They told him to think back, maybe you were looking to visit a friend and didn't realize you were in the wrong building.

But Anthony wasn't going for it; he still denies he was in the building. So, after a couple of frustrating hours, they are forced to let him go. They do a void arrest report, and he is reluctantly cut loose. There is nothing they can do at this point. The next day, they take Anthony's statement down to the DA's Office, and they lay everything out, along with the fact that he denied they were his prints and his denial that he was in the building. Once again, after laying everything out, the Chief tells them that he is not authorizing an arrest. They explain to the Chief that Anthony denied that they were his prints and that he was never in the building. But once again, the Chief tells them you don't have enough, all you have is a LIE, and it is not enough to sustain a conviction for a robbery/burglary or a Homicide, for that matter. Again, the Chief states he could have been in the building visiting a friend, or maybe he had some personal dealings there he didn't want anyone to know. Maybe a girlfriend, a secret lover, or maybe he deals with someone in some kind of illicit conspiracy. Either way, he repeats that you don't have enough to prove anything that would sustain a conviction in a court. There is just not enough for an arrest. All you have is a lie. Once again, he tells them to come back when they get more evidence. So again, they leave the DA's office feeling frustrated. They have given it their all; there is nowhere else to go. Also, the fact that Anthony knows that they are on to him will only make him more careful when he commits another push-in.

NOTE: In another jurisdiction, the DA's office may convene a Grand Jury to investigate further. They may subpoena Anthony before the Grand Jury. Usually, when a person who is being investigated is called before a Grand Jury, they must be given immunity, unless the person waives their immunity. Which, when you are the subject, is not advisable to do. The questions are generally narrow and specifically related to the crime that is being investigated. Since he has been given immunity, if he admits to the crime, he cannot be charged because of immunity. However, when asked if he was in the building where the push-in was, he stated that he wasn't; this is a lie because of his fingerprints that were found there. He then can be charged with Perjury, lying to the Grand Jury, as there is never immunity from Perjury before a Grand Jury. But the case of the Homicide, or the push-in, will still be unsolved. The reason they didn't convene a Grand Jury is that, at some time later, they may come up with enough evidence to make an arrest for the Homicide or the push-in. His being before the Grand Jury previously may jeopardize the case by some technicality.

Another reason, in some cases, if not most, the DAs want an IRON-CLAD case. So, they pick and choose their cases, picking the case with the strongest evidence. One where they feel a conviction is almost guaranteed. They do this so they keep their conviction rate up. Or as the Police would say, as they say in baseball talk, "keeping their batting average up". This way, when they have a press conference or when someone investigates their conviction rate, they can answer that we have a (hypothetical answer) conviction rate of 85%. This is most likely the main reason they won't take a case that has a low probability of gaining a conviction. They don't want to bring down their high conviction rate.

CHAPTER TWELVE

ANTHONY GOES UNDERGROUND

Apparently, Anthony knows for sure the Police are on to him. He is not around his usual haunts, and not around East Flatbush. It is very strange that he has just suddenly disappeared. The push-ins have stopped completely, and surveillance at his home produces no results.

Could he be lying so low that he is nowhere to be found? Could it be that Anthony has moved out of the area? Could he maybe have overdosed on drugs and gone DOA? Or could he be incarcerated for another crime? Wherever he is, he is certainly not around his normal hunting grounds. So, they start checking around, and a check with the Department of Corrections discloses that Anthony is incarcerated at Rikers Island (NYC JAIL) I on a high bail. The charges are a surprise to the SCRU officers. He has been arrested in his local neighborhood for a crime that is not part of his usual M.O. So now an investigation is being conducted to check further what the details of his arrest are. They contact the DA's office. They find that the DA's office is prosecuting Anthony for a nighttime residential Burglary/Robbery/Att. Rape.

The following events of the evening of his arrest, which led to his incarceration, were supplied by the uniformed police involved with his arrest. This is the best scenario that can be gathered for his last arrest.

Apparently, what has happened is that Anthony knowing the Senior Citizen Robbery Unit is on to him and they know his hunting grounds he has changed his M.O. He is hunting in a different area, he is hunting in a new territory to him, which is virgin territory to him. This is the story as best as can be pieced together since there were no witnesses other than the victim, and the fact that Anthony made no statements.

He has turned to nighttime residential burglaries. As he always does, he surveils the area he has chosen. Apparently, one day he observes this young female who lives in an apartment house, who appears to live alone, as every time he sees her, she is alone. So, one day, when he felt sure she was living alone, he picked her out as his next victim. To assure himself, he follows her into the building and observes which floor she goes to. He goes to the same floor and pretends to be looking for an apartment. He pretends that he is confused as he is looking for a certain apartment; he does this to make sure of which apartment she goes to. He observes that when she goes in, she uses a key to enter, and there is no one there to greet her. So more than likely she lives alone, as he suspected. He is satisfied that this would be his next victim, but this one was different. This was a much younger victim, and for some reason, he threw caution to the wind. He must be desperate, because he broke from his usual pattern of picking on the weak and the elderly. He selects someone who can possibly identify him. Someone who is young, stronger, and sharper. Is there the possibility that he was stalking her for some time, and his desire grew so strong that he eventually felt he had to have her? Possible feeling he stretched himself to the limit with older people?

Knowing the SCRU officers are on to him, especially after carelessly leaving fingerprints behind. Also, the fact that they confronted him and basically told him that they knew he did many push-ins. Knowing this, he must feel it's time for a change; he must stay away from East Flatbush and Senior Citizens. The area is too hot for him. So, one night, this is possibly the scenario in which he decided to make his move. After surveilling her several times previously and sure she lives alone. He makes his move; in the early morning hours, he climbs up the outside fire escape and breaks into the apartment of the female he has been stalking. He does this by forcing the window open. She is asleep; he immediately wakes her up and overpowers her. He then ties her up. Then he starts searching for valuables, rummaging through her dresser drawers and night table as well as the closet. He then attempts to Rape her; he warns her not to scream, "or I will kill you". As he is trying to Rape her, she breaks free of her bindings and starts fighting him off. But she is frightened, and she starts screaming and fighting for her life. Her next-door apartment neighbors heard her screams and immediately came to her door. They also call 911 and report the screams. They are calling out, asking, "What's going on. Are you alright?" As they are pounding on her door. But she keeps screaming louder and harder. Her screams are so loud they echo through the plaster hallway walls of the apartment house. Now, several more people in other apartments hear her screams and come to her door. They have no idea what is going on, but are also calling out to her. He is assaulting her and trying to shut her up. Now, several other people in the building who hear her screams also immediately call 911. So now, with all the neighbors calling out to her, he realizes that the Police must be on the way, he must make his getaway, but he can't go out the door because her neighbors are in the hall still calling out as to what's going on in there. They are asking if she is alright, and it sounds like several other people have joined them. They also tell her the Police are on the way. He realizes he must get out of her apartment. So now he figures if he goes out the door, he will have a confrontation with her neighbors, which sounded like there were several of them at this point. So, he has no choice but to go out the way he came in through the fire escape.

THE POLICE ARE ON THE WAY

It's a slow night in the precinct, and about this time, cops are bored and tired of driving around in circles. They are just looking for something to do. If they make an arrest on a midnight to eight tour, it will bring several hours of overtime (O.T.). To a cop who is aggressive, this would be right up his alley; this would be his "dollars for collars". So, when this call comes over as a Burglary in progress and calls for help, they are more than eager to go. They know this is a nighttime Burglar and, by the address, know it's an apartment house. As they are on their way, they receive additional information from the dispatcher. That there are numerous calls, and it is a female who lives alone. This makes their blood pump harder, as well as causing an adrenaline rush. This is a bad guy that they want to get. A nighttime occupied residential burglary is one of the most dangerous crimes there is. Usually perpetrated by desperate, vicious thugs. Picture yourself being sound asleep in the sanctity of your own home. Then, suddenly, in the middle of the night, you are awoken by an intruder. This must be a terrifying feeling for someone who lives alone, or even with family, for that matter. Then, being tied up by this vicious thug and being helpless, your mind must be racing as to what is going to happen next. It must be terrifying, knowing you are at the thug (skells) mercy. So terrified as she fought back, and screamed at the top of her lungs, awakening her neighbors who came to her aid, and thankfully called the Police.

LIGHT TRAFFIC

The streets are nearly empty in the early morning hours, so traffic is not hampering them from getting there quickly. On their way to the scene again, additional information is given: "Female lives alone, calls for help". So now, armed with this additional information, several cars respond. This must be a heavy job, a found job because by now several other callers are calling in. The officers know it's a serious job; this is not just some drunk stumbling into the wrong building, and confused thinking this is where he lives. So, it's lights and sirens blaring all the way. More than likely, just about every car that wasn't on an assignment is responding. There is always a cop working a midnight tour who is looking to make an arrest. Because with an arrest comes O.T. and usually a decent amount. This is one of the reasons many cops volunteer to work midnight to eight; it helps pay the bills, especially if the spouse does not work. There may also be two officers who are aggressive, and both are looking for that extra O.T. So now it's competitive on who gets there first, who will be the first to put the cuffs on this vicious skell. They may even have to choose between themselves. But no matter who has the honors, the bad guy is the loser; he is going to jail. This is a normal thing with cops; a hot job breaks the monotony and boredom. Even with a cop who is not looking for an arrest, this gives him that adrenaline rush until he gets there, and the tension is relieved.

With this additional information, the cops know it's a hot job. Just as the cops arrive, Anthony starts to come down the fire escape. A couple of cops run upstairs, and the neighbors direct them to her apartment. Now that Anthony has gone out the window, she has opened the door. Anthony sees all the cops on the street, so he starts to go back up. As he does, a cop appears at her window. So now he is trapped like a rat, in a giant rat trap, like the rat that he really is. Again, he starts to run down the fire escape, but he can't; there are too many cops waiting with open arms. But he has no choice, so he continues down. When he gets down, there are several cops waiting for him. He decides to try to fight his way out to freedom, so he is fighting violently. But the cops must use

force to overcome force, the harder you fight them, the harder they will fight you. There was no way they would let him go. He is finally subdued and cuffed after a violent struggle. He is charged with Attempted Rape, Burglary, Robbery, Assault, and Resisting Arrest at his arraignment. After a hearing in Criminal Court, there is enough evidence to send the case to the Grand Jury. Where he is eventually indicted by the Grand Jury on all charges. Bail is set at a very high amount, much too much that he can afford. So, he remains in jail.

Now the SCRU officers have the answer to why he hasn't been around. They also take note that since he has not been around, there have been no push-ins in the East Flatbush/Remsen Village section, especially where there were allegedly two perpetrators. Now that Anthony is indicted, he has a hearing at the Supreme Court. After the hearing, the judge heard how serious the crime was and the evidence against him, and he continued the high bail. With Anthony incarcerated on such serious charges, things go back to normal in the SCRU. The pattern case is closed. Apparently, with the bail being extremely high and with the charges so serious against Anthony, he is not getting out of jail any time soon and is hopefully going away for a long time. Assuming he gets convicted, which is more than likely, since he was caught right on the scene. He is facing many years in prison, maybe as much as twenty-five years, especially since he has had a previous felony conviction in the last ten years, which makes him a predicate.

He has been incarcerated for a while, but no one in the SCRU was following his case because it wasn't an arrest of the SCRU. This would be up to the arresting officer to follow up on, or if there was a Detective assigned. Our pattern was closed with his recent arrest. Also, knowing the charges were serious, and he couldn't raise bail, there was no reason to check on his status. As far as the officers of the SCRU were concerned, Anthony was gone for good with the charges he was held on. He was arrested right on the scene and identified by the complainant to the officers right there. There is no way he is beating the identification, especially the fact that it was done right on the scene within minutes of the assault. No way was he making bail; it's too high, he was in for good.

BUT IT WASN'T TO BE

One day, I am at court for a hearing on one of my old cases. When my hearing is over, I go to the sign-out room to sign out. The Sergeant tells me call your office. When I call the office, my Sergeant tells me we had a Push In in the Prospect Heights section, which is near Prospect Park, the largest park in Brooklyn. I am told to respond to the scene and do a preliminary for the team that has the area that will be coming in later that afternoon. The area is a safe area with a very low crime rate for Brooklyn. I will do the preliminary this way, when the team comes in this afternoon, they will have a head start. I respond to the location, and I speak to the woman, another elderly victim. She tells me she came up on the elevator after shopping, and there was a young man who got on with her. He was a gentleman, even pushing the button for her floor. He got off the floor before hers. She proceeds to her floor, and as soon as she opens the door to her apartment, she is pushed in. She is immediately dragged to a chair while he is covering her mouth, she is terrified as he tells her not to make a sound, and "and you won't get hurt." Out of fear, she willingly complies. He ties her to the chair. A cloth is put over her head so she can't see. She then hears a male say hurry up, we have the car double-parked, while the other says, ok I am. (or something to that effect) There is very little conversation between these two robbers, just a word or two every few minutes. However, even though it was supposed to be two people, she said it seemed like only one was moving around. When he/they leave, she says she only hears one set of footsteps leaving. After a short while, when she feels sure that they/he has left, she is able to free herself. She immediately dials 911 to call the Police. She looks around and, on the table, she notices 2 half glasses of juice. As soon as she tells me this, I say to myself OMG "Anthony is out." I immediately call my Sgt, and I tell him Anthony is out. I then tell him all the facts. He says impossible, Anthony is on high bail, he can't be out. The case is too strong against him for the charges to be thrown out or for bail to be reduced to an amount that is affordable for him. The bail was too high for him to make to get out; he was caught right on the scene; he must still be incarcerated. So, then I say, maybe there really were two guys all along, and we were wrong because this is the same exact pattern. If Anthony is still in this, maybe the other half of the team that we really never knew. Could there really have been that there were two of them? So, now on my way back to the office, I am thinking to myself, how could we be so wrong? We were so sure it was one guy playing a game. Is it possible we really screwed up, and there was a second guy? When I get back to the office, as soon as I walk through the door, the boss immediately says you are right, it must be Anthony. We checked with corrections, and Anthony apparently got out on a technicality. He goes on to say he had a court appearance today and was let out on a technicality. The area where the latest push-in occurred is not a far walk from the courthouse in downtown Brooklyn to the Prospect Heights section, where the robbery occurred. Especially for someone who does a lot of walking as he does. So apparently, he saw an easy victim and decided this was too good to pass up. Being incarcerated, he could not make money; he apparently was flat broke. Not having money for transportation, he had to walk home. Or maybe he wanted to walk so he could look for a victim. As he was walking, he was also stalking. So, this could have been someone he stalked, or maybe this was just a by-chance opportunity. He may have observed her walking alone and decided this was too easy to pass up. This was a victim that fit his true M.O., in that she was elderly and frail and apparently alone. So, he follows her right into her building and gets on the elevator with her, and like the usual gentleman that he is, he pushes the button for her floor. Everything about this Push In fits him perfectly. The only difference was that this neighborhood was more of a middle-class area. Where the area where he did most of his push-ins was a poorer area, where the victims were living on just Social Security for the most part. While this victim, although not wealthy, was living a little more comfortably than his previous Push In victims. But this is understandable, considering he was just let out of jail and was walking home. Or maybe possibly walking just for the purpose of looking for someone to prey on, another elderly weak person.

This apartment house was in a higher-rent part of Brooklyn, so there was a good chance this victim had something of value. In this one, he did get some cash and jewelry, which was more than he got from most of his other victims. The result is more of Anthony's handywork. This is another case where there is the strong possibility that Anthony did it, but again no proof to tie him to it. Once again, the victim can't identify him. Even though she is shown a photo lineup, she cannot pick him out. She never got a good look at his face because he kept close to the front of the elevator. When she was pushed in, it was from behind as he dragged her to a chair; she could not get a good look at his face. Given the fact that she was probably too scared to even look. Once again, Crime Scene finds nothing of value that would aid in this case. We called the DA's office again, and they verified that Anthony was out on a technicality, and we asked what it was, but they were reluctant to say what it was. (Possibly someone made a mistake which caused him to be released on a technicality, and they were embarrassed.) But they added that they were trying to correct this technicality and get him back in as soon as possible. We explain to them that more than likely, he is back up to his old tricks. They say that they are preparing to go back to court to reverse this situation. So now we are on high alert for Anthony again, the decoy team is apprised of this, and to be on the lookout for him when they are working East Flatbush. The officer who originally had Anthony's case is in constant contact with the DA's office just about every day. Finally, after a week and a couple of court appearances, we are notified that they were successful in correcting that technicality, and Anthony is back in, with the same bail conditions. While he sits in jail waiting for his trial date, as he is doing so, he is apparently trying to think of ways to get this weight off his back and, once again, gain his freedom.

Now that he sits in jail waiting for his Trial Date, his thoughts probably turn to the night of his last arrest. His aggression escalates as he realizes how his plan fell apart. The pounding on the door and the echoing scream of his victim create a cacophony that drowns his own panicked thoughts. He knew he must escape quickly, but he also knew that fleeing through the fire escape was his only option. Because of all her neighbors in the hallway, He scrambles towards the window, his movements frantic and desperate.

Meanwhile, the neighbors are persisting with their calls, growing more frantic themselves. The police cars arrive at a screeching halt outside the building, and a couple of officers rush up the stairs, their adrenaline pumping as they prepare to face the unknown assailant. At this point, they are unsure of how many there are. The dispatcher basically said numerous calls for help, but never said how many suspects there are. They are determined to catch the perpetrator/perpetrators, driven by the urgency of the situation and the collective call for justice from the community.

Just as Anthony goes out the window and heads down the fire escape, one of the officers spots him as he looks out the window. The officer shouts and alerts his colleagues below, and they converge under the fire escape, blocking Anthony's path of escape. He has no choice because he can't go back up, so he tries to fight his way to freedom. Trapped, Anthony's desperation turns into a violent struggle as he reaches the bottom and attempts to break free. The officers, resolute and unwavering, overpower him, ensuring he cannot escape the consequences of his actions.

Anthony's arrest brings a temporary sense of relief to the community. The charges against him are serious, and his high bail amount ensures he remains in custody. The SCRU officers feel a sense of closure as the pattern case is eventually closed. Anthony's incarceration leads to a period of calm, with no more push-ins in the East Flatbush section. The streets feel safer, and the community can breathe a little easier.

But the story doesn't end there. As his trial approaches, Anthony tries to find ways to escape the weight of his crimes. His attempts at appeals and hearings drag on. Anthony's actions have left a deep scar on the community, but his imprisonment provides a measure of justice for his many victims. Now it's up to a jury to apply that final measure of safety by finding him guilty. In doing so, hopefully, the judge can see fit to keep him behind bars for a long time.

The dedicated officers of the SCRU continue their vigilance, knowing that their efforts have made a difference, even if the path to justice is fraught with challenges. Challenges that have been overcome. There is the possibility that, because of their persistence, Anthony was driven away from his personal best criminal acts of picking on the elderly and changing his M.O. (Modus Operandi) of prowling East Flatbush. Acts that he was apparently quite well versed in, especially where he tried to pretend it was two skells, and they arrived by car, and left by car. Which in no means was the case. Because he has changed his M.O. and decided on another vicious act of criminality, in a different neighborhood, which now hopefully caused him to be faced with many years behind bars, where he so rightly belongs.

CHAPTER THIRTEEN

THE TRIAL

As his trial approaches, Anthony applies different appeals to have his charges thrown out. He is looking for that one mistake, that one technicality, which caused him to gain his freedom in the past. Maybe this time it will be a more serious mistake that will cause him to gain his freedom permanently, with all charges being dropped. He heard of things like this before from Jail House Lawyers/ in conversations he had with them. Maybe he may be one of the lucky ones.

Eventually, after several different appeals and hearings, he has a Wade Huntley hearing that he loses. (There was no Miranda Hearing, as Anthony did not make any statements.) It was just a Wade hearing for purposes of identification. Which really was no problem, as Anthony was arrested at the scene by the Police and identified by his victim right there. He is offered a Plea, but against the wishes of counsel, Anthony decides he wants a trial.

Anthony goes to trial, and the victim testifies, as well as some of the neighbors. Even though they never saw Anthony, they were used by the ADA to show how they heard her frantic screams and show how terrified she must have been as they were at her door. The arresting officer testified as to Anthony's desperate attempt to break free and escape. This is because of the faith of what he feared the most, which was going back to jail. Especially that he knew it would be for a long time, given his past criminal history. After a not-so-lengthy trial, Anthony is found guilty of all the charges. When it comes time for sentencing, even though none of the other cases he is suspected of can be brought up. Only because there is no way they can be proven. However, the Judge sentences Anthony to 30 years in prison. Due to the severity of the crime, which is a nighttime residential Burglary of an occupied dwelling, and the Attempted Rape of the female occupant. Due to his previous history, in that he has a previous felony conviction for robbery, which was in the last ten years, he is considered a predicate felon. So, he is sentenced to Thirty Years in prison, which is not considered cruel and unusual punishment, given the severity of his crime.

In his appeal, he appeals the length of the sentence. However, it was noted that if he had taken the plea at the time, he would have been sentenced to substantially less time. Because he did not take the plea, he is sentenced to the maximum, Thirty Years in jail.

HE APPEALS HIS CONVICTION

After his conviction and sentencing, while he is in jail, Anthony tries to appeal again, this time, it's his conviction. His appeal is based on the fact that he was convicted by an all-White Jury. However, an investigation by the court found this was not the case. It found that there was one Black as well as one Hispanic on the Jury. There was also one Black as an alternate juror, so that blows that appeal out of the water and cements his conviction. Besides the fact that his victim was a black female, this also didn't help his appeal. The court has proven he had a fair trial by a jury of his peers, and his appeal was dismissed.

Just as an afterthought, can you imagine how the victim would feel if he won his appeal and he was set free?

She probably would live in fear for the rest of her life. She probably still has frightening thoughts when she recalls that night, even though he is sentenced to 30 years. The fear is still there, a night she will probably never forget, possibly for the rest of her life.

THE AFTERMATH

A recent check reveals that Anthony served 29 years of his 30-year sentence. He was then let out on Parole. He is now a free man and young enough to commit crimes again, unless he has been rehabilitated. Which could be possible, as they say life sometimes has "many strange twists and turns." The sad part is that neither Anthony nor anyone else was ever convicted or even arrested for the murder of the woman (Harriet Goldberg), who was tied to a chair. Even though homicide cases are never closed, most Detectives know that the first 48 hours are crucial to solving a murder case. To use the Police term Homicides are never closed; they are put on the back burner". If someone wants to give up info on it after all these years, it will be pursued. If it is prosecutable, the DA's office will prosecute. But the more time that passes, the less chance you have of closing it with an arrest. The other problem is that this incident was so long ago that all the Detectives that were familiar with the case are long retired, and many have probably passed on. So, there is no one left on the job who would even know about this murder. It would have to be someone retired and still around, and of sound mind, to bring it up to the current administration. Even then, it would have to be good, strong evidence to make an arrest and for the District Attorney to bring this case to trial.

But until that happens, unless there is some strong new evidence, this case will be kept on the back burner in the Cold Case files. There are many other Homicides, more recent Cold Cases, not as old as this, that can be addressed.

 At this stage of the game, it's highly unlikely that Anthony or anyone else will ever come forward and confess. As previously stated, unless someone knew of it at the time and has been arrested recently and facing serious jail time. He/she may decide to come forward and look for leniency in his/her case. Even though it is so long ago, it will be addressed. As previously stated, if it's prosecutable, the DA's office will prosecute.

Until then, it will be just another unsolved Murder case, and someone has gotten away with Murder. Or maybe Anthony has gotten away with Murder obviously, we will never know. But at the same time, there is also the possibility that Anthony did not commit this murder and someone else got away with murder; if so, like other cases, it will remain on the back burner.

CHAPTER FOURTEEN

SUMMATION OF THE BIRTH OF A NEW UNIT

It's somewhat satisfying to know that at least he has given up 29 years of freedom for all his misdeeds and crimes he has committed all his adult life, and the harm he has done to his victims. So, for 29 years, when he was incarcerated, he could not continue with his monstrous acts. Acts that not only terrified the elderly but possibly even murdered one.

At least there is some satisfaction to the police that investigated Anthony, he paid for some of the monstrous acts he committed against his helpless elderly victims. This is because of his recent arrest. But then, when you think of how many he probably got away with, you must say, "There is no justice". He should spend his entire life in jail. But the element that is needed to sustain a conviction for any crime is that the jury must find the suspect guilty.

GUILTY BEYOND A REASONABLE DOUBT.

In each of the crimes, there was never enough evidence to arrest him and to hold a trial to reach that conclusion.

On another note, upon Anthony's release from prison, he was signed up as a LEVEL ONE REGISTERED SEX OFFENDER, which he will be for the rest of his life. Hopefully, this will keep him on the straight and narrow until he meets his maker.

I LEAVE THE SENIOR CITIZEN UNIT

So after twenty-six months, I got my transfer back to my old command and on patrol. One day later, I am back in Anti-Crime doing what I like best, making those observation robberies, burglaries arrest with great Anti-Crime partners. But I must admit I did learn a lot about investigations and patterns and dealing with the D.A.'s office.

In my opinion, the Senior Citizen Robbery Unit was a necessary unit with great cops, both investigators and decoys. But for whatever reason, it was later disbanded. Senior Citizen Robberies would be back being investigated by the precinct detectives or Central Robbery Squad Detectives, who just didn't have the time to do a real, thorough investigation, as the SCRU did. Especially when it came to transporting them around or trying to help them get reimbursed by the Social Security Department for stolen S.S. cash. Or get them help from the crime victim's compensation board.

So, in closing, besides a couple of stumbling blocks, I will say the Senior Citizen Unit was a great and necessary unit. It is one that the department should never have done away with. Today, there are still many senior citizen robberies being perpetrated against seniors, as they are still the easy prey of these street urchins (skells). The reason is that no squad detective or a specialized unit detective can devote as much time to it as the SCRU investigator. The other investigative units (Central Robbery) have too many other cases to deal with. They could not devote the time to the case as a SCRU investigator could.

However, it was just too slow for me. I was too used to making those on-the-spot arrests, with all the adrenaline rushes that come with it. Also, without all the paperwork that goes with an SCRU arrest. I was used to that on-the-spot satisfaction, knowing you caught a miscreant (skell) right in the act of committing a felony. This also made it easier to deal with it in court; most of the time, the lawyer would advise his client to take a plea. This was done because most of the time the crime was observed by the Anti-Crime cop as it was being committed. The Anti-Crime cop was the best witness that an ADA needed. There was no way he was going to beat the case that was observed by a sharp Anti-Crime Cop. When you made that on-the-spot arrest, there was no need for a Wade hearing or a Miranda hearing. Unless the defendant makes a statement trying to justify his crime. It was like when you caught the hand right in the cookie jar, as he was stealing the cookies. There is no way he can say this is not my hand.

THE SENIOR CITIZEN ROBBERY UNIT

SCRU

THE ULTIMATE MORTAL SIN

TABLE OF CONTENTS

CHAPTER ONE

THE CRIME

CHAPTER TWO

THE INVESTIGATION BEGINS

CHAPTER THREE

A TASK FORCE IS FORMED

CHAPTER FOUR

FOUR YEARS HAVE GONE BY

CHAPTER FIVE

THE PHONE CALL

CHAPTER SIX

DEBRIEFING OF THE PEDDLERS

CHAPTER SEVEN

75 SQUAD DETECTIVES QUESTION HIM

CHAPTER EIGHT

THE CONFESSION

CHAPTER NINE

THE ADA IS NOTIFIED

CHAPTER TEN

IT'S TIME TO GET THE SHOOTER

CHAPTER TEN

THE TRIALS

CHAPTER ELEVEN

THE SENTENCES /APPEALS

CHAPTER TWELVE

THE AFTERMATH

ABOUT THE AUTHOR

CHAPTER ONE

THE CRIME

It was just a normal cold day on the afternoon for the average person on that day of February 3, 1976. But as cold as that day was, it could not cool the burning fires of Hell. For this was the day one of the most heinous crimes in the history of the city of New York was committed. It happened in what most people would call one of the safest places on earth, a sanctuary safe from crime. It was a day that would go down in history as one of the evilest crimes ever committed. For this was the day when the murder of an elderly Priest in the House of God occurred. The murder occurred within the rectory of the church, St. Michael's in Brooklyn, NY. The rectory is the place where priests live; this is their home, this is where they reside while serving God. This was a place where you would never in your wildest dreams believe that something like this could happen. But it did, and it put fear into the community as well as the members of the clergy. Even though it was in the rectory of the church, it was still a part of the church. You might even call this a Home Invasion, because as stated, this is where the priest live. This is where they eat, sleep, pray, and serve God and the community. The second and third floors are where the bedrooms are for the priest. However, the church rectory not only serves as a residence for the priest. But the first floor also serves as the business office for the church.

There are two elderly females who are employed by the church to do all the administrative work. They are there every day, faithfully working to keep the records of the church in order. There is also a volunteer worker who is part of the staff. She gets paid nothing but is there because of her faith in God and the church. These workers handle all the business transactions that go on in the church. They also do all the bookkeeping for the church. There are many types of business transactions. Some transactions that are conducted include special masses for the living or deceased. This is also where wedding arrangements are made as well. This is where you set your date and ask for the mass that you desire. It can be high mass or normal regular mass. With each one, the church is like any other business; the more special the mass, the higher the price. Just like any other business, you get what you pay for. They will set the schedule on the date you desire and for the mass you desire and collect the fee.

JUST A NORMAL DAY

The day started like any normal Monday in the Church of St Michael on Jerome Street in East New York, Brooklyn. The Priest served the early morning mass as he would on any regular day. After mass, he then had some breakfast in the kitchen, where the priest and staff had their meals. After breakfast, he had some free time, so he would return to his room on the second floor of the rectory. There, he would maybe read the bible or take care of some personal business via telephone. He then may even take a nap before his next chore. As he was elderly and not as young as the other priest, he needed that nap to reenergize himself for his next chore. This was his regular routine. Downstairs on the first floor, where business is conducted, everything was moving along normally, nothing was out of the ordinary. Suddenly, there was a knock at the door, which is not unusual, after all, this is where business is conducted. It may be a parishioner who was in dire need of help and needed to speak to a priest to help relieve his/her mental pain. Or maybe a parishioner who may want to make plans to have a special mass said for a family member, usually one who has just recently passed away. Some in the Catholic faith have a mass performed every year on the anniversary of a loved one's death. Or sometimes have a Mass said for someone who is gravely ill, hoping prayers may help. Or maybe someone just wants to make plans for a wedding. So, one of the staffers immediately opened the door and was greeted by two males who were standing there. One of the males stated that he wanted to speak to a priest about being baptized. The receptionist was more than willing to oblige him. So, she invited the two of them in, and she then immediately called one of the younger priests on an intercom system that was also upstairs in the rectory, where the bedrooms are. She asked him to come down to speak to this young man who wished to be baptized. The Priest immediately complied. Once the priest appeared suddenly, these miscreants (skells) turned out to be the disciples of the devil. He was no longer a young man who wished to be baptized. This man, who stated he wanted to be taken under the wings of God, is now nothing more than a street thug. As he immediately drew a handgun and announced a robbery. His accomplice immediately drew a knife. Now they proceeded to demand money. They are no longer wishing to be baptized into the Catholic Church. But are there to break the Seventh Commandment "Thou Shall Not Steal." As this was occurring within a few minutes, one of the thugs who was outside suddenly ushered in two young females. Once he delivered them to his cohorts, he immediately brandished a knife and joined them in the robbery. While another stood outside as a lookout. Unfortunately, the two females walked right into a holdup. One of them was there to make wedding plans for her church service, while the other was just a friend who came along to keep her company. But now they are also victims of this holdup. Now that they are victims, they are robbed of whatever little valuables they had on them. But the thieves were after more than just money from the victims. Apparently, they were attracted by the sign outside of the rectory, advertising One Thousand Dollars cash as prize money for Bingo. This is what they really wanted; they then started demanding the $1000.00 cash that was advertised. However, they were told there was no money on hand, which made them furious. They told them the money had been just sent to the bank for safekeeping. They then ordered everyone to lie on the floor. Faced with three armed men, the victims immediately complied. Now, one of the brothers came down from upstairs, apparently because he heard the raised voices of the robbers. Not knowing what was going on, he came down to investigate. He is immediately greeted by the gunman, and he, too, is ordered to the floor. Now they start ransacking the place looking for $1000.00. Again, they are told there is no money on hand, and again they are told the money has gone to the bank. Due to the threat of a Snowstorm the night before, and in the interest of safety, the Bingo was cancelled. No one would want to walk or drive to the Bingo if the streets were icy and snowy. Because the rectory did not have a safe on its premises. The money was taken to the bank for safekeeping by the bookkeeper and the handyman. This was the normal procedure. But the skells kept demanding the money, apparently not believing them. Just then, the bookkeeper, who was only a volunteer, and the handyman came back from the bank, where they had gone to deposit the money. Back then, there were no ATM's; if there were, the money could have been deposited on Sunday. So going to the bank on Monday was not unusual in an emergency situation. It will only be there until next week's Bingo. As it was only put there to keep it safe until next week, so it did not have to be kept in the rectory.

Upon arrival back from the bank, they had come in through a side door on the other side of the building, so they never saw the lookout on the front steps. The handyman took a back stairway that led directly down to his workshop, while the bookkeeper walked to the front office. She walks right into the stickup and is immediately confronted and ordered to lie on the floor alongside the others.

The elderly volunteer bookkeeper, who was wracked with arthritis throughout her body, said she couldn't get down because it was too painful. She pleaded with them not to let her get on the floor, almost to the point of begging them. But the thugs would hear none of it and kept on screaming at her to get down, shouting, "Get down, or you will be hurt." Still complaining that she couldn't get down, the thug now forcibly threw her down. While she screamed in agony as they continued with the threats. Apparently, in excruciating pain, she screamed even harder. The thug now shouts, "Shut up, or I will kill you," but she is still crying out loud. The Priest lying next to her tried to comfort her because this thug sounded like he meant business. So, he did his best to keep her quiet to prevent her from getting hurt. Now she has quieted down and is just whimpering. Now the victims are pleading with them, they are still trying to tell them there was no money on hand. But the thugs apparently do not believe them and become more menacing. They kept threatening them, telling them, "We know there is money here." Tell us where it is, and no one will get hurt. Where is it? The victims tried emphatically telling them there was no money on hand, as it had just been sent to the bank. But the thugs were so desperate to get what they came for that they refused to believe them. They just wouldn't take no for an answer as they kept demanding the money. Again, there were no ATMs, and banks were closed on weekends, so the money had to be sent to the bank on Monday morning. It was sent because, as previously stated, the rectory had no safe box. So going on Monday was not unusual. This was their normal routine in situations when the Bingo was cancelled. It would only be there until the next bingo session, then retrieved. Now, one of the brothers who was also in the rectory on the second floor heard the commotion, and he came down to see what was going on. He was immediately greeted by the man with the gun. He was also told to get on the floor. The handyman who was in the basement also now heard the commotion and came running up with a very large screwdriver in his hand. He, too, was greeted at gunpoint and was immediately told to drop the screwdriver; seeing the gun, he quickly complied with the gunman's demand. Then he, too, was ordered to lie on the floor. Meanwhile, the other culprits were ransacking the desk drawers, desperately searching for money. Determined to get the money, which is what they came for. They rob what little money the female workers have, as well as the young girl and her friend, who innocently walked into the holdup.

While the holdup is going on, there is also another priest on the second floor who heard the commotion, so he decides to come down and see what's going on. As he is coming down, he is confronted by the gunman who was just going upstairs because he heard noise. The priest asks him what's going on, but then apparently sees the gun, so he realizes this is not good. Now he informs the priest of the robbery and walks him down and orders him to lie on the floor along with the others. They then search all the priests for money. The handyman had a few dollars on him, which were taken from him. The priest, as well as the brother, being in the rectory, had very little money on them, if any at all. Being at home in the rectory, there was no need to carry any money. But they were also searched by these two desperate skells. With all the noise going on, there was a priest on the third floor who also heard the commotion. At first, he didn't think too much of it, since he was up on the third floor, and the sounds weren't really very clear. Because it was also three o'clock and school was letting out (St. Michael's Catholic School), and kids being kids were always goofing off and a bit noisy. He assumed it was the kids clowning around and goofing off. So, he didn't think anything was wrong. But as the noise continued, he realized it was coming from within the building, not just kids on the streets. So, he started to come down, but thought it must be something more serious; not knowing how serious it was, he returned to his room to call 911. Thinking it was some kind of fight or dispute of some kind. He reports to 911 that there is some kind of dispute in the rectory of the church. The 911 operator acknowledges the call and location and notifies the dispatcher, who assigns a car to the job as a dispute in the rectory of St. Michael's. Not knowing that the priest on the third floor called 911, the suspects continued with the robbery. If they had known the priest called 911, more than likely they would have fled at that point if they fled, things would have turned out differently. It would have been just an ordinary robbery. But they didn't, so now the next few minutes change the whole direction of the robbery and their plan. With everyone on the floor, they continued to demand the $1000.00 as they continued searching for it.

A VIOLENT ROBBERY TURNS MORE VIOLENT

Now the gunman hears more noise once again from upstairs on the second floor. Again, he tells the others he was going upstairs to see who else was in the building; his intention was to round them up and bring them down. With all of them down, one of them will tell them where the money is hidden. So, he quickly ascends the stairs to see who is there. As soon as he reached the second floor, within seconds, two shots rang out, immediately followed by two more. He then comes running down the stairs, yelling, "Let's get the f@%&* out of here, I had to take somebody out," or words to that effect.

All three of them immediately ran out the door, joined by the lookout, who was the fourth stickup man. They are all running together down the block. With 911 already being called, the police were already on the way for what at first was a dispute call or an unknown disturbance. However, as soon as the thugs leave the building, one of the clerical workers calls 911 again. But this call is about a priest getting shot, so now a second call goes out as a priest is shot. Now, from a simple run-of-the-mill job of a dispute, it turns out to be a serious assault, one of the highest degrees, a confirmed shooting, a "Shots Fired "job. Now, not just the Police who were assigned the dispute job are responding, but all available units that are not on assignment are responding from everywhere within the confines of the 75precinct. (The 75 precinct is a large, busy precinct that turns out anywhere from 10 to sometimes as many as 15 cars on a day tour). While the Police are responding, the brother and the two Priests who were caught up in the robbery run upstairs. The handyman runs out the back door looking for the local cop, who he knows usually has the foot post nearby.

TO BROOKDALE HOSPITAL

When the trio arrives upstairs, they see Father Craige on the floor, lying face down, bleeding heavily. Just about the same time, the first of many Police cars arrived on the scene. The first two officers run in and are directed to the second floor by the office staff. They immediately ran up the stairs. When they arrive at the 2nd level, they see how seriously the Priest is injured, they wrap him up in a blanket, and everyone grabs a piece of the blanket. The Priests, the brother, and the two Police Officers carry him downstairs to the next level. Father Craige was a large man, well over six feet. So, it was no easy task carrying him down to the first floor, without the proper equipment. Once they got him down to the first floor, an ambulance hadn't arrived yet. It was obvious that he was seriously injured, so realizing how serious the injury was, they carried him down the outside four or five outside steps. Hoping an ambulance will arrive. When an ambulance still had not arrived, a decision was made to put him in the back seat of the RMP (RADIO MOTOR PATROL) Police Car.

Even though he looked like he was at death's door, they are trying their best to save his life. Being that Father Craige was a large man, well over six feet, it was no easy task to cram him across the back seat of the RMP. One of the officers goes to the other side of the car and folds his legs up to squeeze him in. Once he is in the back seat of the RMP, it's off to Brookdale Hospital. That decision was made by the responding officers. A supervisor hadn't arrived yet, so the officers made their own decision. Unlike other jobs where subordinates wait for a supervisor to make the decision, the Police Officers often make their own decisions; they take matters into their own hands.

(When you attend training classes, especially promotional classes, they always tell you a quote direct from one of the textbooks: "even a wrong decision is better than no decision.")

NOTE: (However, even though this is what they teach you in the Academy, sometimes when they feel you made a wrong decision, especially in the use of force cases, that teaching goes out the window.) Sometimes they have compassion, but other times you will be dealt with severely, whether it is administratively or criminally.

Now the officers direct the dispatcher to have Brookdale standby "we have a SHOT PRIEST in the car". They also put out over the police radio to have all main crossings on Linden Blvd kept open (the hospital is on Linden Blvd and Rockaway Pkwy, in Remsen Village). At that time, it was in the confines of the 69th precinct. Every available car from the surrounding precincts, 69, 67, 71, as far away as the 63, responded to Linden Blvd to help clear the way. So down Linden Blvd they go, lights and sirens blasting.

The cop driving that car couldn't make that beat-up six-cylinder car go any faster, with his heart in his throat, he kept that gas pedal to the floor. Every intersection that wasn't opened where the light was against him, he would have to brake the car to safely get through. Then immediately stomped that gas pedal to the floor. As the engine slowly regained power to top speed again. He was driving a car that probably had seen better days, a car that was most likely driven 7 days a week, 24 hours a day, with many, many miles on it. A car that was driven by a variety of different drivers who each drove the vehicle in a different way, some with heavier feet than others.

 The reason he slowed down at uncovered intersections was despite what most people think that drivers automatically yield when they hear a siren, it's not so. Some people are unaware of what's going on around them as they are driving. While others had the windows closed, after all, it was the middle of winter. They also had the heater up full blast and maybe the radio on. Thereby making it almost impossible to hear a siren, or a horn for that matter. But then there are also some drivers who are just incompetent and have the attitude that they can see me, he has brakes. Making it that much harder for the police to navigate through the tangled mess of vehicles on one of the busiest roadway in Brooklyn, NY, Linden Blvd.

 My partners and I, in 69 Anti-Crime (plain clothes and unmarked RMP), Frank Kelly and Joe Daley, immediately respond to the Brookdale emergency entrance where the ambulances bring patients in. We are the first to arrive at the hospital. We clear the way for the radio car with the Priest in it to make sure no one blocks the bay where the ambulances deliver patients. We also notify the staff of a shot priest coming in. We then wait for the radio car with the injured Priest to arrive. Soon, several other cars that had the same idea arrived. As soon as the radio car carrying the Priest pulls up along with several other units, we immediately open the doors, and everyone grabs an arm or a leg of this large man and starts pulling him out, while another cop goes around to the other side door to help slide the Priest across the back seat. The officers are struggling to get his almost lifeless body out of the car; he is still in his Priestly garb. As we are pulling him out, you can see that he looks like he is gone; he is all ashen and lifeless. But you do what you are trained to do, you do what you think is right, you do your best to try to save a life, no matter who it is.

One of the other officers runs up the ramp and into the hospital, and he immediately comes out with a gurney. As he is coming down the ramp with the gurney, we immediately rush to meet him and put the Priest on it and push it up the incline and into the E.R. (Emergency Room). Even though it was announced that it was a shot priest on the gurney, several officers are yelling "shot Priest "shot priest", maybe it was nerves or just the adrenaline acting out. But it couldn't have been made any clearer that the victim was a priest. A team of doctors and nurses immediately takes over and wheels him into a cubicle and pulls the curtain around it. Doctors and Nurses come running from all over and entered the curtained cubicle. All the cops are standing around waiting, hoping for the best, even though most felt in their hearts it was a lost cause. Even though it was announced to the hospital staff that we had a shot priest on the gurney when we ran in for the gurney, some of the other officers repeated that this victim was a priest. However, it was obvious to everyone in the E.R. that this elderly gentleman was a Priest by his clergy outfit. One of the doctors asked what happened and how it happened. He is given a short version of the incident. Before you know it, in those few minutes, the entire E.R. staff knew how it happened. Now everyone, including the hospital staff, is waiting on pins and needles as the doctors are working on him. Finally, within a couple of minutes (with the pressure on, it seemed like an hour), a doctor comes out of the cubicle and confirms what we all feared, "He's Gone". Suddenly, a cloud of sadness and silence comes over the busy E.R. Then this nurse, Carol whom we had known through our many visits to the E.R. on all different types of aided cases, breaks out crying. Here is a nurse working in a busy E.R., where every day she is witnessing just about every kind of injury, illness, or death you can think of, who loses her composure and breaks down crying. My partners and I, along with a couple of other cops, immediately start consoling her; she is consoled the way she would console a loved one who just lost a family member. Just the thought that it was an elderly Priest who was in his Priest garb and was killed for no apparent reason was too much for her to deal with. But when you looked around, there were several Police Officers who were also on the verge of tears. These were cops who worked in a busy precinct with a high homicide rate, and more than likely, even if they only had a couple of years on, they had seen or heard of several homicide scenes already. But never have they seen a man of the cloth murdered. This was a first for the busy 75 precinct, a priest in his priest garb being murdered in the house of GOD. Even though most cops learn to adjust and move on, and do not dwell on it, the murder of a priest is not an ordinary murder of a drug dealer/user. It's a lot harder to deal with.

Now the skells did not only break the Seventh Commandment Thou Shall Not Steal. But have also broken the Fifth commandment, Thou Shall Not Kill. They have now committed the Ultimate Mortal Sin.

So now it's official, the 75 precinct detectives, as well as the 12th Division Homicide Squad, have a Homicide of a Priest to deal with.

TO THE O.C.M.E.

The body will have to be removed to the Morgue, more specifically, the O.C.M.E. (OFFICE CHIEF MEDICAL EXAMINER). There, the M.E. will perform an autopsy to determine the cause of death. Even though he died in the hospital and a hospital Doctor declared him dead, the M.E.

in a criminal matter will make the final determination of the cause of death and the manner of death.

MEDICAL EXAMINERS DIAGNOSIS

VICTIM: PAUL CRIEGE M/W/76

CAUSE OF DEATH: Gun Shot the Chest Internal Organs Damaged /Also Arm Wound

MANNER OF DEATH: Homicide.

The M.E. will determine what parts of the body are damaged, meaning internal organs, which apparently caused his death. He will remove the projectiles from the body, if there are any. He will then write up an official report and supply it to the police, as well as any projectiles removed from the body. If there is a trial, the M.E. will have to testify to his findings of the cause of death. The projectiles will be vouchered by the Police and delivered to the Ballistics section of the NYPD to have their markings (rifling, lands, and grooves) read and identified. They will be compared to other projectiles of the same caliber they already have on hand from previous shootings to see if there is any match. If there is no match, they will be stored, and every gun that comes in the same caliber, its projectile will be compared with the ones from the murder victim.

NOTE: Hospitals by NYS law are not allowed to do an Autopsy on Murder victims; only the Medical Examiner is allowed to do the official Autopsy. Which will be the official record   for   the   Courts.

In the case where the M.E. cannot determine if it is, in fact, a Homicide the case will be sent back to the Police for further investigation. At which time the M.E.will label the case a C.U.P.P.I (Cause Undetermined Pending Police Investigation)? Which means the Police will have to dig further to find if it is, in fact, a Murder or an Accidental death, or Suicide, depending on the circumstances. They will then send their findings to the M.E., who will, after the Police investigation will determine if it's a homicide, accidental, or natural death, or suicide.

CHAPTER TWO

THE INVESTIGATION BEGINS

The witnesses who are questioned separately give different statements. One witness said there were three of them, while another said there were four of them. One witness said they were Black, one said they were Hispanic, and yet another said they were Hispanic and Black. They all agreed that they were too frightened to look directly at their faces, as they were told by marauders not to look at them. Also, the fact that when a gun is pointed at you, you tend to look at the gun and not the face. One also said two of them had guns, and the other had a knife. While another said only one had a gun, and two had knives. Also, two, or maybe all three, were wearing hoodies with the draw string of the hood tight around their faces, thereby not showing much of their faces.

NOTE: It's a known fact among seasoned investigators that this is common, where at the scene of a crime, there will be different versions of the crime, as well as different descriptions of the suspects by the victims. So, the best way to handle this is to interview each victim separately. After they are interviewed, all their statements are compared for similarities. They can then get a better idea of what happened and what the suspects looked like.

The case is assigned to the Detective in the 12 Division Homicide of Brooklyn South, Det. Bieder is assigned. At the time in 1976, the Homicide Squad was divided into zones. The 75th precinct was in the confines of the 12th division/zone. The Detective in the Squad is usually given 3 sets of tours to work exclusively on that case only. He is basically taken off his normal work schedule, or as the detectives call it (off the chart). If the case is not solved within the three sets of tours, even though it is still assigned to him and his team, if another Homicide comes in and he is up, he has another case on his hands.

But for the most part, this is a high-profile case, so all the stops are pulled out. The Detective that is assigned to this case does not follow the normal procedure. He and another member of his team work exclusively on this case for the next six months. During this period, all other Homicides in their zone are handled by other team members. The other team members, when they don't have a fresh Homicide to work on, will help with the Priest Homicide. There are usually 3 to 5 Detectives in a team. Each detective, when he does any investigation on the case, reports back to the detective who is the case officer. Each time they take any investigative action, they notify him/her of every step they take, which is documented on a DD5 (Detective Division 5), which is a follow-up report. This is done to avoid a duplication of effort.

In any Homicide case, the first 48 hours are crucial to the investigation of a Homicide. If it is not solved within the first 48 hours, then it will be more difficult to solve.

It's a known fact in the Police Dept. that the75 precinct is known to some of the cops as the killing fields. The reason being, at the time of the 70s and 80s, between the heroin and the crack epidemic, they had numerous homicides each year. Most of the homicides were drug-related; this year would be no different. It had several already, even though it was February, the beginning of the year. This one was not the first for the year. However, this would be the one who was not a drug dealer or user. Even though all homicides are investigated equally, this one would generate much more publicity. Thereby causing more pressure to be put on the NYPD. The 75th precinct was always one of the busiest of all the precincts in NYC. It would one day have the distinction of being one of the precincts to log over 100 Homicides in a year.

Being the case is such a high-profile case (the murder of a priest, on church grounds) A decision is made to form a Task Force. There are additional detectives immediately assigned, because this homicide of a priest is one that will surely get much press. Especially when it happens on church grounds, it will get more than the normal media attention. Also, given the fact that it was in the rectory of the church, which is considered their residence. The higher-ups in the Police Department will get pressure from City Hall, the media, as well as the Catholic Diocese, and the public in general. It will also get much pressure from the deeply religious working-class community. Many of whom are Hispanic, who are the new immigrants to the neighborhood. The neighborhood which is now in the process of undergoing change. The Hispanics are the new settlers. The feeling among the people was, this is our Priest, our Church, our neighborhood, how can this happen? If the priest is not safe in his own residence (the church rectory), are we safe in our homes?

NOTE: Looking back in history, it reveals that the original ethnic group that settled in the area was the Dutch, many, many generations ago, sometime in the 1600's. When you look back into history, you will find that New York was called New Amsterdam. In fact, many of the streets in the area were named after the rich Dutch settlers, who owned lots of land. This is apparently how the area became known as New Lots. Many of these settlers were selling off their land by the lot. To this day, there is an old Dutch Cemetery right next to the Dutch Reform Church, not far away from New Lots Ave, between Schenk Ave and Barbey St. If you look, you can see the names on some of the Tombstones. They are the names of some of the rich Dutch settlers, the people who owned lots of land that some of the streets were named after. Such as the Van Sicklen's, the Van Sinderens, the Snedikers, the Elderts, to name just a few. The church, which is now maintained by the local community, is one of the oldest churches in Brooklyn, if not the oldest. This is in the New Lots section of Brooklyn, which is an integral part of Brooklyn known as East New York. However, in the year 1664, the English moved in, and New Amsterdam was changed to New York, which was named after the Duke of York. But as time went by, the neighborhood made some more changes, and several different ethnic groups moved in. With the Dutch moving on, English, German, Italian, and Irish immigrants moved in. Like almost all neighborhoods in New York City, it was also eventually undergoing change again. Even though there were still some Italian and Irish families living there, the neighborhood has undergone a change once again. Now, it was the Hispanic and the Black ethnic groups that were moving in as the previous settlers moved out. This area was known officially as the East New York section of Brooklyn, which bordered the Brownsville section of Brooklyn. Which eventually would become two very tough neighborhoods where a hard-core group of youths was raised on the streets of hard knocks.

Father Craige apparently came from a religious family. His two sisters were both nuns. He also had a brother who was a priest who was also in semi-retirement. Father Craige, who had spent his younger days in this neighborhood, left for a couple of years. Eventually returned several years later, only to find out the neighborhood was changing. He found out the hard way. For one day, while out for a stroll in his cleric garb, he was attacked and beaten. In a typical street mugging, however, when they found out he only had a few cents on him, they beat him some more. Since then, he learned that the friendly streets he knew from his younger days had changed, so he very rarely left the confines of the church grounds. He only left when relatives came to pick him up to take him out for a night on the town or maybe a movie, but otherwise, he stood close to home, safely on church grounds, where he was at the time of his killing. Which, apparently, turned out to be not so safe.

CHAPTER THREE

A TASK FORCE IS FORMED

As previously mentioned, a Task force was formed, besides the Detectives of the 12 Division Homicide working on it, a task force of about fifty more detectives was assigned. The detectives were drawn from Detective Squads all over Brooklyn. This is not unusual in a case where there is a lot of pressure as well as notoriety. A Homicide of a Priest on church grounds is a high priority, especially in a neighborhood like East New York, it doesn't get much higher. The detectives interviewed and reinterviewed everyone who was involved in the incident, hoping someone would remember something they hadn't thought of before. The two females were re- interviewed just to be sure that it was just a coincidence that they came to the rectory just as the Robbery was taking place. But they were quickly eliminated as suspects and were just two more innocent victims. No one knew or saw what happened on the second floor, for it was just the gunman and the Priest alone in that upstairs hallway. The detectives theorized that Father Craige, who was a bit hard of hearing, may have possibly heard some kind of commotion downstairs. So, not knowing what it was, he came out of his room to find out what was going on. He came out just as the gunman arrived on the second floor, where he had gone up to investigate the noises he heard. The theory was developed that Father Craige may never even have observed the gun in the suspect's hand. He had extremely poor eyesight due to cataracts in both eyes, as well as poor hearing. Not knowing what the male was on the second floor was there for, the possibility existed that he may have reached out, possibly to greet the visitor by shaking his hand, thinking it was a Parishioner. With information gathered from the other Priest and the brother, the detectives learned that Father Craige was a docile man, and not aggressive; it would not be his demeanor to confront or challenge an armed suspect. Whereas the gunman, on the other hand, may have been intimidated by the large man and thought he was trying to take the gun from him.

There was a possibility that he panicked, and he shot him. But trying to take his gun would not have been the case with Father Craige. If he had known what was happening, he would never have tried to take the gun away. As stated, he was not an aggressive man, and he would have complied with the gunman's demands. This was the only logical explanation the detectives could think of for why he was shot. Even though other detectives may have had their own opinions, this is the one that seemed to fit best. Why else would the gunman shoot a man who was a Priest in full Priest garb and in his mid-seventies with failing sight? He apparently did not realize the priest had failing eyes and was really no threat to him at all. It was just a cold, senseless killing, the taking of an innocent life for absolutely no reason.

The Detectives canvased the area where the Homicide was committed. Remember, this was 1976, long before DNA and Cameras existed. There were no private cameras in private houses as there are today. There were also no city cameras on poles at traffic intersections, as in today's day and age. So, it was a good old-fashioned pounding of the pavement that the investigators did. (As the saying went "hitting the bricks") That was the only way to do it back in those days, seeking any information they could get. Remembering, as they say in the textbooks, "information is the lifeblood of an investigation." Detectives nowadays have a lot more help getting information with the advent of scientific development of DNA, and the numerous cameras all over the city, both public and private. But it was different back then, so the detectives started by knocking on every door on the block where the church was and several surrounding blocks. They ascertained the fact that, apparently, the robbers were on foot. The reason is that most of the time when criminals commit a commercial robbery or burglary, there is usually a getaway car involved. It is usually parked nearby. The car almost always would have a driver waiting for his cohorts and would be double-parked or parked close by. But in this case, there apparently was no getaway car. The detectives had gathered information from their interviews that put the bad guys several blocks away on foot. At one point, a witness who saw them running saw one of the suspects as they were running, hitting one of the other suspects. This immediately put the thought in the investigating detective's mind that this is one suspect's way of saying to the other, "This was just supposed to be a simple robbery." Why did you have to shoot someone? You screwed the whole thing up; now we will be in real big trouble if we get caught. (At that point, it was possible they did not know they killed the priest). This also put the thought in the detective's mind; we may have a weak link here; we have someone who wants no part of a shooting. There is the possibility of a chance he may give himself up, in hopes of getting some consideration from the DA's office as far as prosecuting him for his part of the case. If need be, they can turn him around, and he may give the others up. But that was wishful thinking, but as time went by, no one ever came forward.

In doing the canvas, the detectives found themselves further from the actual crime scene in tracking the suspects. For each block they canvassed, they came up with witnesses who saw them running, which was what the people noticed: a group of at least four running. So, it was obvious now that they did not have a vehicle. From the information from witnesses, the assumption by the detectives was that they were locals. Because they were several blocks away on foot, then suddenly, they just seemed to disappear. They must live in the area and made it safely to their homes or their hideout. So, the manhunt focused on locals from the immediate area.

This was the starting point of their investigation. They saturate the area with members from the Detective Task Force. The detectives are turning over every stone, seeking information. Now weeks have gone by, and with no arrest, the department was feeling pressure from the community as well as the church. The Task Force of Detectives, that were drawn from other precincts in Brooklyn were still actively investigating the case. The detectives employed their usual tactics during their investigation. Mug shots were shown to the victims and witnesses who lived on the street where the skells were seen running. This was done with the hope that maybe someone may recognize one of them; a photo may jog someone's memory. The mug shots were of local criminals who were arrested in the area for various crimes. But once again, it was met with negative results. The neighborhood had two known gangs, which were mostly Hispanic. One was the Sex Boys; the name was derived from Essex Street, a local street in East New York. If you looked at the street signs in the area, you would see that the first two letters (ES) were blacked out. Thereby changing the street name in their minds and on the signs to Sex Street, which to them meant this was their territory. This was to serve as a warning for other gang members to stay out, or else. The other gang was the Montauk Chest Breakers, another name taken from another East New York Street, Montauk Ave. Pictures of those gang members who had previously been arrested were shown to the victims; this was also met with negative results. During one of the showings of photos to the young female who was there to make her wedding arrangements, she made a statement to the investigating detective to the effect, "For the rest of my life, I will never forget the face of the one with the gun". That statement gave the detectives hope that they had a person who could identify when there is a suspect or an arrest made.

Everyone arrested in the area who was arrested for a felony was brought into the Homicide Squad or the 75 Squad for the detectives to interview. Or when notified, the detectives would go directly to the precinct where the possible suspect is being processed. Detectives on the Task Force would also interview all the people arrested. This was done with the thought of having someone with information willing to give it up in hopes of getting consideration for his/her crime. The Anti-Crime officers in the 75, as well as the surrounding 69 and 73 precincts, also brought in persons who were arrested to be debriefed for any useful information. Suspects who were arrested for a violent robbery, especially where a gun was used, were given high priority regarding being debriefed.

Any gun that was confiscated of the same caliber, the rifling on the bullets was also tested against the bullets removed from Father Craige. Of the many guns that were tested, all were met with negative results. Also, pictures of any recent arrest for a felony were also shown. Again, this was also met with negative results. Time is going by, and there is no arrest. Every time they have someone who has the potential to be a suspect, he is quickly eliminated. So, it's always back to square one. A substantial reward is offered by the Diocese, hoping that someone will be encouraged and eager to collect the reward money and come up with some much-wanted information. This was also met with negative results. For no one ever came forward. The clock keeps ticking, and they are no closer to making an arrest than they were on day one. So, after several months, a decision was made by the Chief of Detectives as well as other high-ranking members of the department to disband the task Force.

After all cases were still coming in within their respective commands, as the saying goes among some detectives in the NYPD, "there is no shortage of crime in New York City," so along with crime come cases, and there is no shortage of cases in most squads in NYC. With all the Detective Squads working shorthanded, their bosses, as well as teammates, were desperate to have their investigators back to bring the manpower levels back up. As it was, the Detective Squads as well as the Patrol Force were all working shorthanded already. For this was February 1976, and back in the early seventies, New York City was on the verge of bankruptcy. So, on July 1, 1975, to help save the city, a decision was made by the mayor's office to cut the city workforce. The police dept. was no exception. It was told to cut Five Thousand Police Officers from its force. The department found itself furloughing 5000 of its officers. No one believed they would do it; everyone felt like the city would come up with some last-minute plan to save the 5000 jobs. Or as others thought it was a bluff from the city, a scare tactic to let the Federal Government bail the city out. Most of the cops, as well as firemen, thought, "Our job is essential," they cannot lay us off. That is why several cops and firemen were in a state of shock when it happened. They believed that the Federal Govt would bail the city out. But it wasn't to be, for whatever reasons, the then President of the United States, GERALD FORD, basically stated you are on your own. So, the city was denied the money to bail itself out. As the infamous words on the headlines of the front page of the N.Y. Daily Newspaper blared in June 1975

"FORD TO CITY DROP DEAD".

So, at midnight, July 1, 1975, five thousand Police Officers were laid off.

To fill the vacancies that were left in the Patrol Force, Police Officers from details were put back in precincts on patrol. Some of the officers came from the Organized Control Bureau, others came from the Warrant Squad, and many other places where some officers worked inside jobs or jobs where they didn't do regular uniform patrol. The order was to try to keep the Patrol Force strong, because they are the backbone of the department, and they do all the Calls for service (Radio Runs). They are the first line of defense.

Sometime within a year, some Police Officers were called back. As they were called back, some of the others were sent back to their respective assignments. But the majority of laid-off officers did not come back until 1979. So, between 1975 and 1979, the whole Police Department was working shorthanded. Every Command had to make do with what they had." Do more with less." So from 1975 until 1979, other than the few that were brought back within the first year, there were no new hires in the NYPD. These were tough times in the NYPD. In those days, the department cut corners every way they could. One way was to cut overtime wherever possible. The men and women in the NYPD at the time, as hard as it was for them, rose up to the occasion. Even though it affected their personal family life, they did what they had to do. Some took part-time jobs as cab drivers, truck drivers, or security guards. Others who were more skillful took jobs in construction or did handyman work. As far as the cops who were laid off, they all had to find new jobs, for no one knew how long they would be laid off. Nobody was guaranteed they would come back to the job. When the time came four years later, most came back to the job, but some had found careers in Law enforcement by moving out of state and found jobs there, while others took Federal jobs. After all, most of these cops were young and just starting out in life with a family. There were families to feed, mortgages to be paid, children to raise, and in some cases, school tuitions to be paid. There were others who were a bit luckier; they had spouses who worked, so the burden wasn't as bad for them. But the belt was tightened, and you made the best of what you had.

THIS WAS NOT THE USUAL MURDER

No matter how you looked at it, this was not a usual crime, as it was a shooting over a drug deal gone bad. Or a local Bodega (Spanish Grocery Store) is getting held up, and someone is killed. Homicides of those types were almost normal homicides and were worked on as seriously as any other to try to solve them. But this was a crime that really struck deep into the heart of the community, a Priest in the rectory of a church. This reached all the way up to the Police Commissioner's office, as it surely went all the way up in the Catholic Diocese. So, the pressure was always on the Police Department to solve this crime. Bring these monsters to justice. This had to be solved; it just couldn't be left without a successful conclusion. However, even the cash reward, which often jogs a memory for someone to come forward, apparently was not aiding in gaining any information. Even though, with many Homicides in the past, the investigators had brought in useful information, but in this case, it was not to be. There was always the thought by the detectives that maybe if the bad guys told someone, the reward would encourage that person to come forward. But so far, it wasn't to be; no one ever came forward. Or maybe that person who knew may get arrested for another crime, so to save himself/herself, he/she would give up the information on the Priest Homicide. Or maybe one of the perpetrators themselves would get arrested for another crime and look for leniency, so he may give it up if he wasn't the shooter. There were many thoughts along those lines. Four people involved in such a dastardly crime like this, one of them surely would open his mouth. It was like the old saying in the Police Dept. "Two men can keep a secret as long as one is dead." The feeling was that out of the four, one would talk, tell a friend, or tell a relative. Some people cannot hold something like this inside; they must relieve themselves by telling someone. Maybe someone would tell another, maybe it would be someone who has respect for

God and the Church and could not stand the thought of a priest getting killed. So, they would come forward and give the Police the much-needed information. But in this situation, up to this point, out of the four, no one has come forward or told anyone. But there was always the thought among the detectives that one day, somehow, someway, they would get that break. Someone would talk, even if it was barroom or jailhouse talk, or a braggart who would talk about killing a Priest and getting away with it. But as time went by, it didn't look that way; they had absolutely nothing, and no one ever spoke about it. Apparently, the secret was buried deep down in their evil souls.

Tips kept coming in from locals as well as from far away. Someone who knew or thought he knew who it was would call in, usually anonymously, with the name of a suspect. The Detectives would immediately address it, but the tips led nowhere. They even received tips from out of state. One that looked promising was from a small town in South New Jersey, where one department had a similar type of commercial robbery with the arrest of a suspect wearing a hoodie with the draw string drawn tight, with just a small portion of his face showing. A conference call was held with the New Jersey authorities, and the suspect sounded good. NYPD Detectives then went out to Jersey and questioned the suspect, but they also met with negative results. Frustration was growing every day. This was the type of crime that certain detectives brought home with them. It was, in away a personal matter, one that the detective, especially the assigned detective, lives and breathes. Some of the hardcore detectives, detectives who have seen many different Homicides would fall victim to the emotional stress of working a case of this magnitude. This goes without saying: the pressure from the Diocese, as well as the public, was on the Police Department itself, right down to the investigating officers. Days turned into weeks, weeks turned into months, with still no reliable information. The clock kept ticking, time does not stand still, and the case is getting colder. Month after month is going by, with the months eventually turning into years. Also, during this period, many guns were taken into custody. Every gun of the same caliber was given special attention to the identifying, lands, and grooves. Hoping to get that match from the projectiles that were taken from the priest's body, but this, too, was met with negative results.

There were many other Homicide cases coming in; the Seven Five precinct was one of the busiest precincts for Homicides. Today, it is still one of the busiest precincts in the City of New York, especially for Homicides. It had many Homicides that had to be investigated as time went by, with newer, fresher Homicides that took place. Some were what they called ground ball Homicides i.e., husband kills wife, next door neighbor kills' neighbor. These require very little investigation, if any at all. But the murder of a Priest was one that always stood out, that was by far not a ground ball. As homicides were coming in, less attention was given to the Priest Homicide. The Detective / Homicide squad was just too busy a squad to have one detective assigned to the Priest Homicide exclusively. However, the interviews of prisoners were still conducted on a regular basis in search of information regarding the Priest Homicide, as well as any other felony. Although the other felonies were not investigated with the same aggressiveness. In the NYPD, as it is in many other Police Departments, they say, "Homicides are NEVER CLOSED." They are, as they say in the NYPD, "Put on the BACK BURNER."

With any Homicide as the assigned detective retires, if the case is not solved, it is passed on to another detective. His job is to review the case and maybe do some reinterviews with the witnesses. Also, to see if he can locate any possible new witnesses. Maybe with the passing of time, as they rehash it in their minds, they may have thought of something that may be of help. Even though it may be years old, there is still some kind of follow-up on it. The case is never closed until it has been met with a successful conclusion

Time is going by one year, has gone by without anything useful towards solving the case. They are no closer than they were on day one. They have been coming up on two years, but still nothing has developed. Every time they get some information that they feel may be helpful, it turns out to be a dead end. Now, year two has arrived again, and nothing new has been developed. During the year, there is very little information as far as tips go. Now two years have passed, and still nothing substantial. Now three years have passed, and again they have no new information. During these years, it was still the same, de-briefing all the prisoners, reaching out to informants, but to no avail. Now three years have gone by, and they are still no closer than on day one. In between all the years that are passing by, prisoners who are arrested for serious crimes are interviewed, hoping they will give some information that will break the case wide open. But they never came close to getting any useful information to aid in solving this case. Now the fourth year has arrived, and it seems to be passing like the first three years. With nothing of any value coming in. As the years pass by, the hopes are slim, so it seems, not one bit of information has come across any detective's desk. In the four years, each time they thought they might have a suspect, their hopes were let down when they cleared the suspect. In all that time, there were thousands of arrests for violent felonies. With many interviews. Many of the arrests had gone through the court system, with not one real solid tip coming in regarding the Priest Homicide. There may have been one or two tips from someone who said he knew of someone who could be capable of committing it. But most of the time, it was just someone giving some false information, hoping he could get over on the Police and get consideration on his case, but as previously stated, no one gave any information of any value. Many of the arrests were for violent felonies. There were also thousands of arrests for non-violent felonies or misdemeanors. But still, no information was offered that was useful to help in solving this case. The Detectives still couldn't believe that with a crime like this, someone did not come forward with any useful information. There was always that feeling that, with the four people involved, especially with a crime that was so vicious that it just can't be that these perpetrators were never involved in any crimes before. Or after, for that matter. Could it be possible that they were never arrested before or after this crime? Could it be that after this crime, they just never committed another crime again? Possible, but more than likely not probable. Perpetrators like this are just too violent-minded to just lie back and live a law-abiding life. There must be a time when one of them will get caught for something else and give up the needed information, looking for leniency on their new arrest. Or maybe, as previously stated, tell the wrong person who will give him up. Or maybe even go on a guilt trip and come forward. Knowing a priest was killed for no reason during a botched robbery must weigh heavily on a normal person's mind. So deep down inside, there was always hope that someone would come forward, something would happen to break the case wide open. The odds are that one of them will break and tell someone. But so far, the odds are in their favor, because the detectives still don't have a clue who was involved. But they keep hoping, waiting for their ship to come in, hoping for the one big break. As one of the detectives said, "Maybe it was somebody who was keeping it in the bank" as insurance if he got arrested for a different crime. He could use it to barter for leniency for his recent arrest. As time goes by, detectives are retiring. The detective in the Homicide Squad, who had the case all these years, is preparing to retire. After putting in 25 or so years, it was that time, a time to, as they say, "pack it in". Although it will be a happy retirement, it was also a bittersweet retirement, given the fact that he hadn't made an arrest in the priest homicide. So, he will retire, but will not be completely satisfied because he has that unsolved Priest Homicide on his mind.

When a cop who has that kind of time on the job retires, even though he may put down the gun and badge, in his heart and mind, he is still a cop. For many cops, they live by the saying "Once a Cop Always a Cop," and in a case such as this one, especially when you put so much work into a case like this, you just can't forget it. Some detectives take these types of cases to the grave with them. Even though you are told now is the time of your life where you live for yourself and your family, it's always in the back of your mind. Try as hard as you might, you just can't forget it. These are things the average person doesn't realize. Being a dedicated cop is a part of your life you just can't forget. You want to solve the case so badly, not only for self-satisfaction, but also you want to bring some kind of closure to the victim's family. In some cases, the victim's family wants the detective to solve the case so much so that it puts added pressure on the detective. Making the detective feel like" I must do right for the victim's family." Many dedicated cops who spend a quarter or more of a century as a cop just can't block that part of the job out. And in some cases, it may even ruin your family life if you let it get the best of you. This is why a smart person tells you to retire when you are ready, not just because you have your time on. Retire on your own terms; don't retire because your buddy did. This is especially true when you speak to someone who thought he/she made the right move when they hit his 20 years and got out. Although some are happy, they got out; others are not and will tell you how much they missed the job and are sorry they got out. But after 25 plus years, it may be time to move on, and in some cases, start a new career. So, as broken-hearted as he was that he didn't solve this case before he retired, it was time to move on, so as hard as it is, he is going to retire. Knowing the killer was still out there, and although he and his fellow Detectives did their best, he/they could not mark this case,

CLOSED WITH AN ARREST.

But maybe someday the next detective who inherits the case will have more luck and make that arrest. Because, as previously stated, unsolved homicides are never closed, they are put on "the BACK BURNER"; if any new information comes in, it will be addressed, no matter how old the case is. Especially a case like this where it happened right in the house of GOD. It will always be a sore spot for the detectives who put their hearts into it, especially the original case detectives from the Homicide Squad.

CHAPTER FOUR

FOUR YEARS HAVE GONE BY

Now it's past four years, and they are no closer to solving it than they were on day one. The detective who was the lead investigator on the case is counting down to retirement, and many other detectives who were involved have already retired. Even though many retired, there were still a few of the younger detectives on the job who were part of the case or knew of it. But there was very little follow-up work being done on it. All tips or leads that had come in the past were investigated, and no new ones had recently come in; all the tips had negative results. In fact, the further it got from the original date of the homicide, the tips were barely coming in and had just about dried up. The clock keeps ticking, as the saying goes, "Time waits for no man." It's almost four and a half years that have gone by, and people forget things, but surely someone who was directly involved would not forget. Some day they will get the break, someday their ship will come in. There was always the feeling that someday one of them would come forward, whether he was arrested for something else, and he could use this information to barter for a reduced sentence on his new arrest. Or maybe, just maybe, it was a guilt trip to cause him to give it up. Or maybe some family member that they told may come forward because he/she cannot deal with the heinous secret they were entrusted with. If they were religious, maybe their fear of going to HELL because of keeping this secret from the police would get the best of them. It was always thought that out of four, one of them had to tell somebody. Four young men commit a crime like this and never tell anyone, it just didn't make sense; someone had to tell somebody. It's just human nature to tell a best friend, a wife, a girlfriend, a brother, maybe even a parent. They would just have to wait because obviously, they have nothing else to go on. No witnesses, no info, no suspects, so they would have to wait for that much-needed break. Maybe, as previously stated, someone who has gotten arrested and is looking to cut a deal and give up what he/she knows about the priest killing. Hoping that if he gave up the information, he would get a better deal when he is sentenced on his case, or maybe his case may be dropped altogether. Something that would take the case off the back burner and bring it back to life. Just that little bit of information that would break the case wide open and start the ball rolling to hopefully bring the case to a successful conclusion and end this dreadful mystery. With a Homicide of this nature, it is not forgotten so easy, beside the Police Department, the people on the block know that an arrest has not been made. Even though four years have gone by, the people of the community, as well as the parishioners, still have the fear that was instilled in them by the killing of a priest right in the rectory. The feeling at the time was that most people thought they were locals. Locals who may be living right among them. If they were cruel enough to kill an elderly priest, what would they do to my family? was their thought. So as much as the Police Department wanted an arrest to be made, the community wanted it just as much. Every time the people saw a stranger on the block, the first thought was to call the Police; this stranger may be one of the suspects, and he may be up to no good. But these calls were always unfounded; no one was even close to being a suspect. Even though it was four years, the people on the block were always vigilant for any strangers coming and going on their block. When you live that close to a murder scene, it's something that is hard to forget. The thought in some people's minds always goes back to the day, when the normally quiet block was awakened by the sounds of many sirens, numerous Police Officers running around in and out of the rectory. The priest was rushed away in a police car, at that point not knowing what had happened. Then, with many Police/ Detectives going in and out of the rectory. Also, many detectives were knocking on doors, canvassing the block, interviewing the residents, hoping to come up with any information that would help with the investigation. Once this happens, when the detectives canvass the block, the residents know for sure what happened. They know it before it hits the media; they find out firsthand. But now it's four years later, and the Police still haven't made an arrest, so there is still no feeling of safety on the block. Most feel there is no safety until an arrest is made of the killers of our priest.

CHAPTER FIVE

THE PHONE CALL

Finally, it happens on just a regular, normally busy day of July 1980 in the 75 Det. Squad, the phone rings, Detective Gallo answers, thinking, here comes another case in this already busy squad. Or a complainant wanting to know if there is any progress in his/her case. Or just a crank call of some kind, like kids playing loud music. Why don't the Police do anything about it? Because all kinds of calls like that do occasionally come into the Squad office. But this call was different. Maybe this is the call they have been waiting for, for almost four and a half years.

The conversation went as follows;

He answers with an almost beaten down voice, Det Gallo 75 squad, can I help you. Yeah, this is Police Officer Graziose from Midtown South Precinct. Let me ask you did you guys have a homicide of a priest a couple of years ago? Now the detective answering the phone is excited, his ears have perked up, and his whole demeanor has changed. His mind is racing, thinking back to that day. Could this be the phone call they have been waiting for, for over four years? Is this the break we have been praying for and dreaming about all these years? Did our ship finally come in? Is this the real thing? Because he knows of the Homicide all too well.

On the day of the homicide, he happened to be working and was on the scene. Even though it was not his case, he has a vivid memory of it. After all, the murder of a priest in a rectory is just something that's not easy to forget. Of the many homicides that have happened in the 75th precinct over the last four years, the homicide of a priest is one you don't forget. He has also just inherited the case, with the recent reorganization of the Detective Bureau, where the Homicide zones were done away with. Homicide cases would then go directly to the precincts of occurrence, and a new detective would be assigned. The 75 Squad was such a busy squad for homicide, especially unsolved homicides. They had their own Cold Case Squad. (There was no official Cold Case Squad at the time). There's was called the S.H.I.T., "Special Homicide Investigation Team". Having the team proved to be beneficial; one day, they picked up an old case of a murder of a sixteen-year-old girl who had been murdered right in her apartment almost two years ago. She was strangled and had apparently been sexually abused. At the time, the entire building was canvassed, including the super. No one could provide any useful information. They had no suspects, so the case went into their Cold Case files. Now, two years later, they decided to give it another look. They started by talking to the super of the building, who was the super at the time, to see if he could recall any info that would be helpful. No sooner than they start talking to him, he immediately blurts out, "I did it". Apparently, he is thinking they are coming there for him; he has been living with this guilt all the while. So, the first time a detective speaks of it, he can't hide his guilt any longer. They immediately give him his Miranda warnings, and he gives them a full confession. It was a pre-arranged date that went bad. Apparently, she didn't want to have sex, and things got out of control, which resulted in her death. But like they all do, he throws in that self-serving statement, "She assaulted him first, so I defended myself." But the point was that just a reinterview of a person who is hiding under a guilt trip changes the whole investigation and solves a cold case.

So, when he gets this call, Det. Gallo excitedly says, "Yeah, whadda ya got?" The cop on the other end states we have a guy here who says he heard about a priest getting killed in a church in Brooklyn several years ago. He says he thinks it was East New York. The detective, without hearing anything further, immediately says, "Hold on to him, we'll be there as soon as we can." This is the first phone call in all the years where someone says they heard about the Homicide of a priest in a church in Brooklyn. Mostly all other calls stated they knew who may have committed it and threw a name out. Each was investigated and each was deemed unfounded. As time went by the call stopped coming in. But this was not some news that the papers recently wrote about, or was it talked about on the TV news. This call was about an ICE-COLD CASE. This call was about an incident four and a half years ago, and someone was stating they knew of this Homicide from back then. This was not a story of a Homicide that was recently revived in a special on TV, which is sometimes done when the Police have some kind of new information. Where someone may have seen it on TV and now, they thought they knew who might have done it. So, with the cooperation of the news media, the Police Department is doing a TV special hoping it will spark new information.' But this wasn't the case, this was a phone call out of the blue, where someone mentioned an old homicide. More specific the Homicide of a Priest. This was a phone call regarding a four-and-a-half-year-old case. This was something that had to be addressed immediately. He tells his partner Det. Consolazio suit up were going to Mid-Town South. He also tells his Lieutenant Campy of the call. The LT. states "get right down there." Could this be the phone call they have been waiting for for almost four and a half years. Finally, the day comes when they hopefully are catching that long-awaited break. After almost four and a half years, it has happened. Hopefully, this is the break they were waiting for, when no one at least expected it, from some part of the city where you would never expect it to come from. This is not a run-down neighborhood; this was from an upper middle-class neighborhood. There must be something to this call they are thinking. So, they are eager to get down there and find out if this call will solve their long-held mystery.

JUST A NORMAL DAY IN MID TOWN SOUTH

It was a bright sunny day in the Mid-Town South Precinct in New York City, located in Mid-Town Manhattan. This area of New York City is the heart of City where some cops, as well as civilians called it the CROSSROADS of the WORLD. For it had visitors from all over the USA as well as foreign countries visiting just about every day, every hour of the week. Almost all visitors who come here to NYC want to see the Statue of Liberty, St. Patrick's Cathedral, Rockefeller Center, the Empire State Building, the World Trade Center,

Madison Square Garden, as well as Times Square. Not necessarily in that order. They also want to see the Theater District, with all the bright lights of Broadway. Which is in the Mid-Town South Precinct/Mid-Town North Precincts of Manhattan. This is the area where the vendors/peddlers can make a lot of money, especially from tourists, most of whom are foreign. So, on this bright sunny day two Police Officers of the Mid–Town South precinct went out to do their job. It wasn't a particularly exciting job, but it was a job that had to be done. It was just a routine job, one that was done just about every day of the week. Their job was to go out and round up the street vendors, also known as peddlers. At the time, Manhattan, as well as other parts of the city were getting overrun with these vendors/peddlers and business owners were complaining. The city government at the time turned a blind eye toward it. The attitude was that these are just poor people trying to make a living. But many of these vendors took kindness for weakness and like wildfire it just spread, the vendors were just taking over the sidewalks, they spread their wares all over the sidewalks. Pedestrians could barely walk without zig-zagging around the items they were selling. Even on the bridges connecting Manhattan to Brooklyn that had a pedestrian walk over, the peddlers took that over. It had just gotten out of hand. So finally, after numerous complaints by the store owners, the Police Department created the Peddler Unit. You couldn't blame the merchants after all they were paying rent, insurance, employee salaries, and of course several different taxes. While these street vendors come along with no permits, they set up a table or put their items on the sidewalk and set their wares out for sale. Paying no rent, no salaries, and above all, very little or no taxes at all. They would set up right in front of the stores that are paying taxes, as well as paying rent, and paying whatever necessities to stay in business. It's not surprising that the merchants were complaining, they were scarcely making a living. Even though some of these street vendors were legal in that they had legal permits, usually given to disable vet/vets, however, most of them weren't disabled vets. So, on this day, the officers Graziose and Campisi went out and, as usual, picked up a couple of the illegal vendors that had no permits. They brought them to the Station House, which is the normal procedure, along with their wares, which were then vouchered. They were the usual belts, handbags, costume jewelry, just about all of it were knock offs of brand-name products. Although they looked good, they were cheaply made and usually fell apart after a short time of use, and of course, these vendors gave no warranty. Besides the fact that they were violating certain Laws, especially trade infringement laws, by selling their items under their brand names. Names like Gucci, Armani, and Rolex, just to name a few. These manufacturers didn't want their items copied to look like theirs. Because these items started falling apart within a short time, making their authentic brand look cheap. Some people may have been foolish enough to believe they were buying a $5000.00 Rolex for a mere $500.00. or even $50.00. They may have looked like the real thing, but were really made with poor workmanship and low-quality material. But basically, all the

Police Department was interested in was getting the peddler off the street. They were not interested in trade infringement rights. Or whether the product was real or fake, they just wanted the vendors/peddlers who were becoming a nuisance off the street. Their main objective was to confiscate their wares and send them on their way with a summons. This would ease the complaints that were coming in from the store merchants. Merchants who were happy, as well as the NYPD Manhattan Borough Command, where most of the complaints went. But to be honest, at the time, it was a never-ending battle. In a short while, the vendors would be right back with the same knockoffs, and there would always be someone to buy from them, be it a visitor or a born-and-bred New Yorker. Especially those who wanted to impress their friends with an expensive-looking watch.

CHAPTER SIX

DEBRIEFING OF THE PEDDLERS

After vouchering the property part of the process was the debriefing of the person in custody. The officer would ask him/her if they knew of any crimes, past or present. They also did a warrant check on the vendor, and if he/she came back without a warrant, they gave him/her a summons under the Administrative Code, which usually meant he/she had to pay a fine at a later scheduled date. Once the summons was issued, he/she was on his/her way home. Doing their job as a normal routine, they brought a peddler in who was selling without a license. They processed him as they normally would. After doing a warrant check, which was met with negative results. Officers Graziose and Campisi started debriefing him regarding any crimes he knew of.

It was during this debriefing he started to tell them of a crime he heard about several years ago. This was possibly the shooting of a priest. This happened many years ago which he believed may have been a Homicide. Of course, now the officers are all ears, because they usually hear nothing at all or maybe just some petty crimes. Or many times they would hear from a peddler of someone who is selling drugs, which was very common back then. Usually, this kind of info leads nowhere.

However, they never heard anyone say that he/she knew of a Homicide. So, this was someone they wanted to pay attention to. The peddler starts telling them that it must have been a priest because it happened on church grounds. When asked how long ago this was, he answered several years ago, and it was somewhere in Brooklyn, not sure where, maybe East New York. As they question him further his information sounds credible, compared to most other times where the tips from other vendors usually don't amount to anything, or maybe some insignificant crime. Or maybe a made-up story hoping the police will believe it and cut him/her some slack. Or maybe even give up another peddler for some minor infraction, possibly trying to get rid of him/her because they are selling the same product as they are. But this sounds like it could be the real thing, this could be the info that could lead to solving a Cold Case. Officer Graziose, and Campisi were two sharp cops they knew the area of East New York was covered by the 75 precinct. It was decided by the officers to immediately call the 75 precinct detectives. These cops were sharp, whereas maybe another cop may have let him go because even though he has his info he was not under arrest. Then give the info to the detective squad after they sent him on his way. By the same token, maybe another detective on the receiving end may have said, ok get his info, we will go talk to him at his residence when we get a chance. The feeling may have been just another false tip, of which there were many of after four and half years, there's no rush. But we will go talk to him anyway, the first chance we get.

But it was a lucky day all around with Graziose and Campisi calling the squad directly, and with the detective who answered the phone. The detective who knew of the case firsthand, he was on the scene the day of this atrocious murder. He immediately stated, "Hold him there." We will be there as soon as possible. Call it luck, say it was the hand of GOD, whatever it was, out of at least sixteen or so detectives assigned to the 75 Squad, the one that was on the scene the day of the murder picks up the phone. So, he knew of the case firsthand, and knew it well.

Questioning him at home would not be advantageous to the detectives; being in his home may have given him a sense of security in his own residence. He may change his mind and not be willing to talk, especially if there were family members around. So, it was luck all the way around that this detective had knowledge of it and was aware of it being the Homicide of a Priest. This was a piece of luck for the puzzle, a puzzle that was getting colder by the day. They told the Mid-Town South cops to hold on to him even though he was not under arrest. The Midtown -South cops explained to the vendor that some detectives from Brooklyn want to ask you some questions about the incident. He states that it is no problem he will talk to them when they get here.

Meanwhile in Brooklyn Det. Gallo and his partner, Det. Consolazio gather up the case folder with all the paperwork in it and start to Manhattan. Det. Consolazio, who is new in the Squad, knows very little about the homicide so he is driving.

While he is driving, Det. Gallo is perusing the case to remind himself of the events of that day. Armed with all the information they had gathered over the past four and a half years, they headed out to the big city, to the Mid-Town South precinct.

On the way there, they are wondering just how good his information may be, because in four and a half years, they had all kinds of false information. Is this the real thing or another dead end? They are theorizing it may be something of value because after four and a half years, the case has been at a standstill. No one in the last four and a half years has really given any credible information on the case. Suddenly out of the blue a peddler has information on a four-and-a-half-year-old homicide? So, could this be the break they have been waiting for? Or is it going to be another let down, another dead end. But until they question him, they are still not sure if it is good information or not. On the way to question him they formulate a plan as to how they will approach this informer, if he is in fact one. They would have to ask him a few questions regarding the homicide just to start him off. Then they will let him tell his story. As he is talking, they will analyze what he is telling them and take notes. Does he have good information, or is he just another crackpot seeking fame by making a story up? They will have to decipher whether he really heard something or if he is just repeating news accounts of what he read or heard in the media. They want to get there as quickly as possible, before the informant changes his mind and says he wants to go home. Which he can do, because he is not under arrest. So, all the way there their hearts are beating faster, and their minds are racing even faster. As they are traveling through the streets they are thinking, do we finally have something good or is it another dead end. They want to make sure he is still there, so they are traveling, with lights, and sirens, all the way there.

THEY ARRIVE AT MIDTOWN SOUTH

Upon arrival they are greeted by the two officers who informed them of what the peddler had told them. The officers stated that without any real coaxing, he voluntarily started talking about the Priest Homicide. The peddler stated it was a long time ago, and somewhere along the line, he had heard about it. He wasn't sure where or when, but he knew he heard it somewhere. The homicide was somewhere in Brooklyn, maybe East New York. It was at this point that the officers stated that they would contact the detectives from 75 precinct, the precinct that covers the area. Checking to see if they did have a Homicide of a Priest several years ago. Once they speak to the detective, they find that there was in fact the homicide of a priest several years ago. So this much is true, the conformation of a homicide of a Priest. If his information is any good, it is yet to be seen.

CHAPTER SEVEN

75 SQUAD DETECTIVES QUESTION HIM

Now that the detectives from the 75 arrived and have been debriefed by the Mid-Town South cops, it was their turn to debrief the peddler. They start out by mentioning the priest homicide to him, to start him off. These two seasoned detectives started out slowly, asking him to repeat what he told the two officers. They ask him where he heard this information, and he answers "I don't remember, who did you hear it from, he doesn't remember. Was it in a bar, was it on the street, where was it, who was it? His answers are vague and evasive and non-committal; he says he really doesn't remember when or where. Or how long ago it was he answers he doesn't remember. He just knows he heard it somewhere. So, they go over what he told the officers from the peddler unit. After talking to him for an hour or so, they can tell he is telling them half-truths. So, they go over it again, and each time he adds a little more information, each time he seems to recall more facts. As they are questioning him, he still insists he doesn't remember where he heard it or who he heard it from. Yet he seemed to know a lot about it. So, with this in mind, the detectives feel he knows a lot more than he is saying, so much more that he may really know who is involved in it. Or maybe he himself is one of the perpetrators. But they are still not sure if he is a witness or a suspect. They just don't have enough to arrest him. They still aren't truly sure if he was involved or if he just knows who was involved. Whichever it was, he knew a lot more than they had heard from anybody in the last four years. But after a couple of hours of going around with him, they are convinced he knows more than he is saying but he is not under arrest. So, when he says he is tired and wants to go home, they are forced to let him go. They return to the 75-detective office and confer with Lt. Campy and bring him up to speed what they have learned. They also tell him they are confident that he knows more than he is telling them. The Lieutenant tells them to give it another shot, have another go around with him; he seems like he knows more than he is saying. They then start reviewing the case again. Looking for anything they may have missed previously. Going over these reports was time-consuming, as there were over five hundred or so DD5s. Many of these DD5s were prepared by detectives who were assigned to the Task Force that was created at the time. But after several months the Task Force was disbanded, and the detectives were returned to their own commands. Many of them have retired by now, with some moving out of state, and a couple may have even passed on. So even though there were many reports to go over, as painstakingly as it was, it had to be done. Most of the reports were just the interview of a civilian who could add no information that would help. Some were prisoners, or people arrested with regard to any information they may have, but again, it was all met with negative results. But there were a couple of 5s'(DD 5) that would be beneficial to the detectives as they read further. These were 5s' that described their manner of flight as some civilians noticed and were recorded by the detective. This would also prove to be crucial information to help in solving this case. They studied the whole case folder for over a week, going over every DD5, absorbing any piece of information that looked like it might be promising. So, after almost two weeks of going over the whole case folder it's time to question him again. Before they do, they do a record check on him to see if he has been arrested recently or in the past, if so, are any cases still open? A check reveals he has been arrested previously for some minor cases, but all his cases have been disposed of and are closed. This means he is not represented by Council/Lawyer. Sometimes, a detective may want to go a step further, in that he may call the NYPD Legal Bureau for advice. NYPD has a Legal Bureau with a staff of lawyers on hand who will advise you how to handle your situation, whether it is Civil or Criminal. Once you confer with the Legal Bureau, you are bound by what they advise you, whether it is beneficial to your case or not. However, if you disregard their advice and something goes wrong, you may find yourself in hot water. Because you will not be backed by the Department or the Corporation Council should you get sued.

The Corporation Council handles all lawsuits against the officers as well as the Police Department itself. If you disregard the advice of the Legal Bureau, then it is most likely you will not be indemnified, meaning you are on your own. In this case, they have followed the proper procedure and are able to attempt to question him again because, as it stands right now, he is still being treated as a witness. There is not enough evidence to arrest him. They are still not sure if he was involved or just knows somebody who was. This also means that as a witness, his Miranda Warning does not have to be given. By the same token if he refuses to answer questions, at this point as a witness he has the right to refuse. If he wants to leave, he is free to do so as he is not under arrest. So now it's off to the Bronx they go, as this is where he resides. Keeping their hopes up because this is the closest they have ever gotten to any information-wise in almost four and a half years.

However, before they go to the Bronx to question him the second time, they call the detective who had the case when he was in the Twelfth Division Homicide Squad, Det. Bieder. He was just about to start his retirement from the Police Department. They tell him we have someone who looks like he has some credible information on the Priest Homicide. Right now, the feeling is that he is just telling us half-truths, but we are sure that he will tell us more with this second questioning. They go on to say that at this point, we aren't sure if he is a perpetrator or a witness. But from our previous interview with him, we are sure he has some good, credible information. So much so that he must know more than what he is saying. He either knows who did it, maybe a friend or a relative or maybe he was really a part of it himself, this is where it stands right now. At this point, we are not one hundred percent sure, either way. Would you like to join us when we question him again?

Detective Bieder, without hesitating, immediately says COUNT ME IN. He was about to start his retirement but gladly paused it to be part of this newly developed information. After all, he had this thorn in his side for over four years. Almost four and a half years of frustration, four and a half years of disappointment. Four and a half years of taking it home, four and a half years of sometimes losing sleep. Over four years of never coming close to solving it, yes, he wanted in without hesitating.

So now it's off to the Bronx they go. Hopefully, something positive will come out of this visit, with this newly developed information. The feeling always was that with four perpetrators, one of them had to tell someone. Could this be the one they told, or is he part of the murderous crew? Or is it just another dead end, but from what he has already told them, it sure seems like he knows more than any other person they have spoken to over the last four and a half years. Over the four years, they have spoken to hundreds of people without ever coming close to solving this mystery. On their way to his house, their emotions are on a wild journey, running from high to low. Are we going to hit a home run or are we going to strike out again? Once again, their hearts and minds are racing, with their adrenaline pumping.

NOTE: What the average person does not understand to some being a cop/detective, especially one who is conscientious it is imperative that he solve this case. So, he can bring closure to the victim's family, as well as to put the criminal behind bars, hopefully for many, many years. He is not a salesman selling a pair of shoes or a new car to a family member of a murder victim. One who has lost a loved one that they will never see again, so it's important to him that he brings the family closure. Even though it cannot bring the victim back, knowing he did the best he could gave him a feeling of satisfaction that money can't buy. Even though the department tells you at the beginning of your career "don't get emotionally involved with your cases" to some detectives it is easier said than done. So, the killing of an elderly Priest for apparently no reason is a case that will haunt a detective until he can bring the case to a successful conclusion. Yes, the twelfth division Homicide Detective was guilty, guilty of violating one of the rules of the Police Department "don't bring the case home with you". But it is the kind of guilt that drives you to work harder, despite what the department tells you.

THE SECOND QUESTIONING

Upon arrival at his residence, they are greeted by the peddler, Mr. Hernandez. They tell him they would like to talk to him again and go over a few things that were said. They just want to clear a few things up. He willingly agrees, so off to the precinct they go. When they get to the precinct, they ask him to repeat what he previously told them. As he is doing so, they are referring to the notes they made of his previous statements. He is basically repeating what he has previously told them but in doing so he is again adding a little more to each question he is being asked. The detectives keep pressing him, trying to get the whole truth from him, not just the half-truths he has been telling them.

Finally, after several hours of being questioned he makes a statement that will turn the tone of the investigation, it will now turn into an interrogation. He now states something that was never disclosed before, that only the suspects or a limited number of people would know.

Now that he has made this incriminating statement, all questioning stops and he is given his Miranda Warnings, which among other rights, are the right to Remain Silent, as well as the right to a Lawyer. He states he does not need or want a Lawyer. Now that he has waived his rights, Mr. Hernandez is no longer treated as a witness; he is now a suspect, he is a possible subject(skell). Now the questioning starts, he is told of the fact of certain statements he made where he contradicted himself.

He is apprised of the fact that he stated as the perpetrators were running one of them was striking one of the others. This fact was never released to the public; the only people who knew were the detectives who took the statement and the witness who lived on the block, who gave the information to the detective. It was then kept under lock and key for over four years. This was the statement to break the case wide open; this is the one break they have been waiting for.

Now he is being questioned as a perpetrator; they are playing (as the detectives say) Hardball with him. However, he is still denying he was involved. They now inform him of the fact that it was never released about one suspect striking the other, only someone who was there would know that or was told by one of the perpetrators. They are going over the fact that he knew so much, and yet didn't remember where or when, or who he heard it from. This just didn't add up, to know that much and not remember anything more. They inform him that he has a chance to redeem himself if he just gives it up, "get it off your chest." They could see the look on his face; he is lying, he knows he is holding back the truth.

When you are a good detective with years of experience where you have questioned many suspects, sometimes you can read facial expressions. Sometimes you can almost read a person's mind, or even read body language. This was one of those times when they knew he wanted to talk. They tell him, let it go, get it off your chest, you know that's what you really want to do.

As they are questioning him, they can tell by the look on his face he really wants to talk about it, but at the same time he is apparently afraid to. But the detectives are relentless; they know he is ready to break, so they keep the pressure on him. They also tell him we can't promise you anything at this time, but if you cooperate, we will tell the District Attorney that you did. There is the possibility that if you cooperate the D.A. may give you a deal of a reduced sentence, based on the extent of your cooperation, but we can't guarantee it. At this point, he is giving it serious consideration. He is now asking the detectives how much time he will get if he does cooperate. They tell him this is strictly up to the D.A., but the Judge must also agree with it. The more they talk with him, the more he seems to be looking to finally give it up. Even though at this point they may have enough to arrest him based on his statement of the getaway, it is still not enough for a good, solid case; they would need a lot more info. Finally, after what seems like an eternity, he states he wants to "give it up". He states he will make a complete confession, and in doing so he will name his accomplices. He will tell them exactly what happened and why it happened.

To make sure it is done right they give him his Miranda Warnings again. Again, he states he understands them and will voluntarily make a statement and does not need or want a lawyer.

Finally, the detectives are going to hear what they have been waiting for the almost four and a half years. They are going to hear the information that they were longing for. Information that they didn't have. Which caused some detectives to bring the case home with them, and in some instances lost sleep over it. They are finally going to hear who committed "THE ULTIMATE MORTAL SIN". Who else was involved and how it came to be. Which had been a secret for almost four and a half years. A secret that at one time would never be revealed, and the case would remain in the Cold Case file. Or as they say in the NYPD would stay on the BACK BURNER and remain there until they finally get

that break. Hopefully, this will be the break they have been
waiting for.

CHAPTER EIGHT

THE CONFESSION

Now that it is established that he was involved, now it's time to unravel this mystery. A mystery that has haunted the members of the Police Department, members of the parish, as well as the people of the community for almost four and a half long years. Four and a half years without ever knowing why it happened and who was involved. With the detectives never even being close to making an arrest. Four and half years of people involved whose names never ever surfaced during this intense investigation. Four strangers to East New York.

The questioning starts:

Q. This questioning is regarding a Murder that was committed in February 1976 in the rectory of a church, that you were involved in, is that correct?

A. Yes.

Q. What is your name?

A. Isreal Hernandez.

Q. Who was with you?

One by one, he rattles the names off.

Mario Diego, Humberto Santana, Bobby Broward.

Q. Where do they live?

A. He answers the Bronx.

Q. Where do you live?

A. He answers the Bronx.

Q. Why did you come to Brooklyn?

 A. He answers to rob the church.

Q. Did someone get shot?

A. Yes, a Priest.

Q. Who had the gun and did the shooting?

A. He answers Mario Diego.

Q. Tell us what happened.

A. He proceeds to give up the events of the day.

He states the following.

We came to Brooklyn with the intent of doing a simple robbery of a church. The feeling was that they were all religious people in the Church, a couple of elderly women, a priest or two. They are not street people; they wouldn't resist. It was supposed to be an easy robbery. We knew there would be a thousand dollars prize money on hand because of the weekly Monday night bingo. There would maybe be some extra administrative fee money on hand also. There would be no resistance; we would get the money and take off. No one was supposed to get hurt; that was not in the plans.

Q. How did you know this church had a Bingo on Monday night with a one-thousand-dollar cash prize?

A. Because one of the guys involved lived in the neighborhood at one time when he was a young guy several years ago. So, he knew they had a weekly Bingo, and the cash would be on hand. It was his idea; he planned it. Besides the fact that there was a sign outside the Rectory advertising the Bingo with a one-thousand-dollar cash prize.

Q. How did you get there by car?

A. No we got there by train.

Q. How did you get away?

A. The same way we got away by train, the Elevator Train on Fulton St.

So that was the answer to the mystery of how they disappeared so quickly, how they got away. Several blocks away on Fulton Street, there is an elevated train. There is an entrance to the train at Cleveland St. and Fulton St. The location is maybe six or seven blocks from the church. They apparently made it to Fulton St., ran up the stairs to the train, and made their escape back to the Bronx VIA the New York City Subway system. This would solve the mystery of how they disappeared so quickly, how they just vanished.

While the Police on Patrol were scouring the streets below searching for them, they were safely standing on the train platform above, awaiting the train to make their escape. As luck would have it, they only waited a couple of minutes before the train came in. Even if the Police did check the train station, chances are by the time they got up there, the suspect were long gone. All the while, the police/detectives thought they were locals. Because interviews with people who lived in the area put them on foot as they were running by them. By the statements of the witnesses, and the distance that they were seen on foot away from the crime scene would make it obvious they didn't have a car. So, the most logical thought by the detectives would be they must be locals. It would be almost far-fetched thinking by a detective to think they would come from a borough so far away by train to do a obbery. The Bronx is separated from the borough of Queens by a body of water, where it would have to be crossed with a vehicle over a toll bridge. Then you must cross the Borough of Queens to get to Brooklyn, where the Church is located which is several miles way. So, this is quite a distance to come from the Bronx by train. You would think they would come by car, even if they didn't have one, the usual would be to steal one just for this purpose. After all, they were going to commit an armed robbery, so what would be the big deal of getting there by a stolen car? This is usually the norm: steal a car, do the robbery, get away, ditch the car. But obviously they didn't. Four perpetrators don't come all the way from the Bronx to do a robbery in Brooklyn and use the train to get there and escape back to the Bronx the same way. It's not supposed to happen like that; it just didn't compute, but apparently, it was so, surprisingly, this was the case. To a sharp detective, it would be highly unusual for the suspects to come from the Bronx by train. Surely there are many places where they could stage a robbery in the Bronx, so why come all the way to Brooklyn? With all the skells/thugs in Brooklyn, it would be obvious to the detectives to think they were locals. This was not the normal getaway using 20 tons of steel, driven by an unknowing chauffeur as their getaway driver.

So now the detectives know why they could never get any ID on them; they were from a different borough, the Bronx. They could have just as well been from Mars; it wouldn't have made any difference. They were not locals as originally thought. So, showing pictures of all the local gang members as well as people arrested in all of Brooklyn was just a waste of time. If they were arrested previously for another crime, most likely it would have been in the Bronx or possibly Manhattan. It was always felt that they were locals, or maybe from another part of Brooklyn, or maybe even from the North-West end of Queens, which was not that far from the border of Brooklyn. But the Bronx never figured into the mix. As it turned out, they were just four skells from the Bronx.

In his confession he describes how they came around previously to make sure they still had a bingo with the cash prize. He describes how they did their surveillance and how they stalked the rectory and watched who came and went.

How many people worked there, and how the front desk was manned by just a couple of elderly females. This was not just a one-shot deal to come from where they reside in the Bronx to Brooklyn do the robbery and go home. They did this stalking several times before they put their plan into action. This was well thought out and planned, including their getaway, and the fact that they were unknown to the people in the area. Whereas if they had done a robbery in their own neighborhood, someone may have recognized them, so Brooklyn was a safe bet. The chances of someone from the Bronx who knew them being in Brooklyn on the day of the robbery would be almost a million to one. As far as the skell who once lived was concerned, he lived there when he was much younger, as he aged so did his appearance change. Also standing outside he had his hoodie drawn tight around his face, so not much was showing. Given the fact that he lived there many years ago, chances are the people who lived there when he did are long gone.

He then describes the events as they happened, again as only someone who was involved would know.

How the first two, Mario Diego and Humberto Santana, entered pretending that they wanted to be baptized. It may have aroused suspicion if I came in with them; three of us may have aroused suspicion if we all came in together. So, I waited outside, as a lookout with my other conspirator Bobby Broward. As we are waiting, two young women have come to the church. Not knowing what was going on they had the unfortunate timing of coming to the rectory just as the robbery was going down. They stated that they wanted to go in to talk to someone about making arrangements. At this point, we didn't know what kind of arrangements they wanted to make, and we didn't care. If we turn them away, it may arouse their suspicion that something was wrong. So, I escorted them in, while my other cohort continues to wait outside acting as the lookout. The two unsuspecting females were just there to make wedding plans. One was there to set the date, while the other was just there to keep her company. They had no idea they were walking into a robbery in progress; now they, too, were caught up in this dastardly crime. The crime that was eventually haunting many people, the detectives as well as the Diocese, and neighbors on the block for almost four and half years. The case that was a thorn in the side of the Det. Bieder of the 12th Division Homicide Squad, as well as the 75 Detective Squad.

He goes on to say that now that they have everybody under control, they demand the one-thousand-dollar bingo money. He then went on to describe how they were told that there was no thousand dollars on hand. That was because of the weather (the threat of a snowstorm) the night before, bingo was cancelled, and the money was taken to the bank for safekeeping. He told of how they didn't believe them and ordered all of them to lie on the floor, including the priest who had come down when they asked about a baptism. How they then frantically searched for the money. Also, how they robbed the church workers as well as the two females, and the priest of what little money they had on them. But this was not enough; they considered this "Chump Change," the thousand dollars had to be there. As this was going on, one of the brothers who was also upstairs apparently heard the noise, and he came down to investigate. He was immediately greeted at gunpoint and told to lie on the floor with the others. He goes on to describe how the older woman, who was just a volunteer, came back from the bank, and also walked right into the stickup. She and the handyman came in through a side door, so they never saw the lookout on the front steps. The handyman had taken a route directly down to his workshop, so he never saw what was happening. Now they ordered her to lie on the floor along with everyone else. However, she was suffering from very painful Arthritis and told them she couldn't do it, but the gunman (Mario) demanded she get down. When she doesn't comply, he physically throws her down. Now she is screaming in pain, Mario tells her shut up 'or I will shoot you" or words to that effect. She is frightened, so she tries her best to keep quiet, although she is still whimpering. The priest that was lying next to her is consoling her, he is telling her to be quiet, and everything will be alright. Now the handy man apparently heard her screams, so he comes running up with an 18 inch screwdriver in his hand. He is immediately confronted by the gunman who orders him to drop the screwdriver and get down on the floor with everyone else. The handy man at the sight of the gun immediately complies and drops the screwdriver and gets on the floor. He then went on to say how the gunman (Mario) heard a noise from upstairs and went up to see who or what the noises were. As he is going up the stairs, he is confronted by another priest who was just coming down, also to investigate the screams he heard. The priest then asked him what he wanted. He immediately told him this was a robbery as he pointed the gun at him. The Priest, at the sight of the gun, knew he meant business. He then proceeded to walk him down the stairs where he is then made to lie down alongside the others. Unbeknownst to them, there is also a Priest on the third floor, who hears the noise, but at first thought it was the kids from the school (St. Michaels school) because it was three o'clock and school was just getting out. So, he figures it's just kids goofing off, so he disregards it at first. But then it sounds more like a dispute of some kind from within the rectory, so he is coming down too to find out what is going on. But he decided against it, instead he went back to his room and called 911 and reported it as a dispute in the rectory. The 911 operator acknowledges the call and relays it to the Police dispatcher, who dispatches the call as a dispute at the rectory, of St. Michaels. By doing that, the police are now on the way to a dispute at the rectory.

Now that the gunman has brought the second priest downstairs, he again hears more noise upstairs. He says that, whoever else was there, his intention was to bring whoever it was downstairs, too. So, he goes to the second floor and within seconds two shots rang out followed immediately by two more. Then he describes how the gunman (Mario) came running down screaming that he had just shot somebody. Let's get the F@#$ out of here. They all run out the door and apparently run all the way to the train station. This is how they made their escape from the scene, the elevated Train Station on Fulton St., which was never figured into the getaway. As they were running, it was he who was striking the shooter (Mario). Because this was supposed to be an easy robbery, no one was supposed to get hurt. Now we could be in big trouble because someone did get hurt; at this point, they did not know that the priest would die. They later found out through news accounts that it was a priest who was killed in Brooklyn. This news confirmed what their suspicion already felt.

This was it; this was the real thing; almost all the details that were known and unknown were filled in; all the boxes were checked off. This was no false confession from someone looking for fame and glory. A person who had mental issues that had been plaguing him for years. This would be the thing that would help him rise to fame, which in the past many people felt it did.. Probably the most recent and famous one was the False Confession of the Murder of the young child in Colorado. The Police had nothing on the case after an exhaustive investigation for some time. Then, suddenly out of the blue, someone confesses to the murder of her. This excited everyone, but once he was brought in and questioned by the investigators, they realized his whole confession was fabricated. The confessor had absolutely nothing to do with the murder. Most of his confession was based on newspapers and TV accounts, as well as some he had fabricated. So, he was immediately released and sent for psychiatric evaluation.

But this was the real thing; this was a cross that he had been carrying for over four years. He had to get it off his chest. He wanted to feel relieved. Now he felt like a heavy weight had been lifted from him. This is what the detectives were hoping would happen, how someone's guilt would get the best of him. How he was so tormented that he couldn't live with himself any longer. That he had to just let it out to someone, how he had to get that relief.

Now the weight was lifted off his chest. He spoke about how they vowed they would never speak of it and how they would never tell anyone because (the investigation would blow over soon enough). They didn't know for sure it was a homicide until it was in the newspapers the next day.

The thinking was that the Police would not know it was them because they lived so far away, and no one from Brooklyn knew them. As time passed, the Homicide would be forgotten about and the Police, they had too many other homicides in the city to be concerned about. Each year that went by they were that much safer from getting arrested. Yes, they were safe from the law, but in his own mind it never went away, it was as fresh as the day it happened; he could never escape his demons. In his mind, he was never safe, never safe from his own tormented memory. It was always on his mind, every time he passed a church, every time he heard the church bells ringing. Every time someone spoke of GOD, it was always there; he could never shake it loose. Finally, it reached his breaking point he had to talk about it. So, when taken in by the police for just the simple violation of unlicensed peddler it was time to let go of it. When he first started talking about it, he was talking about it in the third person. As a person who just heard something about it in the passing from a stranger, an unknown person. He would tell the police of the incident, but he would leave himself out of it. He was getting it off his chest by trying to lay blame on this unknown assailant. This way, his conscience was clear; he had told the police of the homicide, and this would help alleviate the burden that had been plaguing him for almost four and a half years. He would feel better about it mentally because his conversation with the Police made him feel like he had gotten it off his chest. But it may have only been a temporary relief; he may have gotten some relief at the time. But down the road, it may surface again because even though he made up this imaginary murderer, he still knows the true story in his mind. That will never really go away until the truth finally comes out.

But in going over his story the detectives were too sharp to be fooled by this made-up false statement that he heard about the murder. They realized he was leaving a big part out. The part that maybe he knew who the culprits were. Or maybe he was involved in it, and he would know who the others that were also involved in it. So, this is why the detectives were relentless in questioning him. The feeling was that he's not telling the whole truth, just a series of half-truths. The more they are questioning him the more they feel he knows more than he is saying.

Is he a perpetrator or is he still a witness? Does he know who the suspects are, and is he one of them? Or is he just covering for them, a relative, a friend? So, after intense skillful questioning, he finally breaks; he gives up what's bothering him for almost four and a half years. In doing so, he gives up the shooter, the other conspirator, and the lookout. He describes what part each played. Now maybe he can maybe get a good night's sleep, he can be at peace with himself. His confession also cleared up the reason why some of the victims said they were Hispanic, and some said they were Black and Hispanic. As it turns out, the three on the inside were Hispanic, and the lookout was Black. This would only be known to the two young females who came to make plans for her wedding as they were the only ones who saw the lookout.

During the questioning, they asked him who had the gun that was used. He states now that they knew the gun was hot, they had to get rid of it. So, they threw it in the Bronx River by the Waterfall near the Bronx Zoo.

THE SEARCH FOR THE GUN

The NYPD has a Harbor Unit as well as Suba Diver Team, Detective Gallo calls them and informs them of the situation. They immediately respond to the scene with a Harbor Launch as well as the Scuba Team. They searched the bottom of the waters where the gun was disposed of. They did this with a large magnet that is attached to a long rope. They kept dropping the magnet down and dragging it to try to locate the gun. Unfortunately, all they are locating are all kinds of discarded metals, which include, among other things, car rims and metal cabinets. The Scuba Team has also been diving down searching for the gun, but they also have no luck. The problem was that the water was too dark and murky. The possibility existed that the gun was still there, but covered by thick mud from the moving currents over the past four years or so. There was also the possibility that the gun may have been carried downstream with the strong undercurrents over time. So, unfortunately, the gun remained in its watery, murky grave. Now that they have searched for a week, a decision was made to call the search off. They gave it their best shot. Even though there is a confession, the DA's office likes to have as much physical evidence as possible. The ADA would like to have the gun so he can physically show it to a jury. Sometimes showing the jury some kind of physical evidence gives them more of a feeling how the crime went down. Having to see the gun, or maybe it even gives them a more realistic feeling about how the crime was committed. This sometimes has the effect in a juror's mind of what the gun looks like and how menacing it would feel to have the gun pointed at them. But as stated, the gun cannot be located, so the ADA must do the best with what he has.

AUTHOR'S NOTE: The NYPD has one of the best Scuba Teams in the Northeast. They are always in the water, whether it's for training, trying to locate some kind of evidence, or saving a life. They do the best they can under the most difficult conditions, if there was any chance that gun could have been recovered, you can bet your last dollar it would have been recovered.

Now that he has confessed, he has a sense of satisfaction that he has relieved himself of the weight hanging over his head. What he doesn't realize is that other people are even more relieved. They are the detective that inherited the case as well as his partner. But more so, Detective Bieder from the Twelfth Homicide, who for over four years lived with this homicide hanging over his head. Now he can go on and enjoy his retirement knowing the case will be put to rest. His head is clear with this arrest, even more so when Det. Gallo allowed him to put his own CUFFS on the suspect, something he wanted to do all these years. Now that he has done it, he too can get a good night's sleep.

CHAPTER NINE

THE ADA IS NOTIFIED

Now armed with this info it's time to call the D.A.s office. They notified the DA's office and advised him of his confession and that he is in custody. A riding ADA is immediately assigned. The riding ADA assigned comes down to the precinct and he is briefed by the detectives of the suspects full confession. Now the ADA advises him of his rights, this was done as he is being video recorded. He basically states the same story he has told the detectives. His statement is a complete confession to the Murder/Robbery, as well as who his coconspirators were. The ADA authorizes the arrest. The suspect also throws in that self-serving statement, like most criminals do. "If I knew someone was going to get hurt, I wouldn't have gotten involved." But apparently, it's too late. He is involved, and he is involved over his head. Now it's time to round up the others.

THEY PICKUP NUMBER TWO

Within a day, they respond to the Bronx and pick up another conspirator who was identified by the peddler, who is Humberto Santana. They pick him up at his job, surprisingly, he works as a security guard in a government facility. He is a stranger to the justice system, as he has never been arrested before. One would think that he would be the one to come forward and confess, given the fact he has never been in trouble with the law. Probably was a decent person who just got involved with the wrong people. However, he is apparently not the weak one, as you would expect. For whatever reason, he was able to keep it to himself. If he did tell anyone else, they as well kept his little, big secret. With a clean criminal record, he was able to secure a government job. His government job of all things is as a security guard; among his other duties he is to keep peace in his place of employment. Now that he too is in custody, he is told that the game is over, that his partner has confessed and has given him up. It's time for you now to get it off your chest. They tell him his partner's name to let him know they have gotten a confession from him, and he has given him up. He is given his Miranda Warnings, he says he understands them, doesn't want a lawyer, and is willing to talk. Now that he knows that his partner has given him up now it's time for him to relieve himself of his guilt. He then proceeds to tell the story; he basically tells the story just as the peddler did. He admits entering with the gunman (Mario Diego) using the ruse that he (the gunman) wanted to be baptized. How they then announced the robbery on these unsuspecting elderly women and the young Priest who had come down to talk to Mario about being baptized. He stated how he pulled his knife out after Mario had pulled his gun, and stated that it was a robbery. With Mario having them at gunpoint, he joined in by pulling his knife. He states how they didn't believe them when they were told there was no money on hand. Because of the impending snowstorm, they cancelled the Bingo and sent the money to the bank. He said they felt the money was still hidden in the rectory. He also states how the gunman (Mario) was furious when they were told there was no money on hand. He felt they were lying to protect the money from being taken by us. He also stated it was easier to control them by laying them on the floor. He then states how their cohort, Hernandez, brought the two females in, and he, Hernandez, joined in the robbery by pulling his knife. They also made the two unsuspecting females lie down alongside the others.

He went on to say how the gunman violently threw the elderly woman to the floor when she refused to get down. If anyone had any doubts that the wrong people were in custody, that surely changed with his statement. The reason is that his statement mirrors what the peddler has already stated to the Police. However, like almost all suspects when they are arrested, he also throws that self-serving statement in. He states that he went along with the robbery because he was out of work, and it would be easy money. If he knew someone was going to get hurt, he would never have gotten involved. Which may or may not be true, either way it's too late; he too is in over his head. Now that he has confessed, he realizes how he has ruined his life. He has finally gotten a good steady job with good benefits and maybe a future. He now realizes his life really was over almost four and a half years ago. All these years he had been living a nightmare waiting for this day to come, for the axe to fall, now it's finally here, now he as well as the others must pay for their evil deed.

THE ADA QUESTIONS HIM

The ADA is notified and told of the statement to the detectives of suspect number two (Humberto Santana). The ADA responds to the detective's office and is briefed by the detectives of his confession. As with the other suspect, the ADA advised him (Humberto) of his rights while he was being videotaped. He states he understands them and doesn't want a lawyer. He, too, gives a statement that just about duplicates the statement of Israel Hernandez, suspect number one, and what number one has previously stated to the detectives. Once the ADA is done questioning him, and he has given a full confession to the crime. The ADA authorizes the arrest. If, for some reason, the ADA would not authorize the arrest, the detective would have to void the arrest as per the Police Department procedure, as outlined in their manual, the Patrol Guide. But it wasn't necessary; the confession was taken legally, and it wasn't a false confession. There have been cases in the past where the Police arrested someone for a crime, but the ADA felt there was not enough Probable Casuse. If that is the case, then the ADA will not draw up a complaint and will tell the officer to Void the Arrest, or the ADA may handle it as a 343 D.P., Deferred Prosecution.

CHAPTER TEN

IT'S TIME TO GET THE SHOOTER

Now it's time to arrest the shooter; both suspects in custody have named him in their confessions. They are building a case against the shooter. Before they go to arrest him, they confer with the ADA and advise him they are going to arrest the shooter, hoping he will make a statement as the others did. About one month or so goes by after building a strong case (as they say they have all their ducks in line) the detectives make their move. They respond to the suspect's home in the Bronx. When they arrive at his home, they are greeted by Mr. Mario Diego (the alleged shooter) (skell). He does not seem to be surprised that the detectives are there. Apparently, he is aware of his cohorts getting arrested and realizes they must have given him up. He is no stranger to the justice system, as he has served a sentence for a previous felony conviction and is recently out of jail. They take him into custody and take him to the Station House, where the questioning will begin.

Once at the Squad office, they advise him of his Miranda Warnings, and he says he understands them and does not want a lawyer. He is also advised that his partners have given him up, and the game is over. It's time for you to let it go. You are in the batter's box, and you have finally struck out. At first, he is in denial, but the detectives remind him that no matter what he says, his cohorts have already given him up. And they know exactly what happened, but maybe he can explain why he shot the elderly Priest. Maybe he can give some sort of justification as to why? Maybe he can explain it away. Which they really know is impossible. So, he starts talking, he basically tells the same story as the other two, that they went there for the Thousand Dollars cash. How he pretended to want to be Baptized. How once the Priest came down, he drew his gun and announced the robbery. He stated they knew about the money because one of their other co-conspirators told them about it. How he (his cohort) had previously lived in the area and knew they had Bingo with the cash prize. Everything is going in line with what the other two culprits (skells) have told the detectives, as well as what they told the ADA. He also admits to where they disposed of the gun, figuring it would never be found in those murky waters. Which apparently, he was right about in his little charade.

WHY DID YOU SHOOT HIM?

So now the Big Question is what happened with the shooting,andwhy? He states when he heard the additional noise upstairs, he went up to investigate, his intentions were to bring whoever it was downstairs to join the others. He previously brought the other Priest down as he did not resist. However, when he arrived on the second floor this time, he saw this large older man who appeared to be walking toward him with his hand extended. He was intimidated by his size (Father Craige, who was a large man over 6 feet). His thought when he was reaching out, he was trying to grab his gun. So, he panicked and accidentally shot him. (a self-serving statement). He stated the gun went off accidentally when he pulled it back. After he admits to shooting him, and after his complete statement regarding the shooting he is reminded by the detectives he shot him four times. Once, maybe twice, may be considered an accident, but four shots would never be. He is then told that the Priest had Cataracts in both eyes, as well as Bad Hearing, and more than likely had no idea he had a gun pointed at him. There was the possibility that, because of his poor eyesight, he thought that he might be a parishioner, and he was reaching out to shake his hand. Upon hearing that from the detectives if he didn't know it before he knows it now that he took the life of an elderly senior citizen who was a decent GOD Loving man for absolutely no reason. During his confession, he admitted that it bothered him too. At times he thought about turning himself in, but the thought of going to jail for the rest of his life frightened him. Given the fact that he had previously served time in jail for a felony, and he did not like it, and did not want to go back again. For he knew that no judge or jury would believe him that he accidentally shot and killed a Priest. Especially in the house of GOD. Without withstanding the fact that especially for that matter one who was elderly and suffered from cataracts and had bad hearing. So, he just tried his best not to think about it, and maybe with the passing of time, it will go away. But deep down inside, he also knows it will never go away. Also knowing his cohorts have given the conspiracy up, it was time for him to do so. Now that his confession is secure, it's time for the ADA to be notified.

THE ADA QUESTIONS HIM

Once the ADA arrives, he gives him his rights again as he is also being videotaped. Again, he states he understands them and is willing to make a statement without a lawyer being present. He repeats everything he has told the detectives. He corroborated everything his partners had told the detectives, as well as the ADA. That their initial plan was to steal the one thousand dollars cash that was on hand. No one was supposed to get hurt. But he, like the others, also throws in the self-serving statement. That he accidentally shot the Priest. He thought the Priest was trying to take his gun away from him. He was intimidated by his size but had no idea the Priest had Cataracts and Bad Hearing until he was old by the detectives. If he did, he would not have accidentally shot him, because he wouldn't have pulled the gun back. But like the others, it doesn't make the crime any less serious. It is still Murder 2nd during the commission of a felony. Once his statement is taken, the ADA authorizes the arrest.

After their arrest the ADA wants a line up even though he is told that all the victims were shown individual photo lineup of all the suspects, no one was able to pick anyone out. He still insisted on a live lineup with the hopes that seeing someone in person may jog their memory. However, it wasn't to be, even the female who stated she would never forget the face of the one with the gun, had failed to pick anyone out.

ONE MORE SUSPECT TO GO

Now there is still one more to go. But finding him is a little harder; he is nowhere in the Bronx or Brooklyn, for that matter. He is the one who as previously stated was the one who set it up. He was the one who lived in the area as a youth and put the thought in their minds about the one thousand dollars and how easy the robbery would be. They search high and low for him. But he is nowhere to be found. They check with the NYC/NYS Department of Corrections, but they do not have him anywhere in their system. As the search continued, they eventually found out that he is in a County Jail in California serving a one-year sentence on a minor charge. He will have to be extradited back to New York   City. Detectives fly out to California with a Warrant for his arrest and to extradite him to NYC. Eventually, he is brought before a Magistrate, where the judge authorizes the extradition. This allows them to take him back to New York. Once he is done with his extradition paperwork he is flown back to NYC.

Unfortunately, the detective as well as the ADA are unable to question him, the reason being he has an open case and by law he is presumed to be represented by council. His lawyer has invoked his Fifth Amendment right to "Remain Silent". So, he cannot be questioned by anyone, unless he voluntarily gives up that right, which he never did. The only hope they have is to put him in a lineup and hope he is picked out. However, he never entered the rectory, so no one inside ever saw him. Throughout the entire robbery, he stood outside acting as a Sentry as his (skell) accomplices were performing their evil deed. The only two people who ever saw him were the two young ladies who were there to make wedding plans. The detectives put him in a lineup that was supervised by the ADA. The lineup is viewed by the two females individually, but neither one was able to pick him out. Understandably, given the fact that it is over four years later, as the person gains or loses weight, the contour of his face may change. It may be a bit fuller or thinner. He may also just look a little older. Also, the fact that he was on the outside and it was a cold February day, and he had the draw string of the hood tight around his face. Leaving very little of his face showing, and the fact that they only saw him for a minute or two, as they were quickly ushered inside the rectory.

Now he has not been identified and has not made any incriminating statements. Because of a technicality in the law, the statements of his cohorts cannot be used against him in a trial. Unfortunately, he cannot be held responsible for this crime. Even though he is the one who set it up, there is nothing that can be done to prosecute him. So, he must be set free. But he will have to live with the thought in his mind that he was ultimately responsible for the death of the Priest. Because he was the one who set it up, if it wasn't for him, there would have been no robbery by these other three. They knew nothing about a church in Brooklyn with a one-thousand-dollar cash prize. He was the one who put it in their heads about how easy a robbery would be. He is the one who instigated the plan. He was really the devil in disguise. But obviously, it never bothered him to the point of giving it up after four and a half years, so it's doubtful he will give it up anytime soon.

Regretfully, the ADA has no choice but to tell the detective the arrest will be a 343. Which is a Deferred Prosecution (D.P.) Which means at this time the DA's Office will not pursue criminal charges. However, if additional evidence is ever gathered in the future, the case can be reopened, and the person can be re-arrested and charged again. It is unfortunate that he must be set free, as he is the one who set it up. In the first place, it was his plan; he was the cause of   THE ULTIMATE MORTAL SIN.

When you think about it, given the fact that there were four of them, all this would have amounted to two hundred fifty dollars apiece. For that menial amount of money they took the life of elderly sickly servant of God.

Regarding the other three, there is a hearing held in Criminal Court, and all charges are upheld against all three of the suspects (now defendants) (skells). The case is sent to the Grand Jury. After all the witnesses testify, which included the victims of the Robbery, as well as the detective. Even though the victims cannot identify anyone, they testified at the Grand Jury to establish the fact that there was a gunpoint robbery and a shooting in the rectory. After hearing all the evidence, the Grand Jury hands down a True Bill. Which means the defendants are indicted on the charges of Murder 2nd Degree, Possession of a Deadly

Weapon 1st Degree, and several other charges. Bail is set, as this is a Murder case there is no bail to be set.

Eventually, there is usually a conference meeting between the DA's office and the Defense Attorney held to see if there can be a plea arrangement. But if they are unable to reach an agreement, the case is marked for trial.

After wrangling its way through the complicated court system, the case eventually goes to trial.

The Sixth and Eighth Amendments of the Constitution are as follows.

The Sixth Amendment Guarantees the Right to a Speedy Trial. The Eight Amendment Guarantees the Right that Bail shall not be excessive.

Due to the seriousness of this crime (Murder 2nd), there is no Bail set.

As part of the system of due process, the defendants have the right to choose who will decide their fate, whether it will be by a jury, or a bench trial, (judge only).

CHAPTER TEN

THE TRIALS

March of 1982 the defendants went on Trial, it is six years since the date of occurrence, which was in February 1976. It seemed like it was a lifetime ago for the detectives that investigated the case, as well as the members of the Church/Diocese, and the community. But as the saying goes, "The Wheels of Justice Turn Slow," so the day has arrived for the defendants to see what fate has in store for them. In the eyes of the Law, you are Innocent until Proven Guilty. They can be judged by a jury of their peers if they choose, or solely by a judge. Which was more than any choice they gave their victim. He was not given a chance to choose his faith. His adversary made the choice for him. So, the Trial begins.

MARIO DIEGO (the shooter) chooses a Jury Trial, which means he will be judged by twelve of his peers. Apparently now that he has been arrested for the Murder, while awaiting trial he confesses to his cellmate of the crime. His cellmate notifies the authorities, who then use him to testify against Mr. Diego.

HUMBERTO SANTANA (first to enter with the gunman) He chooses a Bench Trial, which means he will be judged solely by the Judge a Bench Trial (Non-Jury)

ISREAL HERNANDEZ (acted as a lookout, then escorted the two females in). He also chooses a Bench Trial.

All the defendants are charged with Murder 2nd Degree, Criminal Possession of a Weapon 1st Degree, as well as several other charges.

When the verdicts are handed down, all the defendants are found guilty as charged of Murder 2nd, and Possession of a Weapon 1st degree. Even though six years have gone by, Justice has finally been served. They are found Guilty "BEYOND A REASONABLE DOUBT."

As the saying goes

"JUSTICE IS BEST SERVED COLD"

What it really comes down to they took the life of an innocent man. A man who dedicated his life to GOD, a man who took on a life of poverty. All his years as a priest he helped many people, whether they were parishioners or not. A man who never had the chance of living out his retirement, to be killed in such a reckless, heinous manner. This was at the hands of a ruthless, cold-blooded, greedy murderer, in the house of GOD.

The fact of the matter is, when it came down to it, his life was taken for One Thousand Dollars, which would have amounted to Two Hundred Fifty Dollars and maybe a few extra dollars apiece. Considering there were four of them, the money had to be divided into four ways. They probably could have gone to any commercial establishment, or any Bodega and gotten the same amount or possibly a lot more. But the cowards they were picked a church where the people would not resist or fight back. Where they would confront a couple of elderly women, and maybe a Priest or two, people who are nonviolent.

People who are just working to earn a meager living to survive, and a volunteer who dedicated her time to serve the church. Which is just her way to serve GOD. No matter how you look at it there is no way anyone can justify this dastardly murder, it was pure evil. It was THE ULTIMATE MORTAL SIN.

CHAPTER ELEVEN

THE SENTENCES /APPEALS

 Now that the defendants have been found guilty, it's time for their sentences to be handed down.

MARIO DIEGO:

HE HAS A PREVIOUS FELONY CONVICTION, HE IS THE SHOOTER, HE OPTED FOR A JURY TRIAL. HOWEVER HIS CELL MATE TESTIFIED AGAINST HIM, IN THAT HE CONFESSED TO HIM THE MURDER OF THE PRIEST. HE IS CONVICTED OF MURDER AND POSSESSION OF A WEAPON AND SERVED WITH A SENTENCE OF 26 YEARS + 6 MONTHS TO LIFE.

HUMBERTO SANTANA:

HAS NO PREVIOUS ARREST HE OPTED FOR A BENCH TRIAL (NON-JURY). HE IS FOUND GUILTY OF MURDER AND POSSESSION OF A WEAPON HE IS SERVED WITH A SENTENCE OF 20 YEARS TO LIFE.

ISRAEL HENANDEZ:

HAS A COUPLE OF MINOR ARREST HE OPTED FOR A BENCH TRIAL (NON-JURY).HE IS FOUND GUILTY OF MURDER. HE IS SERVED WITH A SENTENCE OF 15 YEARS TO LIFE.

(He was the first to confess, giving up his cohorts)

Now that they are Convicted Felons their lawyers file a notice of appeal. They file notice that their clients' rights were violated. Each one had his own reason in the manner that their lawyers stated that their rights were violated.

The Detectives involved in questioning all three defendants were questioned by the Appeals Court Judge as to the legality of the rights that were given to the defendants.

There was a hearing regarding all three defendants, each was held separately.

The ADA was also questioned by the Appeals Court Judge as to his part in giving the suspects their rights. The videotape of each defendant is played for the judge at the hearing.

There Appeals were as follows.

MARIO DIEGO:

FILED AN APPEAL THAT HIS COUNCIL WAS INEFFECTIVE, IN THAT HIS COUNCIL TOOK TOO LONG TO FILE HIS APPEAL. HE ALSO SUES HIS ATTORNEY ON THOSE GROUNDS.

DECISION: The court ruled that he was represented by adequate counsel, and his claim that his counsel took too long to file his appeal had no merit. His appeal was denied. His conviction was upheld.

HUMBERTO SANTNA:

FILED AN APPEAL THAT HIS COUNCIL WAS INEFFECTIVE

DECISION: The court ruled that his appeal had no merit, he had an adequate council, and his appeal was denied, and his conviction was upheld.

ISREAL HERNANDEZ:

HIS CONVICTION WAS APPEALED ON THE GROUNDS THAT HIS STATEMENTS WERE TAKEN BEFORE HIS MIRANDA WARNINGS WERE GIVEN.

DECISION: The court ruled that the first time he was questioned in July 1980 he voluntarily agreed to be questioned as he was considered a witness. Therefore, his Miranda Warnings did not have to be administered.

The second time he was questioned, later in July, once the Police realized he was a possible suspect, he was immediately given his Miranda warnings. He was also given his Miranda Warnings by the ADA that were administered as he was being videotaped. His appeal was also denied.

IN summations of the Appeals the courts ruled in favor of the prosecution, which was affirmed after hearing from all sides. This included hearing from the defendants' lawyers, as well as the Detectives and the ADA. Therefore, all the defendants' convictions were upheld as administered, and the sentences were also upheld.

CHAPTER TWELVE

THE AFTERMATH

Humberto Santana, was sentenced to Twenty Years to Life, was paroled after serving twenty years.

Isreal Fenandez was sentenced to Fifteen Years to Life and was paroled after serving Twenty-Seven Years.

Mario Diego (the shooter) was sentenced to Twenty-Six Years to life and was paroled after serving Thirty-Seven Years.
(However, maybe it was Karma, or the hand of GOD, he (Mario) passed away after only two years of freedom.)

All three convicted felons were placed on Lifetime Parole. The fourth suspect was never brought to trial.

Looking back, as young men, they ruined their lives, which more than likely also ruined their families' lives. Their families, who were more than likely hard-working, God-Worshipping people. Whose hearts were broken by the foolishness of their loved one's action. Those families had to endure twenty and in two cases, more than 25 years, without the benefit of having a loved one to help support a family. Because it had to be just pure greed that they were talked into the robbery of a church, by obviously one of their calculating cohorts. A cohort who had no respect for the church, as well as the elderly woman who worked there. It was the lure of one thousand dollars that brought them all the way from the Bronx to Brooklyn to commit this dastardly crime.

While committing this heinous crime took the life of an innocent God Loving Man, who served his parishioners as a messenger of God. While trying to live the rest of his life in semi-retirement. But was killed to what would have amounted to Two Hundred Fifty Dollars apiece, hardly worth taking a life and spending the prime of their mid-lives in prison, leaving their families to fend for themselves. The families of the skells were also unwitting victims of the crime that this cowardly group executed on church property, taking the life of an elderly priest for no reason. The shame they must have endured when their relatives and neighbors found out that their family members were involved in the killing of a priest. Most likely, since they were Hispanic, they were religious people who had shame brought on them by the actions of their loved ones. Which they were forced to live with.

But in the eyes of the many Detectives/Police Officers, they were just four evil SKELLS.

Skells who took the life of an innocent person. It wouldn't have made that much of a difference that he was a priest because of the mere fact that he was a sickly 76-year-old man to begin with. A man who was living his retirement years, still serving GOD, who had his life shortened by four Skells. To the detectives, it was a crime that they had to live with for over four years. A murder that some detectives did what they were told not to do: take the case home with them. They lived with the misery of this mystery of this case until they were finally able to bring this COLD CASE to a successful conclusion.

THE CHURCH

The church still stands and remains open to its faithful parishioners of the neighborhood, of which there are many.

 However, the school has been shut down due to a lack of student enrollment. Possibly, the new residents in the neighborhood are unable to afford the tuition.

The Bingo was ceased not long after the shooting.

The rectory is no longer exclusively the rectory but has been turned into a home/shelter for young men who need assistance with their lives. So, the building is still being used as a place for people from the neighborhood in need.

The elderly woman who worked and volunteered at the rectory, along with the brothers and the priest, were victims of the robbery. At the time, many remained with the Church, but they always feared the day of THE ULTIMATE MORTAL SIN that was committed. It is in their hearts and minds for the rest of their lives, always living in fear, that it can happen again. For no one can ever forget how the life of an innocent man was taken, for no reason, other than greed, a servant of GOD, a man of the cloth,

THE ULTIMATE MORTAL SIN

CEMETERY NEXT TO DUTCH CHURCH ON NEW LOTS
AVE. WITH NAMES ON TOMBSTONES OF STREETS IN EAST
NEW YORK WRITTEN ON THEM

DUTCH REFORM CHURCH NEW LOTS AVE BETWEEN
BARBEY AND SCHENCK AVE DATING BACK TO THE 1600"s

FEAR CITY PHAMPLET HANDED OUT TO VISITORS BY
POLICE OFFICERS PRIOR TO NYPD LAYOFFS, AS A
SCARE TACTIC

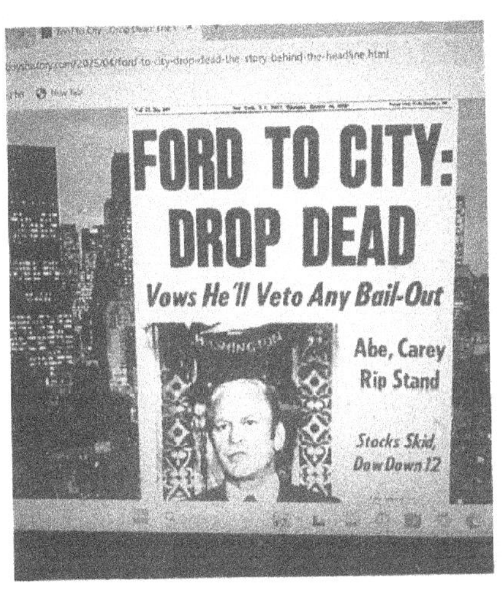

FRONT PAGE DAILY NEWS 6/1975 FIRST DAY OF
MASSIVE LAYOFFS, OF 5000 COPS

1981 69 ANTICRIME LEFT TO RIGHT THE AUTHOR, JOSEPH RAINONE,PO FRANK KELLY, SGT JEFF KRACHT, (GREAT BOSS) PO GENE RAYNOR, EVIDENCE AFTER ARREST FROM A SUPER MARKET STICKUP

NEW LOTS BOYS WRITTEN IN OCTAGON TILES ON THE SIDEWALK, LIVONIA AVE AND ASHFORD ST DATING BACK TO THE 40'S

NO RADIO SIGN IN VEHICLE WINDOW 1970"s NORMAL SIGHT
HOPING TO PREVENT A BROKEN WINDOW

1978 SCRU LEFT TO RIGHT THE AUTHOR, JOANNE DeCESARE, OFFICE MANAGER, PO JOE DALEY DECOY, ROSEMARY CARBONARO DECOY (RIP OFF ROSIE), "A GREAT DECOY", LARRY SALZANO, MY PARTNER

THRASHED CAR NORMAL SIGHT IN THE 70'S

1987 108 ANTI CRIME TOP LEFT PO GEO.KLOUDA, PO CARLINE TORRES,
THE AUTHOR SGT JOSEPH RAINONE, PO CLIFF BIEDER,
BOTTOM PO JOE CAMPANELLA, PO DANNY MAHONEY

1992 PROMOTION. TO LT. PO JOE GALLO, LT J RAINONE
PO SAM CONSOLAZIO, NEPHEWS

ABOUT THE AUTHOR

The author spent over twenty-six years on the NYPD, starting his career in the late 60s and finishing up in the mid 90s. As an old timer said to him, WELCOME to the NYPD, you have just joined the "GREATEST SHOW ON EARTH." And for the next 26+ years he found this to be so true. He came on the job with the aspirations of becoming a Detective to be in possession of the Coveted Gold Shield. During his career, he was let down several times as he saw others getting promoted to Detective while he was passed over (discretionary promotions). He once said to an old-time Sergeant, "This is not fair." His Sergeant's answer was, "Whoever told you the job was fair is either a liar or doesn't know what he is talking about." Which was soon to be proven a true statement.

NOTE: Fifty-some-odd years have gone by, read the New York papers as of recent times, and you will see how true those words are. People with minimum time on the job with very little arrest, if any at all, are being promoted to Detective, doing no investigative work at all. Some are even getting a raise in pay by being promoted to a higher-grade Detective. There are certainly Detectives in Precinct Squads or Specialty Squads who most definitely feel that they should be promoted to a higher grade and were passed over, which was/is an injustice. Just goes to show with all these years that have gone by certain things, such as procedures that are overlooked, and /nepotism/favoritism has not changed in the NYPD, and probably never will.

Eventually he is assigned to Anti-Crime in the 69 precinct. While in the Anti-Crime, the Cops worked hand in hand with the 69 Detective Squad as well as the Detectives in the 12th Division Homicide. The Homicide office was next to the Anti-Crime office. It was during this period that he learned a lot about investigations from seasoned Detectives. He did this by asking questions and reading their reports and just listening. It was then his desire grew even stronger to attain the rank of Detective. At the time the criteria to attain the Gold Shield was to be on the investigative track for several years. Eventually, he went to the Senior Citizen Robbery Unit as an investigator. After 26 months he returned to the Anti-Crime unit. He then served in the Organized Crime Control Bureau (OCCB), Public Morals Division, on the investigative track. He eventually went to the 75 precinct Detective Squad, as they then were called a White Shield Detective, where he was on the investigative track to receive his Gold Shield. However, he was never in the investigative track long enough to get the Gold Shield. This was at a time when it took maybe six, seven years to get that Gold Shield. If you weren't lucky enough to get it on a discretionary promotion. However, he was never on the investigative track long enough. As he was promoted to Sergeant, out of the 75 Det. Squad before he was promoted to Detective. As one of the Cops said to him, because he never got the Detective Shield you were "always a bridesmaid-never a bride". Or as another said to him, "you are like the horse in a two race, you always come in second as far as the detective shield goes.

As a Sergeant, he was assigned to the 108 precinct, where he was eventually assigned as the Anti-Crime Sergeant, which was his dream job in the rank of Sergeant. He had a great team, all good young cops who were eager to learn how to be good Anti-Crime Cops. He was a good teacher because of his previous years as an Anti-Crime Cop. He was the Anti-Crime Sergeant for several years. However it was time to move again, he was asked to return to Organized Crime Control Bureau (OCCB) in the AUTO CRIME DIVISION, a job he was suited for. In Auto Crime, he was a Sergeant of Detectives, supervising a team of detectives, and had a great time, again working with great cops. After several years, he was promoted to the rank of Lieutenant. Then assigned to the 90th precinct as the Special Operations Lieutenant. He was tasked with supervising several different units in the precinct, which included Anti –Crime as well as the SNEU (Special Narcotics Enforcement Unit), Fingerprint unit as well as Conditions Unit, and Community Policing. All of which were under his umbrella. While in the rank of Lieutenant, he still went on patrol with Anti-Crime as well as the SNEU team and made arrests along with the team. His feeling was that Anti-Crime when it was performed right was one of the best units NYPD ever created. The officers were able to stalk the bad guys and arrest them after they observed them committing robbery/burglary or gun possession, or other serious felony. Most of these crimes, if it weren't for the on-the-spot arrest, there probably wouldn't be an arrest. As they sometimes happen so fast, people usually have difficulty identifying the miscreant, or they are just too frightened to ID them. Eventually, after retiring from the NYPD, he worked as an Auto Theft Investigator for a private company, assisting the Police in the investigations and recovery of stolen vehicles. But he was proud to say that he was once part of the NYPD a job he loved. To him, there was no better job. There are some officers who retire and completely forget about their time in the NYPD and must be reminded of it. But there are others who, although they are retired from being a cop, it is still in their blood. As one old timer said on his retirement day, "I MAY BE RETIRED, BUT IN MY HEART, I AM STILL THE POLICE", which is the way he feels.

Although he retired in the rank of Lieutenant, he still felt his desire wasn't fulfilled. He never got that Detective Gold Shield that he and many others felt he deserved. As one of his detectives said to him, "Sarge, this is our shield." If it wasn't for you, I wouldn't have it. This statement has given him some satisfaction in not getting the Detective Shield, knowing a great cop deserved it and he got it because of his guidance. By the same token, he also got some satisfaction, knowing his nephew Joe Gallo as well as his adopted nephew Sammy Consolazio because of his guidance got them their Gold Shields. Which they both deserved, achieved without any nepotism. When he retired, he still felt NYPD was the greatest job in the world. Tanx to all of you I have memories that will last a lifetime.